The New Woman in
Early Twentieth-Century
Chinese Fiction

Comparative Cultural Studies
Steven Tötösy de Zepetnek, Series Editor

Comparative Cultural Studies is a contextual approach in the study of culture in all of its products and processes. The framework is built on tenets of the discipline of com-parative literature and cultural studies and on notions borrowed from a range of thought such as (radical) constructivism, communication theories, systems theories, and literary and culture theory. In comparative cultural studies focus is on theory and method as well as application and attention is on the how rather than on the what. Colleagues interested in publishing in the series are invited to contact the editor, Steven Tötösy, at <clcweb@purdue.edu>.

1. *Comparative Central European Culture*. Ed. Steven Tötösy de Zepetnek. 2002. 190 pages, bibliography, index. ISBN 1-55753-240-0.

2. *Comparative Literature and Comparative Cultural Studies*. Ed. Steven Tötösy de Zepetnek. 2003. 372 pages, bibliography, index. ISBN 1-55753-290-7.

3. Sophia A. McClennen, *The Dialectics of Exile: Nation, Time, Language, and Space in Hispanic Literatures*. 2004. 260 pages, bibliography, index. ISBN 1-55753-315-6.

4. *Comparative Cultural Studies and Latin America*. Ed. Sophia A. McClennen and Earl E. Fitz. 2004. 282 pages, bibliography, index. ISBN 1-55753-358-X.

5. Jin Feng, *The New Woman in Early Twentieth-Century Chinese Fiction*. 2004. 240 pages, bibliography, index. ISBN 1-55753-330-X

Jin Feng

The New Woman in Early Twentieth-Century Chinese Fiction

Purdue University Press
West Lafayette, Indiana

Copyright 2004 by Purdue University. All rights reserved

Printed in the United States of America

Library of Congress Cataloging-in-Publication Data
Feng, Jin, 1971-
  The new woman in early twentieth-century Chinese fiction / Jin Feng.
    p. cm. -- (Comparative cultural studies)
  Includes bibliographical references and index.
  ISBN 1-55753-330-X (pbk.)
  1. Chinese fiction--20th century--History and criticism. 2. Women in literature. I. Title. II. Series.

PL2443.F467 2004
895.1'351093522--dc22

2004000626

I thought of literature as the end of family, and of the society it represented
— Jacques Derrida

For My Parents, Feng Zhende and Yang Jiannong

Contents

Acknowledgments — ix

Introduction: The New Woman — 1

CHAPTER ONE
Texts and Contexts of the New Woman — 20

CHAPTER TWO
Books and Mirrors: Lu Xun and "the Girl Student" — 40

CHAPTER THREE
From Girl Student to Proletarian Woman:
Yu Dafu's Victimized Hero and His Female Other — 60

CHAPTER FOUR
En/gendering the *Bildungsroman* of the Radical Male:
Ba Jin's Girl Students and Women Revolutionaries — 83

CHAPTER FIVE
The Temptation and Salvation of the Male Intellectual:
Mao Dun's Women Revolutionaries — 101

CHAPTER SIX
"Sentimental Autobiographies":
Feng Yuanjun, Lu Yin and the New Woman — 126

CHAPTER SEVEN
The "Bold Modern Girl": Ding Ling's Early Fiction — 149

CHAPTER EIGHT
The Revolutionary Age:
Ding Ling's Fiction of the Early 1930s — 171

EPILOGUE
Ding Ling in Yan'an:
A New Woman within the Party Structure?   189

Appendixes
  Chronological List of Fiction Discussed in Each Chapter   199
   Glossary   203
Works Cited   209
Index   227

Acknowledgments

Many people have helped me in the writing of this book. My parents have always encouraged my intellectual exploration, even as it led me to half a world away. My mentor, Professor Yi-tsi Mei Feuerwerker at the University of Michigan, has remained a constant source of inspiration and support. Special thanks go to Matthew Fryslie, friend and former classmate, who has read various chapters and versions of my manuscript with an eye for style as well as substance.

The Institute for the Humanities at the University of Michigan awarded me a fellowship for 1999–2000, enabling me to complete the first draft of my manuscript with minimum distraction and hassle. Grinnell College has offered generous funds for my archival trips and conference presentations during the subsequent revision of my manuscript. I would also like to thank the class of my "Chinese Women" course at Grinnell in the fall of 2001: Mike Abel, Lura Barber, Jon Cell, Bridget Lavelle, Ilana Meltzer, Jessica Schmidt, Sylvia Techavalitpongse, and Jennifer Wheeler, for keeping my enthusiasm alive with endless questions and challenges.

I would also like to thank my editor Steven Tötösy de Zepetnek, who initiated the project of comparative cultural studies, and therefore provided an intellectual home for my book. Last but not the least, I would like to thank the anonymous reviewers of my book for their most useful and encouraging comments and suggestions. As readers will find out from the following pages, I study early twentieth-century Chinese fiction not as a pure "form" existing in a historical and cultural vacuum, but from the perspective of its dynamic interaction with both other forms of cultural products and with the authorized metanarrative of Chinese modernity. Whether my apparently backward-looking inquiry has provided some insights into the present time is for you to decide.

Introduction

The New Woman

How has the relationship between Chinese intellectuals and radical politics changed over the past century? How can we conceptualize the relationship between the projects for the modernization of Chinese culture and the liberation of Chinese women? What means and methods are open to us to evaluate the agency of Chinese women, especially female intellectuals, in the Chinese revolutions? These questions have not only proven to be of vital importance to recent Chinese intellectual history and of immense academic interest internationally, but are also questions and concerns that challenge national and disciplinary boundaries in the current age. In order to give these questions the full treatment they deserve, this book performs a kind of "narrative archeology" on a number of works of early twentieth-century Chinese fiction. It excavates and examines the recurring narrative patterns that had contributed significantly to the formation of the "new" style of modern Chinese literature but were often stridently denied or conveniently ignored by the authors and the critics. In uncovering these differently inflected layers of narrative practice, my project seeks to trace the nodes and vectors in the web of forces—self-representation, gender negotiation, and literary and national modernization—that constituted the politics of the multilayered narrative forms. Specifically, this project is drawn together by three intertwining strands: the central figure of the "new woman" (*xin nüxing*); the primary theme of the "politics of emotionality"; and a persistent attachment to an approach emphasizing the "reversed" and "oblique," as opposed to the forward and the direct impetus of these texts and their allegedly modern outlook.

The literature under discussion is the narrative and critical literary output of a group of radical Chinese intellectuals in the 1920s–1930s. These authors, including both men: Lu Xun, Yu Dafu, Ba Jin, and Mao Dun, and women: Feng Yuanjun, Lu Yin, and Ding Ling, emerged as leading figures in the May Fourth New Culture Movement (1919-37)—generally held as the first collective Chinese native movement towards modernization that led to pervasive cultural and sociopolitical transformations (Goldman 1-3). Regardless of their specific political allegiances, these authors either actively participated in or manifested strong sympathy towards leftist radical politics. Their fiction and criticism have been canonized in the *Zhongguo xin wenxue daxi* (*General Compendium of New Chinese Literature*, first series published 1935-36), and have commanded an enthusiastic following and scholarly interest to the present day.

In this body of texts, the new woman appears as a highly privileged *urban* figure that can take a number of different forms. These include women who shed the stereotypical domestic roles as the "good wife," "loving mother," or "filial daughter" to become "girl students" (*nü xuesheng*) attending Western-style schools for a modern education; urban drifters with no apparent familial or occupational affiliations; career women (including writers) making a living with their professional skills; and revolutionaries calling for social change through participation in demonstrations, rallies, and other political activities. Furthermore, the new woman possesses a unique and deep emotional interior that sets her immediately apart from the less self-reflective and uneducated female urban proletarians as well as from peasant women.

In view of the general "retreat" from the canon in the field of modern Chinese literature since the 1980s, my choice of such a group of works may seem odd, if not passé. As Rey Chow has pointed out, more and more scholars of twentieth-century Chinese literature are turning not only to noncanonical works (e.g., "popular" fiction of the early twentieth century) but also to nonliterary genres (e.g., film, radio programs, art exhibits, and popular music) (Chow, Introduction 16). These scholars seek to liberate previously undervalued discourses in order to launch attacks on what has been traditionally recognized as the canon of modern Chinese literature, and, as a result, to bring into view a more complete picture of Chinese modernity. However, I argue that the seminal aspect of canonization consists not only in the exclusion it effects but also in its unique mechanisms of inducing cooperation for its own creation and maintenance. The formation of the canon of modern Chinese literature depended not only on the obvious restriction of discourses of modernity but also on furious and multifaceted negotiations between the dominant but unstable ideologies and individual agency, negotiations that both partly enfranchised individual agency for the formation of the canon and exposed the gender and class origin of the canon. Since these complex negotiations particularly occurred within and surrounding canonized work but tended to be obscured in works that received less cultural and critical attention, a close scrutiny of the hierarchical relationships established in the process of canonization—especially those between the interrelated but clearly demarcated center and periphery of the canon as a result of such negotiations—is a valuable means by which we can achieve a more thorough understanding of the process of Chinese modernization.

As an emblematic figure in the canon of modern Chinese literature, the new woman provides a vital tool for the study of Chinese modernity because of her important position in the body of works that played a crucial part in Chinese modernization. The May Fourth intellectuals, would-be architects of Chinese modernity, adopted what Yü-sheng Lin calls a "cultural-intellectualistic" approach (*The Crisis of Chinese Consciousness* 26–27) in emphasizing literature as a vehicle of social change in their project of Chinese modernization. As such, their privileging of the new woman in canonized literature encapsulates the problematic inherent in the May Fourth project of Chinese social and political modernization through literary modernization. In particular, the narrative representation of the new woman reveals an intriguing ambiguity that was both productive and troublesome for the project of Chinese modernization, namely, the fact that it could "neither reconcile the otherness of woman nor exist without it" (Schor). Even as male intellectuals deployed this figure to facilitate both their project of Chinese modernization and self-representation, this fictional "new woman" constantly exposed the ambiguity of their modern position while her real-life analogues, the woman writers within the May Fourth group, adapted to and contested the apparatus on which the male writers and their newly emerged modern subjectivities depended. As such, the figure of the new woman provides a useful analytical focus for the investigation of not only the roles of gender politics and individual agency in the process of canonization but also the meanings and definitions of Chinese modernity, an inquiry that still very much influences ideological and literary orientations in Mainland China today.

In addressing issues facing contemporary China, this examination of the new woman also enables me to contribute to the transnational scholarship on modern Chinese literature and intellectual history. As mentioned at the beginning of this introduction, in this project I will be posing a set of questions to the relationship between cultural and political radicalism through the analysis of the new woman, a figure of subversive complexity despite, or precisely because of its apparent utility for the propagation of radical discourses of Chinese modernity. In the past these questions concerning the relationship between Chinese intellectuals and radical politics have produced both inspired scholarship and bitter political debate. Generations of scholars from diverse disciplines such as political science, history, and anthropology have raised and sought to answer them after each of the major political upheavals convulsed contemporary China: the Chinese Communist Party's (CCP) ascent to national power in 1949 (e.g., Lin, *The Crisis of Chinese Consciousness*), the "Great Proletarian Cultural Revolution" between 1966 and 1976 (e.g., Apter and Saich), and, more recently, the "Tian'anmen Incident" in 1989. In the current age of cultural globalization, these questions have, furthermore, called attention to the political ramifications of applying "international" theories such as poststructuralism, postmodernism, and postcolonialism to the study of Chinese literature and culture. Some scholars, for example, have declared that Mainland Chinese intellectuals have become "complicitous" with a totalitarian regime in adopting postcolonial theories to rationalize their cultural nationalism. This verdict has caused bitter contention between scholars in Mainland China on the one hand, and émigré Chinese and non-Chinese scholars residing outside of China on the other, resulting in cross-examinations of not only individual scholars' intellectual authority but also the very notion of "Chineseness" (Yeh 251–80). Therefore, I have created this backward-looking project not only to shed some light on the continually provocative issue of the relationship between Chinese intellectuals and radical politics, but also to address, through the act of integrating theory into a historically conscious inquiry, some newly emergent concerns in the field of Chinese studies. Towards those ends, I concentrate on the "politics of emotionality" in the narrative construction and utility of the new woman by radical May Fourth intellectuals in the 1920s and 1930s.

Before more detailed discussion of this main theme of my project, a few brief notes are necessary to further elucidate the parameters and focus of my project. With regard to the period under study, in the decade or so between the early 1920s and early 1930s, May Fourth writers not only produced an unprecedented number of fictional representations of the new woman, but also manifested a particularly restless and troubled tone in those representations. This phenomenon bespoke a period of wandering and exploration for modern Chinese writers: between the May Fourth Movement, which violently dislodged traditional mores and moralities and the new political circumstances of the 1930s—such as the rise of the Chinese Communist Party and the war with Japan—which arguably "rechanneled their energies to goals of national survival and revolution" (Lee, "Romantic Individualism" 251). Focusing on this particular period will thus provide us with a sharpened view of both the many contradictions within the authors' narrative representations and the historical exigencies shaping their literary endeavors. The shared political sympathies, ideological inclinations, and more importantly, narrative temperaments of these particular authors also make them an apposite focus group for my exploration of cultural radicalism through an examination of the interplay of tradition and modernity in the literary output of early twentieth-century China. Although far from being the "zealously ideological, heroic" type described by Thomas Metzger (qtd. in Lee, "Romantic Individualism" 240), they nevertheless did proclaim their commitment to cultural and national salvation by radical means. However, they also persisted in representing their modern discontent—their "feelings, moods, vision, and even dreams" (Prusek 1)—more through "realistic" (i.e., lively, authentic) rather than modernist literary techniques in their fiction. In featuring a co-existence of tradition and modernity in both the content and form of their works, these authors presented complex cases of cultural radicalism.

Working within these parameters of time and author, I use the term "new woman"—an integral part of radical May Fourth intellectuals' discourses of modernity—to reveal the unique alchemy of gender and modernity in early twentieth-century China. I attempt this with the consciousness that although widely utilized and circulated by May Fourth intellectuals and their predecessors in the promotion of Chinese women's liberation, the term "new woman" was established on several problematic assumptions. First, it was constructed against the May Fourth intellectuals' own stereotypes of the "traditional" Chinese woman. It perpetuated the picture of unrelieved, monolithic oppression of traditional women while failing to acknowledge that premodern Chinese society was comprised of disparate strata within which women played diverse roles. Furthermore, the term "new woman" privileged male-centered May Fourth discourses of modernity by establishing this female figure as the symbol of "newness" and "modernity." It thus prescribed rather than described what it meant to be a modern Chinese woman by excluding both alternative discourses of Chinese modernity and especially the voice of women as experiencing subjects.

In contrast, my use of the term "new woman" will excavate, rather than gloss over, these problematic premises. I will investigate the cultural context and the discursive mechanisms supporting the politicized uses of the representation of this figure (and her less glorified forebears) for the creation of the May Fourth version of Chinese modernity. The emphasis I place on the constructedness of this figure highlights not only the formal aspects of May Fourth writers' narrative endeavors but also the sociopolitical circumstances that necessitated the creation of new narrative forms. More importantly, I use the "new woman" to bring a close scrutiny to the narrative duplicity underlying the May Fourth intellectuals' representations of women. The dominant May Fourth discourses attributed the emergence of new women to inevitable historical causality, as they alleged that new women should and would replace traditional women in the process of Chinese modernization. However, I will show that the May Fourth writers, especially the male authors, artificially disconnected new women from their premodern predecessors in order to seize power over modern knowledge, a move that, moreover, contributed significantly to their own construction of a viable modern identity. In other words, in promoting the new woman, radical male intellectuals used the gesture of radical antitraditionalism both to mask their own inheritance of the mores and sensibilities of their premodern literati forebears and to marginalize alternative representations of the women of twentieth-century China, often causing the erasure of the particular plight of Chinese women in their experience of modernization. Simply put, we will see that the figure of the new woman played a key role in the May Fourth drama of self-invention and Chinese modernization.

The Politics of Emotionality

The multiple tensions in the representation and use of the new woman by radical intellectuals of early twentieth-century China came to a head in what I shall be calling "the politics of emotionality." I use this term to denote not only the various modes with which May Fourth intellectuals deployed emotions in both their critical essays and narratives for the generation and control of symbolic capital, but also the consequences of such discursive practices: namely, the complex relationships formed both within and between the May Fourth discursive community and its Other (i.e., the allegedly "conservative" and "antirevolutionary" groups).

The politics of emotionality was both a symptom of and remedy to male anxiety about their own precarious grasp of modernity and masculinity. Radical May Fourth intellectuals always integrated the representation of and debate on emotions into their interrelated tasks of national modernization and self-signification. In the early phase of the May Fourth Movement, male intellectuals privileged "sincere" emotions in order to attack the Confucian tradition that they had accused of stifling individual, especially women's, voices. However, in contrast to their proclaimed goals of the liberation of women and the demolition of traditions, male writers also invoked gender stereotypes previously established in the classical canon for the upkeep of their modern and masculine identity, using emotion as an instrument of differentiation to relieve the anxiety about their modernity and masculinity. For instance, in their critical essays they leveled charges of "feminine emotionalism" against women writers (Larson, *Women and Writing* 179–88) for the purpose of marking themselves as masculine modern subjects. Male intellectuals felt compelled to employ the politics of emotionality largely because their narrative representation and deployment of the new woman, an essential part of their projects of national modernization and self-representation, betrayed many irreconcilable contradictions between "tradition" and "modernity."

To be sure, the privileging of the new woman in May Fourth fiction was undeniably a new literary phenomenon. Representations of women in pre-twentieth-century Chinese literature and historiography in the classical language (*wenyan*) generally assigned women to domestic roles. Literati not only produced copious *exempla* of female virtue in the figures of self-sacrificing wives, wise mothers, filial daughters (Mou 109–47) but also, in the case of the "talented woman" (*cainü*), restricted their voices by appropriating them for the reinforcement of patriarchal values such as female "chastity." Vernacular fiction, on the other hand, did produce a crop of "footloose women," including courtesans, matchmakers, and cross-dressers, who enjoyed a certain degree of mobility outside the family structure. However, the authors of vernacular fiction as a rule neither regarded the footloose condition of these women as a particularly commendable state nor did they ever allow the footloose woman to completely sever her domestic ties. Most frequently, she was portrayed as being forced from the home due to the exigencies of poverty or war, or through the promptings of the (ambivalently portrayed) desire to obtain for herself the classical education generally accessible only to men. Nor was her footloose state allowed to continue indefinitely, generally meeting with one kind of authorial rectification or another. Some of these footloose women were castigated as the antithesis of female virtue for their promiscuity, avarice, or shrewishness, while others, lauded for their chastity and loyalty, were re-assimilated into the family and clan system through marriage.

By contrast, May Fourth intellectuals not only created new types of women outside the family, such as girl students and women revolutionaries, but also privileged these new types over the older prostitutes and matchmakers. They also used new literary devices borrowed from Western literature to portray these modern women's complex psychology in their break from the patriarchal family for the sake of self-fulfillment in a modern society, thereby accentuating these women's individuality and agency as well as displaying a markedly different attitude towards the relationship between woman and family. Yet, even as May Fourth intellectuals ostensibly celebrated women's displacement from the patriarchal family as a crucial step both in the realization of the new woman's individuality and in the forward progress of Chinese modernization, their narrative practice betrayed their ambivalent relationship to traditions.

Although generally functioning as an icon of modernity in May Fourth fiction, the new woman under the pens of male writers often appears to possess less moral strength or political conviction when compared to the resurrected versions of idealized feminine sacrifice, especially the "loving and suffering mother." Furthermore, modes of representation prevalent in premodern literature resurface in May Fourth fiction to confirm the genealogical linkage between the apparently dissimilar figures of the traditional and the modern woman; the authorial gaze in May Fourth male fiction commandeered the interior, if not always the body, of the new woman for the illustration of ideologies and the fortification of male subjectivity. Indeed, the patriarchal unconscious underlying the nationalist project of Chinese modernization ultimately guaranteed that the focus on the new woman represented but a transitional phase in modern fiction. Subsequently, valiant revolutionary woman replaced the high-strung girl student as the most visible type of new women in May Fourth fiction starting in the early 1930s. Eventually, selfless women workers and soldiers who were also Marxists replaced women intellectuals as desirable female role models in fiction produced by writers affiliated with the Chinese Communist Party, thus ironically signaling the containment of "liberated" women by the (patriarchal) rule of the Party. Male representation of new woman was not only riddled with irreconcilable contradictions between the alleged progressive message on the one hand and the authors' traditional sensibility and discursive habits on the other, but also, when used as a device of public instruction and social mobilization, called into existence a cadre of real-life new women who proved even more challenging than their fictional prototypes. In view of the unruly females in both fiction and life, it should come as no surprise that a further elaboration of the discourse on emotionality was necessary for the production and regulation of the (predominantly male) discourse on Chinese modernity and female participation within it. Arising from such needs, the politics of emotionality became a discursive interaction performed in two overlapping arenas—fictional narrative and literary criticism—for the purpose of demarcating the gender and class boundaries of membership within the articulating group of intellectuals.

Readers of May Fourth fiction cannot help noticing that psychological depth is regularly aligned with social class in its portrayal of female characters. On the one hand, as Yue Ming-bao has rightly pointed out, male May Fourth writers often emphasized the physicality of the lower-class woman, tending to render her as a silent and suffering body or as an ignorant beast of burden in a process that excluded "women's experience from its own articulation" (54). By contrast, the same writers tended to endow their fictionalized female intellectuals with relatively more psychological complexity. Furthermore, in portraying different classes of women, these authors utilized different narrative techniques that aimed to generate different affective responses in the reader. While they often adopted a third-person narrator and a "case study" approach in their representation of peasant women (see also Duke, "Past, Present, and Future" 45), characterized by an "objective," "realistic," and impassive narrative tone, the situation was different with the depiction of the more intellectual new woman. Here, they took an inward turn and accentuated the emotional turmoil and inner struggle of the male self faced with the plight of his female other. Their practice of conferring differential psychological depth in proportion to the social position of the female character, of course, reflected the promptings of the male authors' own bourgeois background; no doubt more familiar with the women of their own intellectual circles than with poverty-stricken peasants, they were better able to write about their internal experiences. But more importantly, the different degree of emotionality in the May Fourth male narratives dealing with Chinese women proved itself a mark of gender as well as of class.

Compared to the male May Fourth authors' representation of peasant women, their fiction and criticism concerning the new woman betrayed the male authors' inability to leave behind the "discursive habits of a patriarchal tradition" (Yue 54) in more volatile and complex ways. These male authors sought in the narrative evocation of the new woman both an affirmation of the individuality of the male intellectual self in the fictional narrative as unique, emotive human being and a foil for their extratextual performance of modern identity. Female writers in turn responded to and appropriated male strategies of allegorizing the woman as part of their own struggle to establish an independent identity for themselves as well as their characters.

When they produced female I-narrators that spoke primarily of their own emotional experiences, however, they not only exposed the gendered origin of the May Fourth project of modernization but also triggered male writers' anxiety about the bases of their own modern identity.

As Wendy Larson describes it, female "sentimentality" was deemed "bourgeois" or "traditional" by male intellectuals ostensibly because it signaled women writers' disassociation from the context of nation and society (*Women and Writing* 185). However, the much maligned "feminine emotionalism" in fact pointed up the streak of traditional sensibility still visible in the work of the male as well as the female writers; for these supposedly modern male writers inherited and often invoked in their literary works the kind of elegant sensibility characteristic of the premodern elitist literati tradition for the articulation of their subjectivity (Larson, "The Self Loving the Self" 175-93). Furthermore, "sentimental" female writing presented a challenge to the unspoken hierarchy within the May Fourth Movement, a gendered structure based on the premise of a male instructor–female disciple relationship. Last but not the least, it questioned the very nature and efficacy of the male-sponsored project of women's liberation by resurrecting the stifled and trivialized figure of the "talented woman" of old. Consequently, male intellectuals both expressed their anxiety about the issue of emotionality and took counter-measures in the critical literature they produced against the threat it posed.

The late-Qing (1644-1911) reformer Liang Qichao (1873-1929) described "talented women" as essentially the type of traditional woman "who toys with ditties on the wind and the moon, the flowers and the grass [...] who makes ditties on spring sorrow and sad departures" ("Lun nüxue" 39), and summarily excluded them from the project of Chinese modernization on the basis of their sentimental tendency and their lack of contact and concern with pressing social realities. Echoing Liang's judgment, radical male intellectuals criticized the sentimental literature produced by "liberated" women writers in order to secure a superior male position through the essentialization of sentimentality as an exclusively feminine attribute, though ostensibly cautioning modern women to guard against the reemergence of this traditional trait in their literary creation. This strategic use of the new woman in the process of male self-signification becomes even clearer when seen in the light of the relationships the talented women of old forged with their male sponsors.

In the Ming (1368-1644) and Qing dynasties, talented women formed a very real and visible literary and social force through their publication of poetry, distribution of literary anthologies, and, in some cases, their ironical privileging of "female virtue" over literary creativity in the contemporary discussions of female talent and morality (Chang 236-58). Insofar as talented women formed a complex relationship with the dominant discourse of Confucianism, sometimes seeking power through the adoption of the male voice, they disproved the popular May Fourth myth of the unrelieved victimization of the traditional Chinese women. However, radical male intellectuals chose to ignore this revelation while ironically resurrecting the premodern model of male patronization/patronage in their criticism of sentimental female fiction. In other words, just like the liberal-minded yet still "traditional" male teachers and relatives of talented women in the past, radical male intellectuals not only sponsored the production and distribution of sentimental literature by women but also explicitly claimed the position of arbiter and mentor to women writers under the rubric of the enlightenment and liberation of the "second sex" through the introduction of modern knowledge.

The gendered literary criticism coming from male intellectuals made it amply clear that their anxiety about their own modernity was at the same time anxiety about their masculinity. Radical male intellectuals often invoked gender stereotypes in their criticism of female writings and applied a double standard through the creation and careful maintenance of categories such as "rational" versus "emotional," and "social" versus "autobiographical." While male writers' evocative works were hailed either as frontal attacks against traditional morality or as masterful artistic achievements, comparable fiction by female writers was criticized for its lack of social consciousness and artistic control. Male writers who privileged male emotions were not accused of being "effeminate," yet female writers were often accused of being "miss-ish" if they wrote about women's emotions. Simply put, the alleged lack of social consciousness and sentimentality in female literary production were often associated with the inherent inferiority of their gender (Larson, *Women and Writing* 177-88). This kind of gender-inflected male criticism of female fiction led to the creation in the critical literature of May Fourth period of a new form of the new woman: the woman writer. The frequent appearance of the female writer as a target of radical criticism in effect created in the critical discourse of the time a nonfiction counterpart to the new woman of the fictional text, who, like the fictional figure, served as an Other whose expulsion defined the modernity of the radical male intellectual.

Of course, I do not mean to suggest that male writers could not be victimized or marginalized. Rather, it was precisely their marginalized position in early twentieth-century Chinese society—and their keenly felt frustration about the lack of "meaningful" relationships between self and society, between artistic creation and social commitment—that prompted their gendered practice of the politics of emotionality. Furthermore, I will demonstrate that participation in the politics of emotionality enabled male intellectuals to perform their masculinity through the occupation of various and at times even contradictory ideological and gender loci. For instance, sometimes within the same literary piece the male author contrived to have the male center of consciousness vacillate between masculine and feminine positions. But, ultimately, male writers deployed emotions in both fiction and criticism for the sake of strengthening the authorial claim to a modern masculine identity.

Yet the politics of emotionality also proved to be a double-edged sword for the male writers who tried to wield it. Once launched, it gathered momentum and by its own internal logic and power exceeded the intentions of its original creators. As mentioned above, male intellectuals positioned themselves on one side of the politics of emotionality to alleviate anxiety about their own qualifications as modern and masculine subjects. However, the circulation of this discourse on emotionality also turned male writers into the object of its disciplinary force. The particular dilemma faced by radical males who leveled criticism of "emotionalism" against female writers lay precisely in their own practice of the "emotional" narration of new women. Although the evocative narration of new women served to affirm, through its creation of pathos, the writers' modern identity beyond the text as humanistic and modern individuals with a unique, profound, and critical vision of society, it also simultaneously exposed the authorial presence in the process of narration with the production of sentimental overtones. This threatened the male authors with a direct confrontation not only with their own melancholy and pessimism but also with the contradictions inherent in their criticism of feminine emotionalism, and hence the exposure of their patronizing and patriarchal attitude towards women writers. A close scrutiny of the affective residue in male narratives, therefore, would reveal not only the vacillation of their political conviction but also the limits of their self-proclaimed promotion of women's liberation for Chinese modernization. The male writers discussed in this book adopted different strategies to divert such unwelcome attention. Some attempted to displace male emotional weakness onto a female other in their narratives, while others either vigorously denied that their emotionally volatile male protagonists were autobiographical or accentuated their dedication to objective style and to "realism" rather than "self-expression." The most interesting case in this regard is that of Yu Dafu. Unabashed "exhibitionist" though he may have been, he almost never depicted psychologically complex female Chinese intellectuals. Instead, he either formulated a discourse on Chinese modernity in the invocation of Chinese nationalist sentiment through the portrayal of Japanese women or turned his attention to prostitutes and female factory workers, and thus falling back on a more traditional mode of representing male-female relationships.

On the other hand, the politics of emotionality never fully succeeded in annulling women's agency or imposing its entire agenda on women writers, even as it utilized their work and made prescriptions for it. Female writers of the May Fourth generation were, naturally, attracted to the May Fourth discourse of Chinese modernity for its avowed objective of the emancipation of women. As new women themselves, they were free, indeed compelled, to let loose their creative voices and explore women's experience and the possibilities of female autonomy in their own ways, even as their works were also shaped by the austere canons of literary composition dictated by their male colleagues. They not only challenged social norms by bringing attention to hitherto underrepresented female experience, such as romantic relationships between women, but also made ingenious and versatile use of first-person narration in response to the negative literary criticism leveled against them, thus taking important steps in their creation of their own version of an independent modern identity.

Feng Yuanjun, for example, dutifully promoted heterosexual romantic love and freedom of choice in marriage to address the conflict between traditional and modern morality. But at the same time, by privileging first-person narration, she also centralized her female character's complex and ambivalent emotions towards both her native family and her lover, thus subverting the simplistic May Fourth call for the complete demolition of the traditional family. In comparison, Lu Yin more self-consciously changed her narrative style in order to adapt to national and political crises. Early in her career, she produced diary and epistolary fiction focusing on self-contained communities of female intellectuals who used the language of philosophy to explore the notion of romantic love, but in the 1930s she switched from this accentuation of romantic love to that of the love for one's nation in her fiction. However, Lu Yin preserved a strong female consciousness in her fiction, particularly through a unique narrative articulation of temporal experience, even as she sought to survive as a woman writer in a male-dominated world. For Ding Ling, the quest for female empowerment took the form of appropriation of the masculine position through the management of the emotions. In her earlier work, she created heroines who reversed traditional feminine and masculine gender roles; later, during her years in Yan'an, she came to use her authorial position as both a woman and a Communist to defy Party policy and advocate women's rights.

Methodology

The revealing figure of the new woman and the focus on "politics of emotionality" allow a productive juxtaposition of the textual and extratextual, the literary and the political, as well as insights gained from the different narrative strategies used by male and female writers, for the elucidation of the crucial significance of both the "modern woman" and "modern fiction" at an important point in Chinese history.

As I have indicated in the previous section, I have chosen the May Fourth discourse on emotionality as the central theme of my inquiry because emotionality represented a crucial yet vulnerable juncture, one that threatens, under analytical pressure, to succumb and bring down the structured discourses of Chinese modernization and (male) intellectual identity built upon it. To effectively analyze the politics of emotionality, I will examine three sets of interrelated juxtapositions: the fictional and nonfictional (e.g., critical or autobiographical) works produced by these authors; the antecedent(s) and transmutation of this discourse; and the intellectuals' active promotion of their discourse on emotionality and their attempts at restricting practices that opposed or undercut this discourse. In other words, I will excavate through layers of premodern and popular narrative forms, as well as their multiple, ideologically inflected modern successors by crossing and recrossing the boundary between literary text and social context and by integrating findings from historical, psychological, and formal investigations. With this integrated approach, I will be able to explore both the discursive function and the narrative embodiment of the figure of the new woman in works by different authors at different periods, thus making visible broader discursive patterns that emerge from the specifics of each case study.

A systematic study of the fictional representation of the new woman in terms of her realization in the mesh of interests that make up the politics of the narrative form is still wanting in the scholarship on twentieth-century Chinese literature, largely due to the lack of a methodology that takes into full account the complex configuration of history, politics, and literature in May Fourth fiction. Hu Ying's recent book, *Tales of Translation: Composing the New Woman in China, 1899–1918,* provides insights into the earlier representations of new women by tracing Chinese translation and appropriation of Western female role models but does not privilege textual analysis of this figure. By contrast, Lydia Liu's *Translingual Practice: Literature, National Culture, and Translated Modernity – China, 1900–1937* offers many incisive observations about the formation of national literature, Chinese modernity, and nationalism but does not focus on the performance of masculinity and femininity made possible through this figure. Moreover, except for Sally Lieberman's *The Mother and Narrative Politics in Modern China,* the number of scholars who have produced effective comparisons between male and female writers' fictional treatment of the same figure is negligible. I do not mean to promote an essentialist view of writing and gender in Chinese literature, but rather suggest that a nuanced examination of female writers' compliance with and subversion of male prescriptions will enable us to see more clearly the gender negotiations in twentieth-century Chinese literature. Another characteristic of existing methodologies is that few scholars have explored the representation of women in May Fourth fiction by both identifying the narrative permutations of that representation and situating them within a context of historical change and gender negotiation. Some have performed the kind of thematic readings that focused on a female character's significance in a particular work, but this approach fails to reveal either the relevance of the character within the wider canon of May Fourth fiction or the generation of power through the circulation of such a figure. Others, although demonstrating an interest in narratology, nevertheless tend to uncritically accept the May Fourth Movement's own view of modern Chinese literature and thus end up severing the connection between twentieth-century fiction and its premodern predecessors. Still others seem intent on discovering "essential" historical facts rather than discursive mechanisms as the guiding force in the narrative representation of the new woman in May Fourth fiction.

In spite of the current decline in interest in canonical May Fourth fiction and in contrast to existing scholarship on twentieth-century Chinese literature, my project will probe the "politics of form" (Barthes) — denoting both specific formal realizations and general discursive patterns — of May Fourth fiction in order to study its narrative representation of the new woman. I will scrutinize the gendered construction of the new woman in fiction from two perspectives: first, that of the modern authors' complex relations with premodern literary traditions on the one hand and with their own volatile sociopolitical environment on the other, and, second, that of female authors' negotiations of gender roles and voice in their aspiration to enter the charmed circle of the canonized modern writers. Towards those ends, my examination of the formal aspects of narrative construction will not take place in a synchronic, structuralist void; instead, I will bring into view the contextual — sometimes manifested as the intertextual — layers of the narrative practice of both male and female writers.

The authors' nonfictional explanation and interpretation of their own works and their responses to the critical reception of their fiction constitutes the most immediate layer of the context of their fiction. These materials are useful not just because their sheer quantity exposes the May Fourth intellectuals' anxieties about the new identities they were attempting to mold for themselves, but also in that the authors often more explicitly presented their notions of the particular relationships between the author, the text, and the reader in their essays than in their fiction.

Radical May Fourth intellectuals tended to regard themselves as the standard bearers of modern ideas and the educators of the masses. For many of them, priority was laid on the social and reformist effects of their narratives, rather than on artistic achievement. Consequently, they paid close attention to the responses of their readers, for they believed that in order for their works to bring about desired social changes, they must reorient and retrain the Chinese people's reading habits. Their comments on and explanations of their works thus speak to this aspect of their project of "enlightenment." On the other hand, May Fourth writers also used essays about themselves and their work to justify their own or their comrades' literary endeavors, and thus to establish public images for themselves in a tumultuous early twentieth-century China. The May Fourth writers' generally active involvement in politics made it necessary for them to constantly adjust narrative modes in order to better accord with new political agendas. Yet, since not everyone can be a stylistic virtuoso, able to respond with even inspiration to the changing demands of the political climate, their switch from one narrative mode to another often met with far less success than the change of their ideological orientation. As such, the nonliterary explanation of their fiction often served as a means to justify their substandard narrative efforts, demonstrating again the precarious and shifting basis of these authors' position in society.

Another layer of context for May Fourth fiction is comprised of alternative representations of women outside the family both in pre-twentieth-century vernacular fiction and in the popular literature of early twentieth-century China, bodies of writing that were severely criticized by May Fourth intellectuals. Although limiting the introduction of works from these two groups—which were barred from the canon of modern Chinese literature—mostly to chapter one, I hope to formulate a more rounded picture of twentieth-century Chinese literature and to illustrate the way in which the process of canon formation was able to exclude alternative discourses of Chinese modernity.

In the analysis of the narratives per se, I examine not only formal aspects of fictional narratives (e.g., narrator, temporal arrangement, the different modes of summary, description, or narration) but also the significance imparted to these narrative forms by their position in the historical, political, and literary context. I implement the contextualization of narrative forms in two interrelated ways. First, I trace in the larger sociopolitical environment the shift, both in thematic prominence and narrative mode, in the male authors' representations of the new woman—a trajectory that proceeded from the girl student to the woman revolutionary, from subjective to objective modes of representation. Then, against this background, I contrast male writers' fiction and criticism with those of women writers in order to probe the negotiation of gender roles and positioning within May Fourth fiction.

There has long existed a sharp divide of methodology in the study of premodern and modern Chinese fiction. The examination of narratological transmutation in Chinese literature has often seemed to be limited to premodern vernacular fiction. By contrast, modern Chinese literature has time and again been entirely subjected to thematic readings that failed to take into account formal innovations and their political significance (Henry Zhao's *The Uneasy Narrator* and Chen Pingyuan's *Zhongguo xiaoshuo xushi moshi de zhuanbian* [*The Change of Narrative Modes in Chinese Fiction*] are two noticeable exceptions). However, I argue that contextualizing the change of narrative forms of modern Chinese fiction will not only reveal considerable historical continuity between modern and premodern Chinese fiction, but also produce a reading that is not dogmatically ideological but rather exposes the politics that underlie recurring discursive patterns in fictional representations throughout the history of the period.

May Fourth fiction by radical intellectuals bears out the importance of the conjunction of literary text and political context through its changing narrative realization, for changes in narrative forms in this literature invariably echoed political shifts in the larger social context. For instance, in the early phase of the May Fourth Movement, with the promotion of the discourse of individualism in a variety of venues such as modern journals, subjective narrative modes, such as first-person narration and the detailed description of individual psyche, were highly privileged. However, as May

Fourth intellectuals turned from individualism to collectivism starting in the mid-1920s, subjective modes of representation gave way to more objective modes: omniscient third-person narrators gradually replaced I-narrators while collective revolutionary activities, instead of individual psychological development, came to occupy center stage. Furthermore, this engagement of literature with politics was consciously sought after in the May Fourth tradition, as intellectuals wished to facilitate their project of national modernization through the creation of a modern Chinese literature. Their utilitarian view of literature caused many of them to use fiction as a tool to represent and disseminate certain ideological positions that found more forceful expression in their discursive essays. The depiction of the new woman is a case in point, in that it was often tailored to fulfill a variety of explicit political ends.

Precisely because of the convergence of sociopolitical context and literary text in May Fourth fiction, I have not chosen a psychoanalytical approach as the central method of inquiry, even though dealing with "emotionality" in this project. I based this decision, on the one hand, on the "intentionality" of the May Fourth period—i.e., the "social, historical and cultural intention which motivated the production of literary texts" (Denton, "The Distant Shore" 109), which cannot be adequately addressed by only applying a psychoanalytical framework to specific literary pieces. On the other hand, the particular group of radical authors that I examine in this project by and large showed more interest in representing emotions "realistically," namely, in a lively and authentic fashion, than in dazzling their audience with "exotic" modernist techniques such as psychoanalysis (with the possible exception of some of Yu Dafu's works) (J. Y. Zhang).

In view of the complex sociopolitical forces and individual situations that shaped this group of May Fourth fiction, I propose that the contextualization of narration needs to be sensitive to the barter and traffic between text and context, and between the modes and mores of fiction, for ideological messages can often be modified, undermined, or completely sabotaged by narrative forms of the fiction. Ross Chambers suggests a similar way to bring narrative forms into conjunction with their sociopolitical significance in his *Story and Situation: Narrative Seduction and the Power of Fiction*. Chambers claims that every narrative depends on the realization of a "narrative contract," that is, an understanding established between the narrator/author and narratee/reader concerning the "point," or the significance, of any narrative exchange (8). He further explains that the "point" of the narrative is invariably determined by the social and cultural context within which it is produced (20).

The narrative contract aspired to by May Fourth writers reveals that they actually upheld premodern Chinese literary traditions even while vocally rejecting them. Many of these writers borrowed narrative devices from premodern vernacular fiction as well as from Western literature for their fiction writing. Yet even in narratives where authors apparently discarded premodern literary conventions and committed themselves to a complete literary Westernization, they often attempted to resurrect a premodern narrative contract. By presenting themselves as educators of the masses and assigning their fiction as "textbooks" (Chen P., "Literature High and Low" 131), May Fourth intellectuals claimed a textual authority that was based on the hierarchical structure of an instructional writer versus a receiving reader. They were thus striving for a narrative contract modeled after the classical Confucian tradition that advocated the literati's use of poetry to transform people's spirit.

Seen through the lens of the narrative contract, May Fourth writers also forged an ambiguous relationship with the popular fiction of their time. Many of them vigorously criticized popular literature and excluded works by popular writers from the canon of modern Chinese literature. However, the commercial success of popular fiction suggests that despite their vow to educate the masses, May Fourth intellectuals could not match the efforts of their lowbrow rivals in conveying the point of their narrative to a wider audience. While the condemnation of popular literature may already indicate a territorial jealousy on their part, more damaging was the fact that some of the loudest detractors of popular fiction within the May Fourth group made use of similar narrative devices and thus duplicated, even as they imported Western literary devices, the narrative contract privileged in popular fiction that they had previously rejected. As such, popular fiction, just like the women writers within the May Fourth group, proved to be an Other dangerous not for its difference from but for its similarity to the self. After all, May Fourth intellectuals could hardly distinguish themselves from writers of popular literature if they were unable to honor their different, modern narrative contract.

In light of the complex configuration of sociopolitical, cultural, and literary elements in May Fourth fiction outlined above, an approach to contextualize narrative forms—such as Steven Tötösy's comparative cultural studies framework—is by far the most productive methodology for dealing with this body of literature. The nature of the materials and the thrust of my objectives also demand an organization of chapters that can effectively reveal both the narrative changes and gender and ideological negotiations encapsulated in the figure of the new woman.

Organization of Chapters

This book, although concerned with the different realizations of the new woman, does not trace sequentially the various forms of the new woman across different texts, but instead looks at her treatment on an author-by-author basis. Such an arrangement has been dictated by my own analytical objectives as well as by practical considerations. May Fourth representations of the new woman display a great fluidity. In some works, the growth and development of a single woman is depicted in full-length biographical fashion, with the heroine taking on the roles of different types of new women at different stages of her life, thus making it difficult to group specific works under discrete typological rubrics. More importantly, the figure of the girl student proves to be not only the "earliest" type, but also the "archetype" of all new women. That is to say, the narrative representation of the girl student epitomizes the discursive practice of May Fourth fiction, thus anticipating and illuminating the representation of other types.

Late Qing scholars such as Kang Youwei (1858–1927) and Liang Qichao proposed a national self-strengthening scheme that promoted Chinese women's modern education for the sake of national prosperity (Beehan 106–13). Similarly, May Fourth intellectuals regarded education as the first step in Chinese women's emancipation, which, they argued, would also contribute to national modernization. Male intellectuals of the May Fourth period in fact initially focused on the girl student as the quintessential modern Chinese woman, the key witness and primary beneficiary of the success of their push for enlightenment, who would, it was claimed, inspire a widespread modernizing movement among all Chinese women. This practice implicitly consigned all Chinese women to the role of pupils, awaiting initiation into modern womanhood at the hands of male modern intellectuals, who had a monopoly on knowledge of Western literature and ideology. The girl student thus occupied a particularly important position in the metanarrative of Chinese modernization, as she provided a mirror through which the male intellectual was able to "see himself at least twice the size he really is" (Woolf 36). Since the representation of the girl student encapsulates the self-other relationship between male intellectuals and their new female Other, it overlaps with and foreshadows the depiction of other types of new women. Therefore, I will start with the examination of the girl student and follow a relatively flexible typological division in order to draw out the common discursive patterns in the delineation of all new women.

To fulfill most effectively the objectives of this project, chapter one highlights May Fourth fiction's disavowed connections with works excluded from the canon and situates the emergence of the new woman in May Fourth fiction both synchronically and diachronically. On the one hand, this chapter juxtaposes May Fourth literature with works of popular literature in an effort to reveal attitudes towards women shared by both sides. On the other, it brings premodern vernacular representations of footloose women to bear on the literary devices and male-centered consciousness inherited by May Fourth fiction. Chapters two to five examine fiction by the male writers Lu Xun, Yu Dafu, Ba Jin, and Mao Dun, respectively. Chapter six looks at the fiction of Feng Yuanjun and Lu Yin that exposes women writers' problematic relationships to the force of canonization. Chapter seven will be devoted to Ding Ling's earlier fiction such as "Miss Sophia's Diary" ("Shafei nüshi de riji," 1928), and chapter eight to her later works, such as "Shanghai, Spring 1930" ("1930 nian chun, Shanghai," 1930), as she left behind subjective narrative modes for more objective ones. In the "Epilogue," I will first explore new development in the representation of this figure as exemplified in Ding Ling's works within the context of the Maoist discourse in Yan'an in the early 1940s. I will then use that exercise to reflect on the representation and deployment of new women by radical intellectuals that have been discussed in the previous chapters. Finally, I will briefly address the link between radical literature, radical politics, and the Maoist regime in light of the insights gained from my project.

ONE

Texts and Contexts of the New Woman

The scope and depth of radical May Fourth intellectuals' iconoclasm were arguably unique in modern history in general (Lin, *The Crisis of Chinese Consciousness* 6). Yet as is the case with any project redemptive in nature and transformational in objective, their modernization of China was predicated on a reconstruction of the past; they formulated a narrative of a diseased and hopeless Chinese tradition as the foundation to begin "the work of modernity" (Prasad 103). Furthermore, May Fourth intellectuals depended on the representation and deployment of women to both indict a "benighted" cultural tradition and create and consolidate their own emerging modern identity. Such a practice of othering women for the purpose of self-representation, of course, betrayed the radical intellectuals' ties to a patriarchal tradition that they had allegedly rejected, but its capacity to anchor a metanarrative of Chinese modernity demands more than an examination of its ethical ramifications. We must examine both the historical circumstances and the textual productions that provided simultaneously the impetus and apparatus for its operation.

The Intellectual Self in Crisis

The May Fourth metanarrative of Chinese modernization gathered emotional force from a profound sense of dislocation, on both a national and individual level, that had been fermenting since the late nineteenth century. Ever since the "Opium War" of 1840–42, China's every encounter with Western imperialism had brought national humiliation and concession of territory and sovereignty. The defeat of the Qing navy in the 1895 Sino-Japanese war by Japan, a country that had always been regarded as China's tributary state, finally brought home to the educated members of Chinese society the irrevocable loss of China's golden age, when the ancient empire had allegedly reigned as the center of culture and civilization. Within two weeks of the signing of the Treaty of Shimonoseki (April 17, 1895) between Japan and the Qing government, Kang Youwei led more than 1,200 of his fellow examination candidates (*juren*) in Beijing to present to the throne the famous "Ten Thousand Word Memorial" advocating comprehensive institutional reforms (Yü 143). Ironically, these scholars' efforts to strengthen China led to the demise of their own class. With their proposed educational reform spreading nationwide and leading to the establishment of modern schools and programs to send students to study abroad, a modern school system finally replaced the national civil service examination system (*keju zhidu*) in 1905. The abolition of the examination system was more than a change of format in the recruitment of civil servants. Its elimination ended the most widely accepted and time-honored channel to officialdom for scholars educated in the Confucian classics, and thus set the stage for the birth of the modern Chinese intellectual (*zhishi fenzi*).

Growing up amidst China's traumatic transformation from a premodern to a modern society, May Fourth intellectuals witnessed the disintegration of the traditional framework of culture and morality. The dislodgement and erosion of Confucian ideas and values as well as the disappearance of the civil service examination system deprived them of any traditional means of actualizing the Confucian ideal of continuity and harmony between one's inner self and the external world, and between the individual and the divine (*tian ren heyi*). As a result, not only were they compelled to abandon the traditional career path and change their own career choice, they were also embroiled in a profound crisis of the self that was caught between the old and the new.

The crisis of the intellectual self was manifested most noticeably in the radicalization of intellectuals in early twentieth-century China (Yü 147), for it encapsulated their struggle for a radical way to signify themselves as well as to modernize China. Ying-shi Yü observes that May Fourth intellectuals were more susceptible to political and cultural radicalization than their reformist predecessors (e.g., Yan Fu, Kang Youwei, and Liang Qichao) in that the May Fourth anti-traditionalism represented "a paradigmatic change [...] in the development of radicalism in modern China" (130). Indeed, May Fourth intellectuals not only advocated "whole-sale" and "immediate" transformations of the long-established Confucian tradition, the *Way*, into a variety of Western models (Yü 128), many of them also later converted to Marxism, and devoted themselves to political activities rather than literary productions.

However, a close look reveals that their project of radical modernization was deeply ingrained in their "fundamentally traditional desires to empower the self through an organic linkage with the outer world" (Denton, General Introduction 48). In other words, May Fourth intellectuals' totalistic rejection of tradition constituted not only a crucial part of their plan to modernize China, but also a key step in their quest for a modern identity in a world rapidly changing beyond recognition, by paradoxically conceptualizing their new identity through the utility of the traditional paradigm of self-signification.

To be sure, the disassociation of modern intellectuals from state power contributed to their radicalism. Modern education, unlike classical education, did not guarantee state employment, and modern intellectuals, no longer due for lucrative official posts, were not obliged to uphold state ideologies. But, paradoxically, it was precisely their marginalized position in state politics that spurred May Fourth intellectuals to launch a "cultural revolution" that would supposedly revitalize China. In so doing, they sought to gain political power by emphasizing the importance of culture and their status as leaders of a radical cultural movement. Radical intellectuals in fact utilized their iconoclastic stance against traditions to present themselves as leaders of Chinese modernization, thus securing for themselves a way back to the political center through the claim of moral as well as cultural authority. They had vocalized their rationale for thus completely severing ties with tradition: They declared that tradition was due for demolition because it hindered progress and national salvation. This rationale was then transformed into an indisputable proof of the worth of any "modern" project they undertook, and, by extension, established their position as the moral guardian and the architect of modernity for the Chinese nation. Kirk Denton has argued that May Fourth intellectuals' political commitment eventually led them to resurrect "the traditional role of the Confucian scholar-bureaucrat" (General Introduction 11). Indeed, by representing themselves essentially as both "'servant of the state' and ... 'moral critic of the ruler'" (Feuerwerker, *Ideology, Power, Text* 13), May Fourth intellectuals' self-image ironically harked back to the Confucian model of the scholar-official.

As a central part of their project of Chinese modernization, May Fourth literary modernization also demonstrated radical intellectuals' paradoxical practice of replicating the role of the Confucian scholar-official for the invention of a modern self. The rationale for their privileging of literary modernization had a distinct Confucian echo; for May Fourth intellectuals reaffirmed the Confucian emphasis on the cultivation of the mind as an integral part of the transformation of society (Metzger 134) by not only proposing to revitalize the nation through the enlightenment of the people but also particularly choosing literature as a vital tool in their project of nation building (see also J. Liu 106–16). However, May Fourth intellectuals also advocated the importation of Western, and hence "modern," literary theories and devices both for the eradication of native traditions and for the establishment of their modern identity even as they surreptitiously utilized the Confucian model of self-realization to justify their radical views and practices. As a result, the literature that they produced revealed the conflict between the modern and traditional values—embodied most obviously in their discourses of iconoclasm and nationalism—that seemed to be pulling the self in opposite directions. This conflict lay at the heart of the crisis of the intellectual self at the time.

However, the acute sense of crisis also compelled May Fourth intellectuals to seek its resolution in literature, if only by invoking traditional paradigms once again. This can be seen in their attempts at achieving a fusion of

Self and Other through both their fiction and literary criticism as a means to reconcile the discourses of iconoclasm and nationalism. With regard to theoretical construction, such attempts were most visible in the overlapping literary theories of "Romanticism" and "Realism." In the early 1920s, May Fourth participants became divided in their ideas about the new literature with the employment of these two Western literary terms, and formed two apparently mutually exclusive literary groups. While the Literary Research Association (Wenxue yanjiu hui, 1920-32) (Denton, Glossary 503) espoused an objective delineation of reality, the Creation Society (Chuangzao she, 1921-29) (Denton, Glossary 496-97) promoted aesthetic self-expression. However, the theoretical boundary between the two literary groups had never been clear-drawn, for their difference seemed to be only a matter of subject matter. As Lu Xun facetiously observed, "To write a good deal about yourself is expressionism. To write largely about others is realism" ("Bian" 87). Denton has further pointed out "some fundamental assumptions about the origin and function of literature" shared by these two schools of writers (General Introduction 36). He argues that both schools insisted on "a fundamental unity of the subjective and the objective" (36) and therefore, "[a]n assertion of self, interconnected with humanity and the external world [...] is necessarily an expression of the other" (46). By thus connecting the self with the others, the May Fourth view on the relationship of Self and Other, which was shared by the Realists and Romanticists alike, revealed their common bond with the premodern Confucian notion of individual assertion as a way to transform the external world.

In narrative practice, radical intellectuals' efforts of resolving the crisis of the self can be seen not only in their continuous practice of creating a female Other, the new woman, for the formation and consolidation of male subjectivity (Eagleton 71) both within the text and extratextually, but also in their voluntary switch from the subjective to the objective mode of representation in the construction of such a self-other relationship. The May Fourth trajectory of national modernization can be described as one that gradually subsumed individualist autonomy under nationalist political engagement. To be sure, at the start of the May Fourth Movement, a general fixation on the self seemed to have emerged in literature. Yu Dafu's well-known definition of fiction was representative of the common sentiment: "All literary works are the author's autobiography" ("Wuliu nian" 335). This "inward turn" (Kahler) was also evident in their portrayal of new women. Be they male or female, "Romanticists" or "Realists," May Fourth writers privileged not only individual beliefs and emotions, but also subjective narrative modes such as first-person narration, diary fiction, and epistolary fiction in their depiction of new women. The centrality of the individual in the early May Fourth fiction testified to the cultural milieu of the early stage of the May Fourth Movement, when the principle of individualism was being strongly promoted. But even at this stage, intellectuals already betrayed their uneasiness about extreme individualism. Not only did they always anchor their modern subjectivity on the representation of a female Other in fiction, but they also claimed that they were facilitating Chinese modernization through such a practice, and hence the disregard of the artistic independence and autonomy of literature. Starting in the mid-1920s, the fusion of Self and Other manifested itself in literature in more noticeable ways. Radical writers changed their narrative modes into more objective styles (e.g., third-person narration) as well as started to write more about the proletariat and the peasantry.

This objective turn in narrative style reflected changed historical circumstances. Both the increasingly fierce nationalist struggle against Japanese invasion and the rise of the Chinese Communist Party during the Communists' political conflicts with the Nationalist Party (Guomin dang) fostered the May Fourth intellectuals' gradual conversion to Marxist ideology and collectivism. Yet, given the self-other positioning in the fiction about new women, the objectification of narration starting from the mid-1920s was in a sense inevitable. As has been mentioned above, the representation of the male intellectual self, both within the text and extratextually, was predicated on the creation of a female Other, the new woman. However, not only did this practice fall short of its objective of enhancing male subject formation, it also revealed a disconcerting link between May Fourth literature and its stridently denounced others, the contemporary popular culture and premodern Chinese literature. Therefore, the narrative objectification starting in the mid-1920s can be seen as yet another effort to re-invent the intellectual self through literature, this time by fusing Self and Other in the name of Marxist collectivism rather than that of individualism. As such, the self-other dichotomy between the male intellectual and the new female in the early May Fourth fiction signaled both a response to and a symptom of the crisis of the intellectual self in early twentieth-century China.

The Emergence of the New Woman in Print Culture

The cultural milieu in early twentieth-century China, fraught with tensions and confusions, compelled May Fourth intellectuals to seek out feasible means for the reinforcement of their subjectivity. However, their particular choice of the new woman as a tool to fulfill this need must be further explored. What follows is a brief examination of first, the existing cultural market that provided the necessary mechanism and motivation for their narrative practice and, then, the literary precedents that specifically shaped their writings.

The May Fourth project of Chinese modernization was facilitated through the publication of voluminous journals and books. May Fourth intellectuals' privileging of print materials as one of the primary means of propagation was due not only to their shared belief in the supreme power of cultural transformation, but also to the prominent role that print culture played in satisfying the general public curiosity about the mores and modes of modernity. As the material fixtures of modern life had little presence as yet in the daily life of most families in early twentieth-century China, people first turned to textual representations—more readily available than radio, film, and other forms of mass media at the time—as a way of gaining access to modernity. Consequently, a number of large publishing houses became important conduit for the dissemination of modern knowledge, which in turn molded Chinese people's understanding of modernity. The phenomenal success of the Shanghai Commercial Press (Shangwu yingshu guan) presented a good example. In addition to the publication of widely used textbooks for the distribution of modern knowledge, the Commercial Press also launched two well-known "repositories" (*wenku*) to introduce "Western learning": *Dongfang wenku* (Eastern repository, 1923-34) and *Wanyou wenku* (all-comprehensive repository, 1929-34). The *Wanyou* repository alone consisted of two gigantic series containing more than one thousand volumes each. For the category of "Western learning," as opposed to "Chinese learning," the two repositories together included two hundred and fifty titles of translations of "world classics," two hundred titles under the heading of "natural science," and fifty titles listed under "modern problems." The titles covered categories such as philosophy, psychology, sociology, political science, economics, law, education, natural sciences, and various national literatures (Lee, *Shanghai Modern* 55-57).

The involvement of May Fourth intellectuals in such enormous undertakings of cultural modernization seemed obvious. In the preface to the first series (1923) of the two repositories, the chief editor of the Commercial Press, Wang Yunwu, acknowledged help from "friends" such as Cai Yuanpei, Hu Shi, Li Shizeng, Wu Zhihui, and Yang Xingfo, all renowned leaders and activists of the new culture movement (Lee, *Shanghai Modern* 55-57). The circulation figures of May Fourth literature also apparently testified to its wide influence. According to Chen Pingyuan, the twenty-five years from 1902 to 1927 saw the inauguration of some two hundred journals, more than forty times the number of journals published between 1872 and 1897. The most influential May Fourth journals, such as *Xin qingnian* (*New Youth*), *Xiaoshuo yuebao* (*Short Story Monthly*) and *Chuangzao zhoubao* (*Creation Weekly*), each realized large increases in their circulations from 1920-21: *New Youth*'s rose from one thousand to 16,000; *Short Story Monthly*'s from two thousand to ten thousand; and *Creation*'s from three to six thousand ("Xiaoshuo de shumianhua" 224-26).

As for May Fourth fiction, Lu Xun's anthology *Nahan* (*Call to Arms*) was printed thirteen times between August 1923 and 1930, totaling 43,500 copies; his *Panghuang* (*Hesitation*) was printed eight times between August 1926 and January 1930, amounting to 30,000 copies (Chen P., "Xiaoshuo de shumianhua" 226-29). Ba Jin's best-selling novel, *Jia* (*Family*, 1930), first serialized in 246 installments from April 1931 and May 1932, was published as a single-volume edition in 1933, and had gone through as many as ten editions by early 1937 (L. Liu, *Translingual Practice* 219). We do not have definite sales figures for other May Fourth literary works of the time, but according to authors' recollections and contemporary witnesses, Yu Dafu's *Chenlun (Sinking)* sold more than 20,000 copies (Yu, "Jilei ji tici," 326), while *Young Werther's Sorrow*, translated by Guo Moruo, sold more than 40,000 copies between 1922-30 with fourteen reprints (qtd. in L. Liu, *Translingual Practice* 229). At a time when the more widely distributed books sold a little over two thousand copies and most fewer than one thousand (Zhang J. L. 127-28), the popularity of "new" books and journals seems a well-established fact. The wide circulation of May Fourth books and journals indicates that at least a certain group of readers (presumably college and high school students) were eager to receive such writings. Moreover, May Fourth authors became culture authorities through their efforts of disseminating modern knowledge. Lu Xun was regarded as mentor for the youth, and was frequently sought by magazines and newspapers for advice on cultural matters, such as appropriate reading materials for the masses (Lu, "Qinnian bidu shu" 12). Tales of enthusiastic following also abounded. For instance, admiring the neurotic intellectual hero in one of Yu Dafu's stories, young men rushed out to have their suits made of exactly the same material and cut in the same style as that of the hero's (Kuang 28).

Despite the impressive success of May Fourth literature among urban readership, it by no means dominated the book market. Popular literature in fact enjoyed more success among the general audience for at least the first thirty years of the twentieth century (Link 14). *Libai liu (Saturday)* (ed. Wang Dungen, 1914-16, Shanghai), a representative journal of the school of "Mandarin Duck and Butterfly Fiction" (*yuanyang hudie pai xiaoshuo*) had 20,000 subscriptions at its peak (Chen P., "Xiaoshuo de shumianhua" 226). One of the most popular love stories of this genre, *Yuli hun* (Jade pear spirit) by Xu Zhenya (c. 1876-?), was reprinted seven times and sold more than 200,000 copies within a two-year span (Chen P., "Xiaoshuo de shumianhua" 229). Some observers of the time even lamented that of all the fictional works published in Shanghai in the early twentieth century, "eight or nine out of ten are popular love stories" (Yuan J. 250). Just like May Fourth literature, popular culture also circulated the image of the new woman. Through the representation of this figure, both sides offered their vision of and commentary on Chinese modernization. Since May Fourth intellectuals often took the moral high ground by condemning the vulgarity and obsession with entertainment and consumption of popular literature, a sketch of the representation of new woman in popular literature can be very useful. It will serve to illustrate not only *what* May Fourth intellectuals allegedly fought against, but also *to what extent* their discursive practice converged with that of the popular literature in their attempt at producing a radical discourse of Chinese modernity.

Popular culture of early twentieth-century China took advantage of the contemporary cult of the "new," and profited from producing and circulating images of "new women." In most works by popular fiction writers, the new woman represents the two faces of modernity: its power both to seduce and to destroy. Leo Lee has called our attention to the way domestic space was made more accessible to the public through the publication of popular journals in Shanghai in the 1930s and 40s. After an in-depth analysis of *Liangyou huabao* (Good friend pictorial journal), he concludes that "the 'narrative' that can be derived from reading through *Liangyou huabao* is one which revolves around women's new roles in a modern conjugal family, into which are woven other aspects of an evolving style of urban bourgeois life" (*Shanghai Modern* 229). Yet, precisely because "[t]he domestic space of the household [was] now fully, open, 'publicized,' and as such [became] a public issue" (Lee, *Shanghai Modern* 229) in popular culture, male voyeurism and patriarchal oppression were also more effectively masqueraded as the goodwill of finding a proper space for women in order to ensure domestic felicity and cultural advancement. It should come as no surprise that women *outside* the home, a dangerous force inassimilable either to existing social hierarchy or to the discourse of Chinese modernization promoted by popular culture, which was centered on women's proper domestication, were offered up for more blatant forms of voyeuristic consumption and moralistic condemnation.

A case in point is a journal entitled *Nü xuesheng* (Girl student) (starting 1931, Shanghai), edited by the "Butterfly Fiction" writer Bao Tianxiao. Not coincidentally, its inaugural issue enclosed many photos and pictures of women both Chinese and foreign, real and imagined, literary and athletic, and of both noble and common lineage. A perusal of the table of contents yields titles such as "Various Poses from a Girl Student's Daily Life," "The Six Women Athletes of the Shanghai Track and Field Team," "A Queen after the Revolution," "Portrait of Miss Fu Xuewen" (wife to Shao Lizi, one of the founders of the Nationalist Party), "Famous Dames: Portraits of Miss Liu Manqing and Miss Wang Canzhi" (Liu was China's first female explorer, and Wang China's first female pilot and daughter to the Late Qing woman revolutionary Qiu Jin), and "The Goddess of Peace." These images of women extend down to the early childhood and prepuberty, as we encounter pictures entitled "The Kindergarten," "Cartoons on the Eighteen Changes of a Young Girl." In his mission statement, the editor Bao Tianxiao vowed to remedy the situation that "nowadays society is still male-centered, and there are hardly any magazines devoted to women" (1). However, the sole self-proclaimed "Chinese journal for the perusal of young women" turned out to be undermining rather than supporting the endeavors of the various "woman politicians, woman clerks, woman attorneys and judges" (1) whom the editor had claimed to admire. By displaying titillating images of young women and female celebrities, this journal exhibited and trivialized women, belying the lip service Bao paid to the cause of women's emancipation.

Similarly, writers of popular *yanqing* (love story) fiction also plunged into the production and exhibition of modern women, and produced popular romances that ran the gamut of the emotions that the authors harbored for the new woman. Some condemned the destructive influence of modern education on women (e.g., Li Dingyi's *Ziyou du* [The Poison of freedom, 1919?]). Others lamented the tragic fate that befell girl students who received modern education (e.g., Gong Shaoqing's *Nü xuesheng mimi ji* [The Secret tales of a girl student, 1931]). Still others both lauded those girl students who preserved traditional virtues despite their modern education and criticized those who lost their chastity (e.g., *Nü xuesheng zhi baimian guan* [The Many facets of girl students, 1918], edited by Shi Taizhao and others). These tales often proclaimed their intent of didacticism and moral caution, while ensuring entertainment value through the sensational titles and plots, not to mention the surfeit of women's pictures accompanying each story.

Blessed with a robust cultural market but faced with a commercially highly successful rival, modern intellectuals also increased the publication of women's magazines and newspapers. From the 1910s to the 1930s, numerous women's newspapers and journals were published in major cities in China. These included *Funü zazhi* (*Lady's Journal*) (starting in 1915, Shanghai), *Xin funü* (New women) (starting in 1920, Shanghai), *Nübao* (Women's newspaper) (starting in 1909, Shanghai), *Funü shibao* (Women's time) (starting in 1911, Shanghai), *Nüzi shijie* (Women's world) (starting in 1914, Shanghai), *Funü pinglun* (Women's discussion) (starting in 1920, Wuxi), *Funü sheng* (Women's voice) (starting in 1922, Shanghai), *Funü zhoukan* (Women's weekly) (starting in 1924, Beijing), and *Xin nüxing* (New women), to name a few. Moreover, in 1924, only five years after the eruption of the May Fourth Movement, the interest in "the woman question" (*funü wenti*) culminated in a two-volume, ten-section anthology entitled *Zhongguo funü wenti taolun ji* (Anthology of discussions on the Chinese woman question), which was reprinted twice within a decade of its first appearance.

Almost all of the journals controlled by May Fourth intellectuals can be characterized as "culturally critical." That is, contributors to these journals delved into social issues affecting early twentieth-century China, and did not just focus on literary works. A quick study of these journals reveals that the majority of the editorial staff and contributors to the May Fourth women's journals were male, college educated, and supporters of the May Fourth New Culture Movement. This interesting fact, of course, hints at the male sponsorship and male authorization of the women's movement in modern Chinese history. According to Wendy Larson, this was a cross-cultural phenomenon that happened in Greece and India as well: "The pattern of male intellectuals promoting women's rights prevailed in virtually every culture moving toward the modern nation-state form" (*Women and Writing* 20). More importantly, male control of the magazines formed the journals' editorial vision of Chinese women, which in turn influenced the readers' understanding of Chinese women and modernization.

For instance, the inaugural issue of *Xin funü* (New women) contains a mission statement ("Xuanyan") that vows to "reform contemporary society, to make women completely enlightened [*juewu*], so that they can shoulder all major responsibilities in a new society together [with men]" (1). Typically, in this proclamation the editorial staff set up "new women" against women in traditional society: "The reason for naming this journal *New Women* is to make people realize that women in the new society are not like the women of the old society. Women in the new society possess complete personalities, cheerful spirits, and worthy occupations. They are equal to each other, free, independent, and mutually supportive" (1). More tellingly, the editorial staff clearly regarded itself as indispensable to the production of new women. To fulfill its task of "enlightening" women, the staff proposed to accomplish four goals. These were: 1) the elimination of all the thoughts, systems, and customs in society that hinder the new woman's progress; 2) the investigation of approaches and paths that the new woman should adopt; 3) the introduction of the new women's movements and thought from Europe and America for Chinese new women's reference; and 4) the undertaking of research on the current living situations of women in Chinese society to prepare for reforms (1–6).

With a similarly advisory spirit, all the other May Fourth women's journals of the time engaged in discussions of the plight of Chinese women. The more "proactive" male intellectuals promoted women's freedom in choosing their marriage partners, women's right to participate in politics, and women's financial independence; others, reacting more to what they perceived as injustices, condemned the oppression of women in society. During the May Fourth discussion of the woman question in China, the Confucian family came under full attack. When discussing the situation of women and offering solutions, modern intellectuals invariably denounced the "traditional" family and called for its complete destruction. Fu Sinian (1896–1950), the chief editor of one of the most renowned precursor modern journals, *Xin chao* (New tide), labeled the traditional family "the origin of myriad evils" (*wan e zhi yuan*): "Family burden! Family burden! Family burden! Countless heroes have been crushed by this lament" (127). The radical intellectual Chen Duxiu (1879–1942), one of the leaders of the May Fourth Movement and founding members of the Chinese Communist Party, attributed the differences between Western and Eastern civilizations to their different social structures that were determined by the different roles family played in society. He concluded, "The Western society is based on the individual while the Eastern society is based on the family. The various symptoms that speak of the ignominy, lawlessness, cruelty, and weakness of the Eastern countries can all be traced back to this [evil of the traditional family]" (4). It can be seen that Chen's promotion of rebellion against the traditional family was meant, as was the case with so many other May Fourth intellectuals, to eliminate traditions in order to build a more just and prosperous modern China.

May Fourth intellectuals' assaults on the Confucian family were not entirely modernist in nature, since intellectuals promoted individual liberation more as a means to realize national modernization than as an end unto itself. This reveals a Confucian heritage that emphasized an individual's responsibility towards the collective. Moreover, the May Fourth scheme of Chinese modernization often ironically entails the domestication of women in the name of national welfare. The advocacy of "modern motherhood" at one period of the May Fourth Movement is a revealing example (Lieberman 27–34). Even as mothers were extolled for their "happiness and authority" in the education of their children (Feng Z. 1379), the fact that the role of mother was privileged over others demonstrates a move to limit women's mobility.

Furthermore, although May Fourth intellectuals dismissed women who would marry for the sake of financial security as confirmed slaves (Zhang X. 1269–73), some of the most enthusiastically discussed topics in their journals were surprisingly domestic. For example, one topic that ignited heated discussions in 1926 in *Xin nüxing* (New women) turned out to be whether the journal should include recipes to teach women how to make cakes. A distinctly domestic action, making cakes was nonetheless used as a trope to discuss women's education. Sun Fuyuan, for one, derived from this discussion the idea that "education [for women] should be practical," arguing that while teaching how to make cakes should not be an end unto itself, it was certainly better than "aiming too high and offering only impractical suggestions [for women's modern education]" (417). Zhou Zuoren more explicitly voiced his dissatisfaction with the current state of women's education: "Modern women really lack knowledge, let alone practical knowledge [such as making cakes]" (560). Male intellectuals who participated in the discussion certainly manifested a disavowed arrogance and condescension towards women, as was evident in their demand that topics about which they knew very little themselves, such as baking cakes, be included in the curriculum for the education of new women. More revealingly, by in effect requiring Chinese women to learn household chores such as cooking, they betrayed their tacit agreement on the notion that women's proper place should be at home. In arguing that learning how to make cakes would make Chinese women better educated, and hence more qualified members of the modernizing force, they also revealed a rather limited understanding of what modernity entailed for Chinese women. For these intellectuals, cakes, as objects imported from the West, functioned as a form of synecdoche to denote Western modernity. But the fact that male May Fourth intellectuals assigned a domestic image to signify the new women's education not only exposed their inherently traditional view of women's roles, but also broke down the carefully maintained boundary between May Fourth intellectuals and popular authors. Although radical May Fourth intellectuals decried the exploitation of women by writers of popular literature and editors of popular pictorial journals for material gains, they themselves also overlooked women's individual needs and invoked traditional female roles in their discussion of women's liberation, if only for the alleged purpose of promoting their own version of Chinese modernization.

By juxtaposing print materials produced by both the May Fourth group and popular authors, we can see that both male May Fourth intellectuals and male writers of popular literature presumed the right to speak for and dictate to Chinese women. While the former discussed the contribution of women's liberation to Chinese modernization, the latter more often lamented the ruination of traditional values with the emergence of new women. But both groups formulated their conceptualization of Chinese modernity through the deployment of the figure of the Chinese woman. Their allegorical practice of commenting on social changes by representing new women actually elided the particular quandary and interests of the women.

Despite, or, precisely because of this overlap in discursive pattern, May Fourth intellectuals attempted to mask the similarity between their works and popular literature by violently criticizing the latter especially on the grounds of their supposed demeaning treatment of women. This action can be attributed to their deep anxiety about the need to establish their modern identities. When May Fourth writers such as Mao Dun accused popular fiction of "poisoning the people" (qtd. in Mao D., "Zhenyou daibiao" 311), they had two goals. On the one hand, they were trying to exclude an alternative representation of Chinese modernity and therefore establish themselves as the only source of cultural truth. On the other hand, they were hoping to show their complete break from premodern traditions by distancing their works from popular literature, whose "playfulness," according to them, smacked of traditional tastes and hindered the scheme of Chinese modernization through literary modernization. However, May Fourth intellectuals' distinction between tradition and modernity was repeatedly undercut by their own practice.

May Fourth intellectuals often defined modernity as a contrast to and negation of tradition. Thus, not only did they predicate modernity on an unstable *différance*, they also exaggerated the alienness of tradition. All this while they actually often surreptitiously embraced tradition in their discursive practice. For instance, true to the Confucian heritage they had otherwise denied, May Fourth intellectuals often defined themselves as part of a collective cultural force to bring about and maintain profound societal changes through Chinese modernization. As mentioned above, this self-image resurrects the role of Confucian scholar-officials, who had taken it upon themselves to represent the "people" (*min*) and determine the political legitimacy of current regimes (Feuerwerker, *Ideology, Power, Text* 11-14). Furthermore, although May Fourth intellectuals were eager to establish clear-cut dichotomies such as old versus new, and conservative versus revolutionary, such attempts often tended to be undermined by the classical training they had received. Not only did they constantly fall back on a traditional male-centered position on women's nature and roles, their literary productions that represented Chinese women also invoked themes, images, and literary devices that had thrived in and grown out of premodern Chinese literature.

Therefore, a few inferences about the gender politics engaged in by these intellectuals can also be drawn in light of their problematic configuration of tradition and modernity discussed above. As mentioned earlier, May Fourth male intellectuals often positioned traditional womanhood as a category opposed to that of modern womanhood in order to promote women's liberation and Chinese modernization. Their essentialist distinction of traditional and modern Chinese women not only created the myth of traditional women's unrelieved, passive victimization, which has been challenged by recent studies by historians (e.g., Mann and Ko), but also functioned to acquire for them the role of moral and intellectual guardian of new women. With their superior knowledge of Chinese modernity thus established, May Fourth male intellectuals subsumed Chinese women's liberation under the project of national modernization while eliding the individuality of Chinese women they purportedly worked to emancipate. As such, their endorsement of women's appropriate role (e.g., enlightened motherhood) or criticism of women's shortcomings (e.g., feminine emotionalism) must be construed as vehicle not only to promote their scheme of national salvation but also to make possible their performance of a modern masculinity that was ironically based on the traditional model of the Confucian literati-scholars. Such a complex entwining of tradition and modernity, and gender and nationalism, in the construction of masculinity and femininity defies any singular, convenient definitions of "manhood" or "womanhood" in early twentieth-century China. However, it also simultaneously offers up rich opportunities for us to examine the lively performance of and tentative reach for so-called "stable" gender identities.

The narrative representation of the new woman provides just such a valuable venue to explore gender negotiations and definitions supported by a mixture of "traditional" and "modern" praxes. Oftentimes in May Fourth fiction, modern ideologies are juxtaposed with premodern Chinese literary paradigms, while iconoclastic zeal is pitted against nostalgic attachment to fond memories of traditions. Before I examine specific May Fourth literary works, a brief survey of representations of women in premodern Chinese narratives is necessary to reveal the conventions that, though vocally rejected by the authors, had nonetheless shaped the production May Fourth fiction. The representation of Chinese women in narratives written in the classical language, especially in the genre of *lienü zhuan* (Biographies of noted women), the primary means for the representation of women in official history, has been discussed very productively by various scholars (e.g., Raphals), some of whom have also provided insights into the influence it had on May Fourth fiction. Therefore, I will focus my attention on the representation of the "footloose women" in vernacular fiction, the immediate native predecessor to the new woman in May Fourth fiction in terms of both language and characterization.

Footloose Woman as *topoi* in Vernacular Fiction

The figure of the new woman is not entirely a modern innovation, since premodern Chinese vernacular fiction had already produced images of women who wandered outside the Confucian family structure: the "footloose women." They range from high-class courtesans and unlicensed prostitutes to female go-betweens in both the arrangements for illicit affairs and proper marriages—such as matchmakers, Buddhist nuns and Taoist priestesses—to legendary cross-dressers such as Hua Mulan and Zhu Yingtai. These women enjoy partial economic independence, comparatively freer association with the opposite sex, and, on occasion, considerable clout when dabbling in official business. For example, in the *Jin Ping Mei* (*Plum in the Golden Vase*) (c. 1580), matchmakers such as Xue Sao (Auntie Xue) are able to wheel and deal with high officials by taking advantage of the networks they have established with the officials' wives and favorite concubines. Yet, despite occasional examples of subversive texts that challenged the traditional patriarchal norms (Yang 99-152), vernacular works, produced by men and intended for male consumption only, generally attempt a unanimous containment of the footloose women through both themes and narrative devices.

At the thematic level, footloose women are usually portrayed as occupying marginal social positions, and when appropriate, are reabsorbed into the family structure. In premodern literature the majority of drifters are male. The wandering man's Other, the abandoned and waiting woman back home had constituted a time-honored literary *topos* in Chinese literature by the Song dynasty (Samei). By contrast, the wandering woman does not have a male Other who signifies her presence even in her absence. Rather, she often represents an aberration and even a menace in need of containment. With the economic development and the consequent urbanization of the Song (961-1279) and Ming (1368-1644) dynasties, the emergent vernacular fiction featured a group of male wanderers who are adventurous, enterprising, diligent, and frugal, and who enjoy financial success in a big city away from home (e.g., Qin Zhong [Feng M. 4.31-70]). In contrast, in vernacular fiction wandering women (with the possible exception of chaste cross-dressers) are almost always associated with dubious sexual dealings. "Negative" types such as conniving matchmakers and licentious nuns are depicted as avaricious for wealth and sexual gratification obtained through the illicit exchange of material wealth and sexual favors (Feng M. 4.271-97). Even "positive" examples of footloose women—often extolled for their beauty, talent, resourcefulness, and fidelity—are mostly reformed famous courtesans (e.g., Du Shiniang [Feng M. 3.483-99] and Wang Meiniang [Feng M. 4.31-70]) who have worked as sex slaves in the past. There is no shortage of praise for the sexual purity of female cross-dressers who pose as men, of course. However, it is precisely because their sexuality is concealed, and hence contained, that these women are allowed to roam in masculine domains. Furthermore, the very obsession with the masquerading of female sexuality exposes the furtive voyeuristic gaze and desires that female cross-dressers were subject to.

Besides being stigmatized by a sexually risqué reputation, a device of marginalization and control in itself, footloose women are also contained by the structuring of the plot in premodern vernacular stories. In heroic tales, matchmakers who are accused of wrongdoing perish at the avenging hands of male heroes. In happy-ending domestic stories, courtesans give up their trade and cross-dressers their disguise, before marrying into respectable families. The tragic tales, such as that of the courtesan Du Shiniang, of course, depict the bankruptcy of such a self-reform program. Du Shiniang manages to "get out" (*congliang,* literally, following a good man [husband]), only to be resold by her lover and forced to commit suicide. But even her death confirms rather than undermines the notion that *congliang* is the only path to salvation for these sometime *femmes fatales.*

In addition to the plot structure, in premodern vernacular stories authors also employed certain narrative devices to establish a particular narrative contract with their implied audience in order to contain the footloose woman. The realization of this narrative contract first depends on the simulation within the story of a professional storyteller telling the story to his audience (Hanan 1–27). The footloose women in vernacular stories are invariably presented to the reader through an omniscient and impersonal narrator. By citing proverbs, poems, and familiar prefatory stories, this simulated oral storyteller establishes himself both as an authority armed with knowledge to enlighten the less educated masses, and as a fellow member of their society who shares their deeply entrenched likes and dislikes (D. Wang, "Story-telling Context" 133–50). As such, when commenting on the machinations of footloose women, the narrator can always quote numerous well-known proverbs and horror tales to caution the audience against the insidious nature of women's social mobility. In so doing, the narrator not only invokes traditional wisdom to corroborate his narrative, but also consolidates certain cultural stereotypes in an effort to maintain the solidarity between the narrator and the audience.

Authors also resorted to particular narrative techniques to contain footloose women. Most prominent of these are what Keith McMahon calls "interstice" and "recurrence." McMahon observes that in seventeenth-century vernacular Chinese fiction, although the writers were "studiously devoted to illustrating exceptions to the norm and to noting details—minute, obscene, or erotic—that belie the consistency and decorum of the surface" (1), breaches of social norms are countered by formulaic "linkages" that hold the narrative together. He categorizes these devices as two kinds. First, "interstice, a transition between two poles, such as inside and outside, man and woman, nonaction and action, etc. It is the space between two joining things; but, as such a space or emptiness, it is also a bridge or a filler" (18). Under this category he lists certain *topoi*: festivals, windows, or a scene in which a character goes outside to relieve him or herself. Second, "recurrence, [which] refers to a correspondence over a broader range, such as a scene, motif, character type, or word that resonates with another elsewhere in the work, or, in some cases, where there is a semblance of cyclic return" (18).

The device of "recurrence" McMahon has mentioned is similar to Andrew Plaks's notion of "figural density" (*The Four Masterworks* 87), which denotes the parallel of characters, imagery, and *topoi* that helps to unify the narrative. The device of "figural density" is used in the narrative representation of footloose women in order to correct their transgression. For instance, the courtesan in "The Oil Peddler" is restored to the bosom of her long-lost natural parents soon after she is married to the oil peddler. The reinstatement of her as a "respectable woman" (*liangjia funü*) depends on a double restoration: Her attainment of a respectable married name parallels the recovery of her maiden name. As such, her marriage is endorsed by patriarchal blessings while simultaneously perpetuating the patrilineal line; she is said to have produced three sons by this marriage, all of whom enjoy enormous success in the civil service examination. Similarly, interstices can also encumber women's movement in fiction by producing narrative arrest (i.e., nonlinear, usually descriptive segment between major actions). In vernacular stories, interstices often facilitate voyeurism. In the *Jin Ping Mei*, for instance, the opening of a window always solicits a roving eye that witnesses the unfolding of a sexual encounter inside the room. At that point, the narrative comes to a full stop for the audience to better savor every tantalizing detail. With this device, the woman is changed into an exhibition in order to produce vicarious pleasure and/or moralistic preaching.

Briefly stated, pre-twentieth-century vernacular fiction reincarcerates footloose women through the establishment of a male-centered contract between the narrator and the audience. The intention of containment is not only often clearly stated in moralistic commentary, but also manifested in the way the narrator relates the transgression of footloose women. By means of both the plot and narrative devices, the narrator manages to share with the audience the delights of both the women's transgression and his containing of them at narratological as well as thematic levels. The narrative thus achieves balance by absorbing women's temporary aberration of venturing outside home. Footloose women are also strategically presented in vernacular stories to create erotic titillation, righteous indignation, and superior condescension, all of which help to coax the audience into a narrative contract that acknowledges and enhances the narrator's authority.

Images of footloose women also appeared in the immediate predecessors of May Fourth fiction, the late Qing *qianze xiaoshuo* (exposé fiction) and the early Republican popular *yanqing xiaoshuo* (love stories), some of which I have mentioned in a previous section of this chapter. Zeng Pu's (1872-1935) *Nie haihua* (Flowers in a Sea of Sins), a representative work of the exposé fiction, will be particularly examined in this section for its portrayal of a footloose woman with modern flavor; I will use the edition included in *Zhongguo jindai wenxue daxi* (*General Compendium of Early-Modern Chinese Literature*). But first, a brief introduction of the narrative significance of exposé fiction is necessary.

In terms of both themes and narrative forms, exposé fiction appears to be a bridge between May Fourth fiction and pre-twentieth-century vernacular narratives. For example, Wu Woyao (1866–1910), author of *Ershi nian mudu zhi guai xianzhuang* (Strange phenomena witnessed during twenty years), mostly depended on established narratological apparatus for the depiction of modern phenomena. This novel exposes the rampant corruption in the Qing officialdom (*guanchang*) from around 1884 to 1904. It demonstrates the burgeoning of capitalist economy and ideology by contrasting officialdom with the business arena (*shangchang*), and unabashedly endorsing the latter. Although this novel was considered by some as the first work of Chinese fiction to use first-person narration (Dolezelová-Velingerová, "Narrative Modes"), Wu freely borrowed narrative techniques from *Honglou meng* (*Dream of the Red Chamber*) to structure his novel, such as a prefatory frame, a *"xiezi"* (prologue), in which a disillusioned middle-aged man who calls himself "Sili taosheng" (Fleeing death) acquires a manuscript written by somebody named "Jiusi yisheng" (Nine deaths but just one life). Perhaps more importantly, Wu mostly used the first-person narrator, Nine Deaths but just One Life, as a variation of the traditional storyteller. Not only does the first-person narrator in this novel cite the formulaic phrases that are the trademark of the simulated storyteller in premodern vernacular novels, such as *"xiahui fenjie"* ("wait for the explanation in the next chapter"), the novel also emphasizes his function of recording the strange phenomena he witnesses rather than his individual thoughts and feelings.

Like *Ershi nian*, *Nie haihua* also adopts a narrative mixture of the old and new for the portrayal of footloose women. In this novel, the author further added a certain exotic flavor to the depiction of footloose women. Zeng Pu created not just a foreign footloose woman, a female Russian anarchist and would-be assassin of the Russian Tsar Alexander III, but also a Chinese semi-footloose woman, a courtesan-turned-concubine named Caiyun, who uses her feminine wiles in foreign locales. Substituting for her husband's primary wife as his companion on his diplomatic missions abroad, Caiyun learns how to speak English and socializes with high officials and royal families in foreign courts. She clearly outshines and overpowers the purported hero of the novel — her husband, the *zhuangyuan* (top examinee of the national civil service examination) Jin Wenqing, in every aspect. While he appears gullible, she is shrewd; when he falters on social occasions, she dazzles with her beauty and quick wit. Caiyun dominates her husband to such an extent that she eventually brings about his death through her adulterous affair with a German officer. Although echoing the stereotypical *femme fatale* in premodern fiction (McLaren), the image of Caiyun has two distinct new features. First, her husband the Confucian scholar is depicted as coming in a distant second to her competence and confidence in foreign countries. Their relationship reverses the Confucian husband-wife hierarchy and symbolizes the collapse of Confucian order under foreign influence. Second, by demonstrating greater mobility on foreign soil, Caiyun obtains a "modern" veneer. Whereas the *femme fatale* of yesteryear usually used her physical allure and sexual prowess to ensnare and eventually destroy both infatuated men and herself, Caiyun indulges in excessive sex but has the mental capacity to utilize her sexual attractiveness for personal advancement.

However, Zeng Pu explicitly utilized premodern vernacular narrative strategy to contain the footloose woman even as he also invoked the most popular cultural icon of the time, the Western figure of "the Lady of the Camellias," in his portrayal of Caiyun (Y. Hu 41). Not only did he use Caiyun's transgression and the disintegration of the Confucian family order as an allegory of the system malaise of the country, thus echoing old tales of the rise to power of beautiful but evil women as sign of the ruination of the state, but he also reduced Caiyun's individuality, and hence the restriction of her power, by invoking specific techniques prevalent in pre-twentieth-century vernacular stories. For example, Caiyun's name is used in a drinking game at a banquet early in the novel (56–66), even before she appears on the scene, so as to plant clues for future development of the plot, a technique used both by the *Jin Ping Mei* and the *Honglou meng*. In this banquet scene, the guests drink wine and make merry while each reciting a poem that contains a homophone of "caiyun" (meaning "colorful clouds"). Her name appearing as a "play thing" implies her inferior position in a male-dominant environment. Moreover, with each poem the guests quote, the vicissitudes of each character's future life are also foreshadowed (P. Li 154). As Peter Li points out, some of the poems are from *Mudan ting* (*The Peony Pavilion*), a play that tells the story of the death of a lovesick maiden and her resurrection by the supreme power of love. Since in her past life Caiyun had been a courtesan mistreated by a younger Jin Wenqing and now she has been reborn to repay his faithlessness, these poems imply their separation in a previous life and their reunion in this life (P. Li 154). One of the poems cited is a line from the *Honglou meng*, "Colorful clouds are easy to disperse and glass easy to break" (Cao 69–92), foretelling the tragic ending of their relationship (P. Li 156). Caiyun's destructive power over her husband is thus explained by the principle of retribution, and her agency reduced through the revelation that she is only playing out her proper role in an overarching and determinist cosmic order.

In view of the similarity in narrative forms between the exposé fiction and pre-twentieth-century Chinese vernacular fiction, it would appear that May Fourth fiction embodied a dramatic break from its predecessors in formal aspects. However, although vehemently denied by radical intellectuals, the development of May Fourth fiction owed much to its native traditions. Most directly, as Chen Pingyuan has pointed out, the flourishing of print culture since the late Qing privileged the genre of the short story, thus offering May Fourth writers ample opportunities to experiment with the new genre ("Literature High and Low" 220–249). Similarly, Milena Dolezelová-

Velingerová observes that the literary exploration since the late Qing, which led to the appearance of certain "modern" narrative devices in late Qing fiction, also contributed to the narrative innovations in May Fourth fiction ("Narrative Modes").

Perhaps most importantly, May Fourth intellectuals betrayed the commonality of their works with both exposé fiction and premodern vernacular fiction precisely in their utility of narrative innovations to disseminate modern knowledge. Narrative forms and narrative politics are always intertwined with each other. For the expression of radical modern ideologies, May Fourth writers purposely rejected native literary traditions, and imported Western literary genres and narrative conventions, such as diary fiction, epistolary fiction, and first-person narration, to portray the new woman. However, not only did some May Fourth writers also make use of vernacular narrative devices to depict modern phenomena, but even the adoption of Western narrative devices, apparently completely different from conventions of premodern vernacular fiction, reaffirmed rather than disclaimed May Fourth intellectuals' cultural heritage.

Simply put, May Fourth intellectuals borrowed literary devices from Western literature because of their belief that Western nations rose to power through the promotion of special types of literature. This utilitarian view of literature prompted these intellectuals to regard modern Chinese literature as a means to promote modern ideologies. Their project of national modernization through literary modernization demonstrated a Confucian heritage that assigned literature as the vessel of the *Way*, and accentuated the power of literature in transforming people spiritually. Furthermore, male May Fourth intellectuals often resurrected the narrative contract, if not the exact devices, of premodern vernacular fiction. Whereas writers of premodern vernacular stories reassimilated footloose women to establish the solidarity between the author and his audience in a male-dominant society, male May Fourth writers often allegorized and objectified new women to both propagate a variety of political and moral messages and construct viable male identities for themselves. In both literatures male writers designated the author as educator of his audience while depending on the narrative deployment of women as the essential signifier of his power of persuasion. Only in May Fourth fiction, it was a sense of personal and national crises rather than an optimistic view of the innate justice and order of the world that organized the representations of women. Even though the avowed intent that motivated and sustained either narrative contact differed — thus spurring displays of apparently distinctive authorial attitudes towards the same figure — the dynamic relationships between the author, the audience, and the character remained very much the same in both.

In view of the complex and ambiguous relationships of May Fourth literature to premodern Chinese fiction and to contemporary popular fiction, the following chapters in this book will not only "embrace a view of tradition and modernity as 'continuous rather than separate, dialectically related rather than diametrically opposed'" (Denton, General Introduction 4), but also scrutinize the way that the tension between avowed modern attitude and deeply ingrained traditional discursive habits shaped the narrative representation and criticism of new women in May Fourth fiction. Furthermore, I will illustrate that contending ideologies and conflicted loyalties were most dramatically exhibited through the gender-inflected performance of the politics of emotionality in both narratives and discursive literature.

TWO

Books and Mirrors:
Lu Xun and "the Girl Student"

In his 1925 essay, "Lun zheng le yan kan" ("On Looking Facts in the Face"), Lu Xun forcefully stated his view on the nature and function of modern Chinese literature: "Literature is a fiery flame radiant with the national spirit, and simultaneously it is a light illuminating the way along which the spirit of a nation ought to go" (240). However, he remarked, the Chinese had so far produced only "a literature of concealment and deceit under the influence of which the Chinese sank deeper and deeper into a bottomless quagmire" (240-41) because they "never looked life straight in the face [*zhengshi rensheng*]. They had to deceive themselves and dissimulate" (240). In criticizing the existing Chinese literature, Lu Xun actually advocated a particular way of writing and, indeed, of reading literature that would reveal the "fact" and "truth" of life. For Lu Xun, this was an *internal* truth. For it not only revealed what Kant called the "hidden motive powers of human existence or human life" (qtd. in Galik, *The Genesis of Modern Chinese Literary Criticism* 238), but it also both originated from and influenced human psyche: Lu Xun endorsed a modern Chinese literature born out of the author's fearless self-reflection and incisive study of reality, which would in turn facilitate the spiritual awakening of the reader.

In stating the mission of modern Chinese literature as fostering critical self-reflection among the Chinese people, Lu Xun reaffirmed the May Fourth agenda of reforming the Chinese "national character" (*guomin xing*) through the creation of a modern literature. Yet he also in effect defined the role of the modern author as the initiator and organizer of the enlightenment of the masses, and thus established the hierarchical self-other dichotomy prevalent in the literary and critical output of May Fourth writers.

As is revealed in his essay on the nature of modern literature, Lu Xun actually made a claim to both a panoramic view of history and the cultural authority necessary for him to act as the spiritual guardian for the people when declaring that Chinese literature up to that point was one of "deceit and concealment" and advocating the creation of a new literature that would nurture a healthy national spirit. Like many radical May Fourth intellectuals, he held an "aerial" view of the masses; he designated himself as an observer who looked from *above* to dissect the people's spiritual disease. As such, his self-representation was predicated on the "othering" of an inferior Other, namely, the marking off of an Other as beneath and under the power of the Self. However, even as Lu Xun sought to stake his modern identity on the creation of a distinctive Other, this way of self-representation also necessitated self-alienation; he must separate himself from the "unenlightened" masses for the maintenance of this carefully defined and power-generative differentiation of Self and Other, and of the subject and the object of the May Fourth enlightenment project.

When it came to the representation of the new woman, an Other disturbingly similar to the Self, Lu Xun was forced to devise more effective strategies to sustain this self-other dichotomy. He deployed emotions as a mark of not only gender but also modernity in both essays and fiction. In the remaining part of this chapter, I will first outline Lu Xun's position on the role of emotionality in literature, and then focus on his "Shangshi" ("Regret for the Past," 1925), a short story that represents a new woman in the heroine Zijun. Since Lu Xun privileged the revelation of an internal, psychological truth in literature, as mentioned at the beginning of this chapter, his essentialization of emotionalism as an exclusively feminine trait created irresolvable tensions in his conceptualization of the nature and role of new literature. Furthermore, when juxtaposed with his narrative practice in "Regret for the Past," his discussion of emotionality in his essays illustrates the way gender-inflected deployment of emotions generated contradictions even within the same author's experiments with different genres.

I have chosen to focus on "Regret for the Past" to examine Lu Xun's deployment of emotions because it occupies a unique position in May Fourth fiction by representing the archetypal girl student. In this story, Zijun, the heroine, leaves home to "live in sin" with the male intellectual Juansheng, dazzled by modern ideas such as free-choice marriages and women's liberation espoused by him. However, she returns to her family and dies alone as a "ruined" woman after an unemployed Juansheng, under the pressure of financial hardship, declares he no longer loves her. As a fictional counterpart to Lu Xun's famous lecture, "What Happens after Nora Leaves Home" ("Nora zouhou zenmo yang," 1923), "Regret for the Past" creates a Chinese Nora whose tragedy exposes the inadequacy of the May Fourth discourses for resolving the plight of Chinese women. It shows that Chinese women's efforts to achieve independence were not only suppressed by hostile conservative forces, but also hindered by the very modern male intellectuals who had initiated and encouraged women's rebellion against traditions. As is illustrated by Juansheng's example, male intellectuals were unable to live up to their own ideal of demonstrating individualistic courage under adverse circumstances, and in effect became accomplices to a society that destroyed those women who were struggling to break away from the Confucian family.

More importantly, Lu Xun also implicitly criticized May Fourth male writers who similarly "othered" woman for the sake of reifying male subjectivity by revealing the way the male narrator Juansheng manipulates the narration of Zijun's story in order to justify his failings. Although her occupation as student is more implied than stated in the story (e.g., her dress, her place of residency, and her interest in Western literature), the character of Zijun encapsulates the typical role of female intellectuals in the male-dominated May Fourth tradition: that of a girl student. This is because in "Regret for the Past," not only does Juansheng regard Zijun as his devoted pupil, liberated from the patriarchal family by him through his introduction of Western ideas, he also uses her as an indispensable mirror image to contemplate and articulate his own subjectivity. Similarly, male May Fourth writers created the new woman in fiction in order to allegorize their own scheme of national modernization not only for the edification of the people, including their female comrades in the May Fourth Movement, but also for the reinforcement of their own modern identity, often at the expense of objectifying, distorting, and belittling the female subject position.

Lydia Liu rightly credits Lu Xun with the exposure of the deep flaws of the "male-centered discourse of modern love" (*Translingual Practice* 167) through the representation of Juansheng's narrative practice. However, I argue that even as Lu Xun criticized the I-narrator Juansheng's "self-narration [. . .] as an attempted deictic anchoring of the self in the here and now as the narrator guiltily rejects the then and there of his past memories" (L. Liu, *Translingual Practice* 165), his own deployment of this story reveals that he was equally caught in the web of male-centered cultural forces. Like those he had criticized for turning the individual Chinese woman's plight into a national allegory, Lu Xun too ultimately sought to reform the Chinese people's spiritual life, and hence the fulfillment of his public mission of enlightening the masses, through a sacrificial use of the female body in "Regret for the Past." More importantly, the multifaceted narrative form of "Regret for the Past" also undermines Lu Xun's self-proclaimed authorial intention of educating the masses, continuously defying any singular, homogenous interpretation of the story. Using an I-narrator and a retrospective timeframe to accent "regret" and sorrow in Juansheng's psyche, Lu Xun created powerfully engaging emotions that would potentially thwart his attempts at facilitating spiritual awakening even as the same narrative devices also inspired affective identifications. At certain points in the narrative, Lu Xun seemed to be wavering between identifying with and criticizing the male narrator. The particular narrative form of "Regret for the Past" thus both aided and subverted the realization of his avowed authorial intention.

The conflict between the narrative form and authorial intention in "Regret for the Past" can, of course, be traced to the tension between Lu Xun's personal life at the time and his status as an influential May Fourth writer bound by the spirit of public service. Lu Xun chose the format of first-person narration to relate a story that uncomfortably recalled aspects of his personal life in "Regret for the Past," all while trying to disperse public curiosity about his personal affairs and guide his readers to critical self-reflection. It should come as no surprise that he did not always succeed in that mission of enlightenment through the writing of this story. But more importantly, despite his proclamation of his sole objective to be in providing a mirror for his readers with his fiction, this story was also a mirror that revealed Lu Xun's attempt at self-representation. On the one hand, by revealing the problematic in Juansheng's narrative practice, Lu Xun sought to present himself as a modern Chinese writer with an unassailable social conscience and personal courage, who dared to challenge the dominant May Fourth discourse on women's emancipation. On the other, even though Lu Xun wrote under the rubric of exposing social problems, the narrative form adopted in this story betrays the inconsistency inherent in his self-representation.

In view of both the complexity of "Regret for the Past" and his influence in the May Fourth era, it is evident that Lu Xun simultaneously knit together and unraveled the typical May Fourth narrative of the modernization of Chinese women through this story. Therefore, the analysis in this chapter will foreshadow the examination of fictional works by other male writers in the following chapters. Fiction by these male authors either fleshed out precisely the scheme of othering the Other (the new woman), a practice on which Lu Xun had incisively and often acerbically remarked, or shared with Lu Xun similar ambivalence towards this kind of narrative practice. But before analyzing "Regret for the Past," I will first examine the complex treatment of "emotions" in Lu Xun's nonfiction works in order to provide a footnote to both his fiction and the general male literary criticism of women writers of the May Fourth era.

The Performativity of Male Emotions

Although characterizing himself as a writer who "dissected [him]self more mercilessly than [he] did others" (Zuo 142), Lu Xun also manifested an intense aversion to the revelation of his private emotions. He explained his dislike for self-exposure as a resistance to the public viewing and savoring of the personal, and associated it with his goal of enforcing self-reflection among the Chinese people—the same way his revered satanic poets used their poetry to "disrupt people's heart" ("Moluo shili shuo" 71). However, seen in the light of both the May Fourth male intellectuals' dichotomization of tradition and modernity and their criticism of "feminine emotionalism," Lu Xun's distaste for excessive emotions signified a general anxiety about their own modernity shared by radical male intellectuals. This anxiety gave rise to repeated male performances of their modern identity through the marginalization and expulsion of the traditional and the feminine. Furthermore, Lu Xun was a lyrical writer as well as an uncompromising critic. How to draw the line between appropriate and excessive expression of emotions thus became a particularly crucial and challenging task for him.

One strategy Lu Xun adopted was to accentuate the "objective" nature of his writings. He had long been a staunch advocate of "Art for Life" (*wei rensheng de yishu*). Although having never joined the Literary Research Association, the majority of whose members advocated "Art for Life," he is believed to have edited and approved its inaugural declaration drafted by none other than his younger brother Zhou Zuoren. Mao Dun, one of the founders of the Literary Research Association, described the practice of "Art for Life" as "objective observation and unflinching examination of all aspects of society" (qtd. in M. Anderson 33). Similarly, Lu Xun claimed that the goal of all his works was to "reveal the disease [in the people of a pathological society] and draw attention to its treatment" ("Wo zenmo zuoqi xiaoshuo lai" 512). Yet his promotion of an "objective" attitude and of "looking facts straight in the face" played a central role in his self-signification as well as his works to modernize Chinese literature and the Chinese nation. For, by advocating an objective representation of social reality, he also sought to mask the discrepancy between his self-proclaimed modern stance and deep-rooted traditional heritage through an exile of "excessive emotions" to the land of femininity.

Lu Xun fully realized his own precarious position as a link between the old and new culture. He described the dilemma of being "an intermediate object" (*zhongjian wu*) caught between two worlds in a plain verse entitled "Farewell of a Shadow" ("Ying de gaobie"). In this poem, he spoke in the voice of a lamenting shadow: "Yet darkness will swallow me, and light will destroy me" (165). Ironically, it was also in his poetry that the "darkness" of Chinese traditions loomed large, for he demonstrated more proficiency with traditional regulated verse than with modern vernacular poetry (T. A. Hsia 149). In favoring traditional poetic forms, Lu Xun revealed his affinity with the rigid formal requirements of classical Chinese literature that radical May Fourth intellectuals such as Chen Duxiu and Hu Shi had long called for elimination. In using classical verse to "regulate his emotions through rhyme, rhythm, and form" (T. A. Hsia 150), he also confirmed the classical Chinese aesthetics that advocated a constrained expression of emotions. This was the kind of aesthetics that he had denounced in his earlier "On the Satanic Power of Poetry," in which he promoted a new "satanic" poetry—represented by the "stirring" poems written by Romantic poets such as Byron and Shelley—for the revitalization of the spirit of the Chinese people. In order to mask this inconsistency underlying his modern position and legitimize his surreptitious attachment to traditional aesthetics, Lu Xun self-consciously characterized "emotionalism" as a form of traditionality that only belonged to the alien realm of the feminine.

His poem entitled "Wo de shilian" ("My Disappointed Love," 1924) illustrated the way Lu Xun associated the traditional with the feminine through the use of excessive emotions as a barometer. Although written in the vernacular (*baihua*) language and containing a number of modern images, this poem was described by him in its subtitle as written "in imitation of the ancient [style]" (*nigu*) (169) for its apparent adoption of the form of "Sichou shi" ("The Poem of Four Sorrows"), written by Zhang Heng (78–139) of the Eastern Han (23–220) dynasty. Lu Xun later explained that he wrote this poem as a burlesque of the then popular love poems that he dismissed as full of artificial sentiments and effusive expressions such as "aiya, aiyou" ("Wo he Yusi" 166). That Lu Xun should resort to a mixture of traditional and modern forms for the censure of excessive emotions was in itself highly suggestive. But more telling still, excessive emotions were considered by him not only as a sign of "insincerity," and hence traditionality, but also an attribute of "feminine" writings.

Since Lu Xun had defined modern Chinese literature as the author's sincere and courageous dissection of self and others, effusive love poems, labeled "insincere" by him, were clearly denied entry into his version of modernity. But more problematic still, Lu Xun also associated emotionalism with female writings. He explained in a letter to Xu Guangping—then a student of his at Beijing Women's Normal College—that when he said "female/feminine writing" (*nüxing de wenzhang*), he meant more than "the excessive use of [emotive particles such as] 'ai, ya, you'" (Letter no. 10, *Liangdi shu* 40). Rather, he claimed, it referred to a particular style of lyrical essay (*shuqing wen*) in which "women writers use more beautiful words, talk more about scenery, pine more for their families, feel melancholy at the sight of autumn flowers, and burst into tears upon seeing the bright moon, and so forth" (40). Lu Xun's definition of "feminine writing" echoed Liang Qichao's similarly unflattering view of the writings by the "talented women" (*cainü*) of traditional China (see Introduction). Lu Xun also criticized the "feminine" style of May Fourth women writers for the same reason Liang did: that such writings described personal emotions to the exclusion of social reality. Yet by reprimanding women authors for their effusive expression and, hence, insincerity from his privileged position of cultural authority, he actually excluded their writings from the canon of modern literature. In so doing, he also masqueraded his own traditional heritage—his adherence to traditional aesthetics—as a universal standard that would expose the defects of his female Other in order to ensure his own claim to modernity.

Compared to his poetry, Lu Xun contrived this gender-biased designation of emotions in a more complex way in his essays. While he utilized a lyrical style of writing in personal narratives for a direct representation of his modern identity, he adopted an "objective" attitude in essays in which he discussed the issues of women's emancipation. Furthermore, in both cases he performed a "masculine" control of *his* emotions by either instilling heroic forbearance into the image of Self or by advocating unflinching examination of the dire situation of Other.

Lu Xun remained detached almost to the point of cynicism in his "What Happens after Nora Leaves Home," one of the best-known lectures of the May Fourth era, which he delivered on December 26, 1923, at Beijing

Women's Normal College (then called the Beijing Women's Advanced Normal School). Deviating from the usual optimistic view of many May Fourth intellectuals, in this lecture he did not promote Nora, the heroine who leaves home in Ibsen's *A Doll's House*, as a role model for contemporary Chinese women. Instead, Lu Xun painted a rather bleak picture for Chinese women who might have the courage to defy social norms and leave home. He stated that in contemporary China, there could only be two outcomes awaiting a Chinese Nora: "She would either become bad [*duoluo*], or return home" (159). Turning the popular metaphor of a caged bird freed from the cage on its head, he asserted that for a long-imprisoned bird, being released did not guarantee freedom. On the contrary, "there are predators such as eagles and cats waiting outside the cage. If the bird has forgotten how to fly, with its wings paralyzed [by the long imprisonment], it really has no hope to survive [in the outside world]" (159).

In the same lecture, following his diagnosis of the Chinese women's situation, Lu Xun proposed a two-pronged remedy in the same matter-of-fact tone. He apparently believed "economic independence is the most important. At home, there should be equal distributions [of financial resources] between men and women; and in society, there should also be equality between men and women" (161). Yet, curiously, he did not underestimate the usefulness of dreams either. They appear in his lecture as an option other than financial independence: "Dreams are good; otherwise money is important" (160), for "the greatest suffering is to wake up from dreams with nowhere to turn" (159). Many scholars have ascribed such a clear-sighted view on Chinese women's plight and its cure to Lu Xun's incisive analysis of contemporary Chinese society, where gender equality through women's participation in social labor had yet to be realized in any meaningful way. However, his deliberately detached tone also served to validate his modern and masculine identity; for, unlike emotional Chinese women mired down by their own sufferings, he alone seemed to possess the courage and the critical faculty to "look facts straight in the face."

Lu Xun's attempts at consolidating his modern status through the demonstration of a masculine control of personal emotions can be even more clearly illustrated through a juxtaposition of his deployment of emotions in his essays on Chinese women and in his personal narratives. The objective, analytical tone of the lecture "What Happens After Nora Leaves Home" contrasts dramatically with the uncharacteristically lavish description of his own sufferings in his equally well-known "Preface" to *Nahan* (*Call to Arms*), his first anthology of short stories. We can, of course, partly attribute this contrast in tonality to the difference of genres. After all, a public lecture hardly provides a suitable forum for self-revelation, as we normally expect the speaker to self-consciously conceal intimate thoughts and emotions from his or her audience. However, in Lu Xun's case, the "Preface" was no less performative than the lecture. That the personal narratives in both the "Preface" and Lu Xun's later essays were submitted by the author for publication and therefore for public consumption indicates the author's awareness of both his audience and of the ramifications of such descriptions of his emotions. The "Preface" has also always been considered one of the most prominent works in Lu Xun's oeuvre, suggesting that the accentuation of his anguish in this personal narrative well served Lu Xun's purpose of self-signification.

In the "Preface," Lu Xun reminisced about his aborted efforts of facilitating Chinese people's spiritual awakening through the publication of a journal entitled *New Life* (*Xinsheng*) in Japan. He described his keenly felt anguish after the failure of the journal: "this feeling of loneliness grew day by day, coiling about my soul like a huge poisonous snake" (*Selected Stories* 3). He then supposedly plunged into a period of self-enforced silence, using "various means to dull [his] senses" because his loneliness "was causing [him] agony" (4). Since Lu Xun presented this period as a precursor to the explosion of his creativity during the May Fourth period, the years of silence helped to cast him as a *bona fide* modern intellectual. For his past silence, poignantly recalled and integrated into the description of the present, not only distinguished him as an emotive individual whose "loneliness" signified superiority as well as isolation, but also painted him as a heroic figure that both demonstrated stoical forbearance in the face of adversities and eventually overcame formidable social and psychological obstacles to join in the project of literary modernization.

Nevertheless, Lu Xun himself denied any intention of self-signification through his writings. He declared in the same essay that his motives for writing were not for the sake of self-expression, for "[he] no longer feel[s] any great urge to express [him]self" (8). Rather, he claimed, "I sometimes call out, to encourage those fighters who are galloping on in loneliness, so that they do not lose heart" (8). Apparently, his concern for the social effects of his writing determined his style: "This is why I often resort to innuendoes [. . .] I, for my part, did not want to infect with the loneliness I had found so bitter those young who were still dreaming pleasant dreams, just as I had done when young" (8). Lu Xun claimed that he had controlled personal feelings out of pedagogical considerations: that he wished to spare the younger generation the loneliness he had suffered from in the past and to encourage their participation in the new culture movement. He thus characterized his writings as geared towards the needs of others rather than self-indulging outpouring of personal sufferings. In this way, Lu Xun proclaimed not only the moral consciousness underlying his deliberate choice of a more constrained and "objective" style, but also his valuable contribution to the enlightenment of the Chinese people by writing in such a style. The performance of masculinity thus fortified his modern identity.

Such adroit display of both his experience and control of personal emotions from Lu Xun, a writer generally known for his relentless and objective social commentary, was hardly an isolated or insignificant incident in his writing career. For example, at the ebb of the May Fourth Movement in the mid-1920s, he described once again his spiritual sufferings: "The *New Youth* group disbanded. Some obtained official promotions, others retreated, and still others moved forward. I witnessed once again changes among colleagues in the same group [...] I was once again left to wander about in the desert" ("*Zixuan ji zixu*" 456). Furthermore, Lu Xun again used the control of his own misery to signify his modern status. He claimed that in the 1920s he was not allowed to take refuge in silence, for he had been "bestowed with the title 'writer'" and "could not escape the fate of writing desultory words in journals" ("*Zixuan ji* zixu" 456). This statement not only highlights the enormous strain under which he continued his work as a modern writer while being subjected to increased public scrutiny, but, uttered with self-mockery, it also performed his conquest of personal sufferings through the application of irony. At that time Lu Xun occupied an exalted position in the arena of new literature. He was generally revered as one of the most influential leaders of the May Fourth Movement and a "guide to the youth" (*qingnian zhidaozhe*) (Han 3.210). Therefore, his conquest of his emotional agony that was exacerbated by his public visibility would, and did, appear all the more remarkable when this victory was related in an apparently self-deprecatory tone.

From the above analysis, we can see that the apparently distinctive tones of Lu Xun's personal narratives and his more "objective" discursive essays actually both contributed to the same configuration of tradition, modernity, masculinity, and femininity as featured in his poetry. Lu Xun aligned excessive emotions with femininity and traditionality in order to conceal his own resurrection of traditional sensibilities and modes of writing. This male-centered deployment of emotions, when transported into his fiction, created the discrepancy between the narrative effects of his fiction and his proclaimed authorial intentions.

"Regret for the Past"

A sense of futility permeated Lu Xun's second anthology of fiction, *Hesitation* (*Panghuang*), published in the mid-1920s. Compared to his first fiction anthology *Call to Arms*, *Hesitation* mostly portrays intellectuals instead of peasants. Interestingly, the stories in it also adopt a more melancholy tone. This darker mood was both foreshadowed in the quoted lines from Qu Yuan's *Lisao* (Sorrow of Departure) on the frontispiece of the anthology, and echoed by a poem entitled "Ti *Panghuang*" (On *Hesitation*) written by him in 1933. In this poem, Lu Xun described himself as a solitary soldier carrying a spear and wandering aimlessly (*panghuang*) between the "lonely new literary arena [*xin wenyuan*]" and the "peaceful old battlefield [*jiu zhanchang*]" (150) to accentuate his sense of isolation and bleakness. Even though the disquieting sensation of being suspended between two worlds was nothing new to Lu Xun, the particular personal circumstances at the time increased the intensity of his anxiety, thus presenting him with new challenges in his maintenance of a modern and masculine image. With his personal feelings of dejection belying his image of a modern intellectual in possession of rational faculty and stoical forbearance, Lu Xun had to dissimulate his own emotions more than ever. This he attempted through both the narrative forms of his fiction and his own essays that suggested for his readers the "appropriate" ways to read it.

Lu Xun's discursive maneuvering with regard to "Regret for the Past," included in the same anthology *Hesitation*, demonstrates the complex way he negotiated the private and public spheres of his life in the management of his modern identity. As the story delineates a modern romance that recalled aspects of Lu Xun's own life at the time, it naturally caused widespread speculations among his contemporaries. Although Lu Xun denied it, external evidence indicates that the writing of this story had induced intense and not always pleasant emotions in Lu Xun. It was finished on October 21, 1925, and later collected into his anthology, *Hesitation*. Lu Xun was undergoing occupational and psychological crises at the time. Not only was he dismissed from his official position as *qianshi* (section head) of the Ministry of Education on August 14, 1925 due to his support of "riotous" female students of Beijing Women's Normal College, he was also by then romantically involved with one of his female students, Xu Guangping, despite his longstanding arranged marriage (Wang D. H. 324). Highly suggestively, he was very prolific during this period, producing over two hundred short stories, prose essays, and translations between 1924 and 1926, including his collection of literary essays reminiscing about his childhood, *Morning Flowers Plucked at Dusk* (*Zhaohua xishi*); the anthology of prose-verse (*sanwen shi*) *Wild Grass* (*Yecao*); and a number of anthologies of essays such as *Tomb* (*Fen*), *Hot Wind* (*Re feng*), in addition to *Hesitation*. This allows for speculation that Lu Xun was pouring all his pent-up emotions about his personal life into his literary works.

More pertinent to "Regret for the Past" itself, a number of facts concerning the writing and publication of this story show that Lu Xun treated it with more than even his usual degree of circumspection. It was one of the only two stories that he never submitted for publication in a journal before collecting it into an anthology. The other is "The Misanthrope" ("Gudu zhe"), a short story generally regarded as highly autobiographical. "Regret for the Past" was also one of the stories that Lu Xun himself mentioned least. Even though the writing of the eleven stories in *Hesitation* were generally less well-documented by him than the fourteen stories in *Call to Arms*, Lu Xun did usually record in his own diary the date when he finished or sent out a story for publication. Only four of his stories were never mentioned in his diary: "A Happy Family," "Regret for the Past," "Brothers" ("Dixong") and "The Misanthrope." Like "The Misanthrope," "Brothers" was noted for its autobiographical content (Han 3. 33). More interestingly, of all Lu Xun's fiction, "A Happy Family" is the only other story besides "Regret for the Past" that deals with the central theme of romantic love and modern marriage. Lu Xun's reticence concerning "Regret for the Past" thus raises the question whether he deliberately suppressed personal connections to this story because it hit too close to home.

On the rare occasions that Lu Xun discussed "Regret for the Past," he made valiant efforts at concealment and elimination of its personal significance through his essays. Lu Xun characterized "Regret for the Past" as "nonautobiographical" (*Lu Xun shuxin ji* 1.121). His denial of having written an autobiographical work harks back to his customary practice of representing himself as an objective writer who chose to expose social problems rather than indulge in self-pity. However, other than allegedly enabling him to fulfill his public mission of awakening the masses, his painstaking self-effacement was also a means of self-representation. It helped him to keep from public eyes his personal "life that even he could not look straight in the face" (Wang X. "Wufa zhimian" 456–94) for the maintenance of his public image as an incisive and intrepid social commentator.

Lu Xun was aware of the personal implications of his writings. For instance, he admitted that, being the oldest of three brothers in his family, he cast negative characters only as first-born, fourth, or fifth brother, so as to "forestall the poisonous tongues of rumormongers" (Huang R. P. 45; Han 3. 466). More than personal attacks, he was wary of the political ramifications of writing. He pointed out the dire consequences of using real persons as models for one's fiction: "The author would be labeled an 'individualist' [*geren zhuyi*] and regarded as having committed the crime of destroying the 'United Front' [*lianhe zhanxian*], and henceforth would not be able to function in society [*zuoren*, literally, "being a person"]" ("*Chuguan* de 'guan'" 519). It follows that "Regret for the Past," with a plot resonant with Lu Xun's personal dilemma, elicited more strenuous efforts of dissimulation from him even as such efforts created more violent conflicts between the effects and the proclaimed intention of his narration.

In "Regret for the Past," Lu Xun sought to expose the I-narrator's narrative duplicity, thus destabilizing the narrating self and distancing the authorial self from the fictional "I." Despite his best intentions, however, Lu Xun generated two conflicting moods in this piece. His determination to embrace pessimism in order to eliminate uncertainty and achieve closure, called by Wang Hui as his "philosophy of resisting despair" (404–32), accounted for the bleak story he told in "Regret for the Past": For him, to confront reality was to anticipate tragedy. Yet the way he told this story, especially his unique utilization of a first-person narrator, also privileged the pathos of the story over its avowed ethos. On the one hand, Lu Xun exposed the I-narrator, Juansheng's duplicity through both the construction of the plot and the representation of Juansheng's narrative maneuvers in order to deliver criticism of inadequate male modern intellectuals and flawed May Fourth discourses. On the other, with the centralization of the narrator's sorrow, Lu Xun inevitably made him appear in a more sympathetic light. Although it can arguably add to the complexity of Juansheng's character, such a narrative effect also both aided the de-voicing of the woman character, Zijun, and hindered the cultivation of social consciousness and self-reflection in a readership as yet unused to critical interpretation of emotive representations—a fact testified by the many readings of this story at Lu Xun's time or close to it. Leo Lee rightly points out that Lu Xun, a modern Chinese author who employed I-narrators frequently and effectively, in fact often used first person narrative to "avoid revealing himself" (*Voices from the Iron House* 63). In this case, however, the narrative form of the story not only demonstrates Lu Xun's ingenuity at using an individualized voice to express social concerns while concealing himself, it also reveals the inherent contradictions in his act of displaying self-control for the management of his modern identity.

"Regret for the Past" adopts a narrative mode (Frye 33–67) that digresses considerably from Lu Xun's usual style; of all his fiction that represents new women, it alone both features a first person narration and privileges emotions. It adopts the *topos* of an individual looking back on his/her past, and hence the related narrative paraphernalia including an I-narrator, a retrospective timeframe, and an emphasis on psychological delineation.

In some of Lu Xun's stories, he used the figure of the girl student to expose the conservative male characters' hypocrisy (e.g., "Soap" ["Feizao," 1924] and "Master Gao" ["Gao lao fuzi," 1925]), thus turning the new woman into a device of satire rather than presenting a well-rounded picture of her subjectivity. Although "A Happy Family" ("Xingfu de jiating," 1924), like "Regret for the Past," also depicts the new woman and is also told from the perspective of a male modern intellectual, the modes of these two stories remain completely different. Whereas the death of romance is unequivocally and dramatically confirmed by the death of the heroine in "Regret for the Past," in "A Happy Family" it is the everyday unhappiness that gradually erodes the ideal picture of romantic love. "A Happy Family" features a third-person, synchronic narration. The narrative tone of the story is ironic, as "complete objectivity and suppression of all explicit moral judgments" (Frye 40) is scrupulously preserved in order to distance the reader from the object of the author's ridicule. The hero's "power of action" (Frye 33) is tested against ordinary life event through a juxtaposition of quotidian details and his exaggerated vexation and futile efforts to cope, and is subsequently exposed as woefully inadequate. In such a narrative mode, the sense of the absurd rather than that of the tragic comes through more clearly. In contrast, "Regret for the Past" adopts an I-narrator and a retrospective temporal arrangement. The narrator is also represented as more psychologically complex and more lyrical in his expression of sorrow than the hero in "A Happy Family." These narrative features help to reduce the distance between the character and the reader, and to establish a narrative contract of identification rather than alienation.

Therefore, even as Lu Xun partly revealed the narrator's objectification of the new woman, the overall effects of "Regret for the Past" undermined his alleged intention of exposing the moral flaws of the characters in order to foster self-criticism among the Chinese people. Since he attempted at self-representation through alleged participation in the education of the Chinese people, the generation of powerful emotions through a lyrical narration in "Regret for the Past," and hence the hindrance to reader's rational self-reflection, also posed questions to his effectiveness as a modern intellectual. Furthermore, since this story exposed the prevalent male practice of demarcating Self and Other by the degree of emotionality as both artificial and untenable, it also questioned the project of literary modernization anchored in such a practice, undertaken by radical male intellectuals like Lu Xun. Below I first explore the thematic dimension of the story, and then look at the two narrative devices Lu Xun adopted: a frame of reminiscence and an I-narrator who strives for a singular lyrical voice, in order to examine the particular ambiguity and tension represented by this story.

In the plot, Lu Xun exposed the duplicitous narrative practice of the I-narrator, Juansheng. It is shown that he creates an Other in the image of Zijun, his love, by turning her into both his audience and his mirror for the fortification of his subjectivity. Even though their romantic love can be seen as a joint "literal translingual experience" (L. Liu *Translingual Practice* 165) in light of their shared love of translated literature, Juansheng ensures his authority in the relationship, and hence the establishment of a gender hierarchy, by representing himself as the introducer and disseminator of Western literature and Zijun his devoted pupil and worshipper. Not only does he hold forth on the topics of break with tradition, gender equality, women's liberation while Zijun is said to only "nod her head, smiling, her eyes filled with a childlike look of wonder" before their cohabitation (Lu, *Selected Stories* 198); Juansheng also eventually uses Western literature as a facile tool to break up with Zijun, invoking the notion of sincerity while urging her to leave him as courageously as Ibsen's Nora. In an uncanny replay, Zijun is again seen as reduced to silence while "her face turned ashy pale, like a corpse; but in a moment her colour came back, and that childlike looks darted from her eyes" (210). Juansheng thus portrays himself as the determining force in their romantic relationship even as he expresses his remorse for its tragic ending, for he alone possesses the power to provide happiness and cause pain.

Perhaps more importantly than serving as his audience, Zijun also functions as a mirror that both supplies Juansheng with much needed adulation, and hence the enhancement of his self-esteem, and enables him to project his own inadequacy onto her. From the beginning of his relationship with Zijun, Juansheng is paralyzed by his awareness of the hostile social environment against their relationship. He waits for Zijun to come to his hostel, because her uncle has once cursed him for "accosting" Zijun. When walking with Zijun in public, it is also he who recoils from the contemptuous or leering looks of bystanders and must turn to Zijun as a source of courage. She seems to him "quite fearless and completely impervious to all this [public gaze]. She proceeded slowly, as calmly as if there were nobody in sight" (200). When she declares: "I'm my own mistress. None of them has any right to interfere with me" (198), Juansheng is so overcome with joy that he is moved to make a leap of faith from individual experience to nationwide forecast, asserting in ecstatic hyperbole: "Chinese women were not as hopeless as the pessimists made out, and we should see them in the not too distant future in all their glory" (199). What is more important for Juansheng, of course, is not exactly the future of Chinese women or even that of Zijun. Zijun's courage matters to him only in so that it bolsters his own ego: "She was fearless then only because of her love (for me)" (212).

After they move in together, Juansheng continues to use Zijun's expression and behavior as an index of his worth. However, the illusion of Zijun's absolute adoration is harder to maintain when they are living in close quarters. The deterioration of their relationship allegedly originates from his clearer reading of *her* weakness. He is at first vexed by Zijun's dreamy expression when she silently reminisces about their romantic past, supposedly because he does not wish to be reminded of his own shallow posturing at that time but actually more because he is anxious about living up to her romantic impression of him. Later Juansheng feels his wishful placement of Zijun as his worshipper shattered when she becomes completely absorbed in cooking, feeding chickens and her pet dog with no time to "chat, much less to read or go out for walks" (202). He resentfully comments, "I was very conscious, however, that my 'place in the universe,' as Huxley describes it, was only somewhere between the dog and the hens" (206). This marks a turning point in their relationship not only because Juansheng begins to detect the insecurity of his position at the pedestal, but also because in Zijun's ordinariness, he discerns his own. Moreover, while expressing his resentment towards Zijun for stripping away his spontaneous, romantic, and modern façade with her mundane domestic mien, he again reverts to quoting Western literature. This hackneyed practice not only reveals that he clings desperately to his perceived superior knowledge of modernity, but also sheds new light on previous cases when he had cited Western literature to woo Zijun. Was he, after all, twisting the literature he ostensibly revered only for self-serving ends, all while misunderstanding and/or disregarding what those Western writings really signify?

It is perhaps inevitable that Juansheng would project his sense of inadequacy onto Zijun. Zijun's fights with their neighbor over some trifle not only cause her "the look of unhappiness" (206) but also depress him when he ferrets out from her the reason for her grievances. As he has no financial ability to provide a suitable residence for both of them, he can only brood: "People ought to have a home of their own. This was no place to live" (206). When he is dismissed from work, he resents Zijun's reaction more than his boss's action: "What distressed me most was that even Zijun, fearless as she was, had turned pale. Recently she seemed to have grown weaker" (203). Just as Zijun had mirrored his desires of being recognized and idolized before their cohabitation, now she also reflects his fears for his manhood: He is reminded of his own failure to provide for Zijun and realizes his failed ambitions by her waning confidence in him. He counteracts by lashing out and driving her out of his life so that he can avoid facing his own failings looking back at him through her eyes.

When Zijun finally leaves their home, the first reaction Juansheng has is to feel the room "extraordinarily quiet and empty" (211) even before being informed of her departure. The lack of verbal proof of Zijun's absence is very telling. One might argue that according to the logic of the plot, Zijun really has nothing and should have nothing to say here. However, the more salient aspect of her silence lies in the fact that Juansheng can read the material traces of Zijun's existence—"salt, paprika, flour and half a cabbage, with a few dozen coppers"—as a voiceless yet reassuringly persistent declaration of love from her: "These were all our worldly goods, and now she had carefully left all this to me, bidding me without words to use this to eke out my existence a little longer" (211). Yet, even Zijun's perceived last gesture of goodwill proves to be inadequate compensation for the loss of her as the mirror and buttress for his existence.

In discarding Zijun as his sounding board, Juansheng discovers the futility of reciting Western literature. The "quiet" in his room implies the loss of his own voice as well as hers, for Zijun's absence deprives him not only of an audience but also of the object of his vocal interpretation. Furthermore, he feels completely paralyzed after her departure, "I went out now much less than before, sitting or lying in this great void, allowing this deathly quiet to eat away my soul" (211). He is unable to assert his individuality and venture towards all the wondrous locales he had read about in literature and dreamed about during their cohabitation: "high mountains and great oceans below, big buildings and skyscrapers, battlefields, motorcars, thoroughfares, rich men's houses, bright, bustling markets, and the dark night" (210). Whereas the previous entrapment he had felt in cohabitation could be blamed on a hapless scapegoat, Zijun, now he has to turn his gaze upon himself. It is he himself who cannot step into the "new life" that he had envisioned while guiltily wishing for Zijun's death in the past. Without Zijun's presence to bolster his image, Juansheng is slipping into the passive feminine position he had previously willfully assigned to her.

Juansheng's textual approach to Zijun is both his buttress and his downfall. His reading of Western literature only supplies him with a seductively glamorous veneer without offering any concrete means of self-sustenance: His translations are mostly rejected and unprofitable in monetary terms. More importantly, when applying his textual interpretative methodology to their romantic relationship, he invariably misreads Zijun, making her into a silent book and denying a real dialogue between their voices and worldviews. Although claiming to have read her "soberly like a book, body and soul" (201), he actually has not acquired knowledge of Zijun, but rather is unconsciously projecting his own failings throughout their relationship. His willful misreading of Zijun, which handily contributes to his takeover of her subjectivity, may well reflect his similar use of the Western literature that he reads and translates: It helps to present himself in more flattering but no less false colors. But more importantly, she functions more as a mirror that reflects his desire and anxiety rather than as the "book" that presumably provides internal knowledge about her. Therefore, we can see that in his insistence on reading and signifying Zijun, Juansheng also proves that his sense of the Self is in fact predicated on his construction of the Other.

Lu Xun revealed that Juansheng's self is constructed *against* an image of Zijun that he conjures up. In that process, Juansheng assigns all his weakness to Zijun, an alien Other, so that he can more effectively disassociate himself from such weakness. Like Juansheng's narrative construction of Zijun, his exposition of "regret" is yet another device to formulate and consolidate a coherent masculine subject. However, Lu Xun's privileging of Juansheng's emotions through the implementation of a retrospective temporal frame and an I-narrator produced an affective residue that detracted from the stated authorial intention of fostering critical thinking among his readers. First, with the gesture of looking back, the narrator Juansheng can both distance himself from his past guilt and lure readers into an emotional identification with rather than an analytical interpretation of his behavior. For this temporal arrangement grants the narrator effective means to embellish his feelings and thus generating engaging emotions of grief and repentance for the disguise of his moral character. As such, the privileging of *his* rather than her unique psyche provides him with yet another convenient way of establishing his individuality while eliding *hers*.

"Regret for the Past" features a poetic frame that consists of a preface and an epilogue to Juansheng's account of his romantic tragedy. In the opening and ending, Lu Xun gave the narrator ample space to tell beautiful lies, even though he exposed this narrator in the main body of the story. The beginning of Juansheng's reminiscence generates engaging emotions through an evocative and poetic description. It begins with the completion of a circle, as Juansheng moves back to the same hostel he lived in before the ill-fated cohabitation. The sense of lyrical unity is further enhanced as he retouches this familiar locale with poetic nostalgia:

> This shabby room, tucked away in a forgotten corner of the hostel, is so quiet and empty. Time really flies. A whole year has passed since I fell in love with Zijun and thanks to her, escaped from this dead quiet and emptiness. On my return, as ill luck would have it, this was the only room vacant. The broken window with the half dead locust tree and old wisteria outside and square table inside are the same as before. The same too are the mouldering wall and wooden bed beside it. (197)

He uses six "*zheyang*" ("just like this") sequentially to depict his surroundings: the same worn-out small room, the same dilapidated windows, the same half-dead tree and vines outside the window, the same desk in front of the window, the same worn-out wall, and the same shabby bed leaning against the wall. Thus, he not only establishes the rhythm of sameness but also transforms the ordinary scene into a landscape of meditation. Whereas such a beginning already invites the reader to share in the I-narrator's desolation, the ending even more effectively establishes him as an individual struggling against the crushing force of fate.

Juansheng declares at the end of the story:

> Since I am living, I must make a fresh start. The first step is just to describe my remorse and grief, for Zijun's sake as well as for my own. All I can do is to cry. It sounds like a lilt as I mourn for Zijun, burying her in oblivion. I want to forget. For my own sake I don't want to remember the oblivion I gave Zijun for her burial. I must make a fresh start in life. I must hide the truth deep in my wounded heart, and advance silently, taking oblivion and falsehood as my guide. (215)

This ending, as an epilogue to his account of the romantic tragedy, produces mixed effects. On the one hand, it exposes Juansheng's attempt at reinventing himself. After retelling their past, Juansheng envisages hell as a fictional transformative space that would allow him to obtain Zijun's forgiveness: "I wish we really had ghosts and there really were a hell. Then, no matter how the wind of hell roared, I would go to find Zijun, tell her of my remorse and grief, and beg her forgiveness. Otherwise, the poisonous flames of hell would surround me, and fiercely devour my remorse and grief" (215). However, he knows there is no hell, as is revealed by the word "*suowei de*," "so-called," he uses to qualify "hell." This final call for redemption, just as his account of his "regret for the past," signals another move to reconstruct his past in order to usher in a new future.

Nevertheless, even as the ending reveals Juansheng's ulterior motive behind his act of remembering—his wish to describe the past, to contain its effects, and then to forget it, so as to move forward—it also creates a powerful gesture of poignant confession. As such, he emerges from the story not as a common malefactor who repents his past sins, but as a "wounded" romantic hero who rises from the ashes of past failures and moves resolutely towards the future. With the construction of such an image of the self, his use of "oblivion and falsehood" (215) can only be construed as the means that will be unambiguously justified by the end. The discourse time (i.e., the time when the story is told) of the story—which starts with Juansheng's expression of remorse after Zijun's death and ends with his avowal to move forward—in fact simultaneously masks Juansheng's narrative manipulation and aids him to re-signify the events of the story time (i.e., time when the real events happen in the story). In view of both the powerful affect produced by Juansheng's gesture of reminiscence and Lu Xun's contemporary readers' response to "Regret for the Past," we may well argue that Juansheng's mechanisms of othering Zijun could have been revealed more clearly and Lu Xun's didactic intention more successfully realized without the lyrical frame of the story.

More than the accentuation of the narrator's gesture of looking back, the focalization of his voice grants him even more power to silence Zijun through the lyricization and centralization of his own experience. The use of an I-narrator in fiction usually enhances readers' identifications with the narrator, since s/he appears to be the orienting force of the narrative. Moreover, in this particular story, poetic descriptions by the I-narrator prevail over direct representations of characters' speeches, and "sight" is privileged over "hearing," thus more easily allowing him to use his expression of remorse to consolidate his subjectivity rather than exposing his moral defects. Juansheng has to re-organize the past, to "strip the word of others' intentions" (Bakhtin 297), or, to rid his voice of the resonance of Zijun's. He attempts this through the creation of a lyrical univocalism in the retelling of his relationship with Zijun, their cohabitation and separation, and Zijun's eventual death.

As I have mentioned above, Zijun is rarely allowed to speak for herself in Juansheng's narrative. While the sounds made by her heels on the brick pavement are duly indexed by Juansheng to reassure himself of her comforting existence, her voice has to be suppressed, since it has a signifying function that could sabotage his narration. In other words, if told from Zijun's point of view, their story would inevitably take on meanings that he refuses to acknowledge. Consequently, Juansheng feigns amnesia in order to monopolize the right to bestow meanings on the past. He characterizes the days of their courtship not only with the comforting presence of Zijun but also with her convenient silence. He even claims that he has forgotten her response to his proposal: "I can't remember clearly now how I expressed my true, passionate love for her. I did not even see clearly how Zijun reacted at the time. All I know was that she accepted me, although I didn't know what she said, or whether she said anything at all" (199-200). Juansheng's efforts at paraphrasing and silencing Zijun are particularly revealed in the breakup scene that he stages. On that occasion, he finally tells her that he no longer loves her: "You asked me to tell the truth. Yes, we shouldn't be hypocritical. Well, to tell the truth—it's because I don't love you any more!" (209). Upon receiving this blow, Zijun only greets his cruelty with silence: "I was expecting a scene, but all that followed was silence. Her face turned ashy pale, like a corpse; but in a moment her colour came back, and that childlike look darted from her eyes. She looked all around, like a hungry child searching for its kind mother, but only looked into space. Fearfully she avoided my eyes. The sight was more than I could stand" (209-10). In this scene, while Zijun's voice is silenced, her image is invoked not only to convey the sense of tragedy in their confrontation, but more importantly, also to validate Juansheng's subjectivity: he *perceives* the tragedy and is spurred to action, whether by fleeing home at that time or professing remorse later, while she is perceived as immobilized by his act of betrayal.

In addition to the revelation of Juansheng's selfishness, a more important aspect of this scene lies in Juansheng's invocation of Western discourses in order to silence Zijun's voice and to suppress his own guilty conscience. Juansheng's speech is often a parody of the May Fourth discourses of modernity. His courtship has been reinforced by an eloquence originating from his knowledge of the West. In his talk, the foreign, the new, the revolutionary, and the good interweave into a dazzling narrative that help him to seduce Zijun. Moreover, Zijun's death, he reasons, is caused by his "honesty." In the scene of their breakup, Juansheng "deliberately" brings up the past (209). He even quotes the same Western authors he had previously used to seduce Zijun, but this time to issue a break-up declaration: "I spoke of literature, then of foreign authors and their works, of Ibsen's *A Doll's House* and *The Lady from the Sea*. I praised Nora for being strong-minded" (209). When his painstaking "remembering" of their past years rings false, Juansheng invokes the bourgeois idea of individualist, sincere self-expression to deal Zijun the final blow: "Yes, we shouldn't be hypocritical. Well, to tell the truth—it's because I don't love you any more" (209). Under the guise of upholding "sincerity" and "individualism," Juansheng actually reduces his version of "modernity" to an unabashedly social Darwinist message: survival of the fittest at whatever expense to the others.

As I have shown above, in his account of his relationship with Zijun, Juansheng strives for a univocalism by privileging the poetic description of scenes over the representation of direct speeches by Zijun. Lu Xun exposed Juansheng's narrative practice of eliminating other voices for the creation of a coherent narrative of the self by juxtaposing Juansheng's loquacity with Zijun's silence. However, by featuring such an eloquent I-narrator, Lu Xun also granted Juansheng the power to signify his narrative with poetic lyricism while suppressing the voice of Zijun. The use of such an I-narrator potentially allows the narrator's emotional performance rather than the author's alleged rational insights to sway the readers.

By examining the two striking narrative features of the story, its gesture of reminiscence and its lyrical I-narrator, we can see the ambiguity underlying Lu Xun's act of self-representation through fiction writing. On the one hand, he duly exposed Juansheng's elaborate linguistic contortions. By detailing his activity of (mis)reading Zijun throughout the narrative, Lu Xun revealed that the hero's attempts at self-reinvention are both obvious and futile. Since Juansheng is the one who tells the story, it is only his voice that we hear and it is only his voice that shapes his own subjectivity and the chains of causality in his remembering and forgetting the Other. Juansheng's subject-position proves to be only crafted by his false words. Moreover, by exposing Juansheng's egocentrism, Lu Xun also implicitly criticized the May Fourth practice of using women's situations as barometers of the state of the nation. May Fourth intellectuals steered clear of either the cult of women's chastity as a crucial means to preserve "national essence," or the condemnation of "licentious women" as the ruination of the state, two attitudes towards Chinese women often adopted by Confucian moralists. But May Fourth intellectuals' idealistic conceptualization of Chinese women's roles in national modernization produced unexpected side effects. As is shown in this story, the practice of treating Zijun merely as a signifier of women's emancipation and national salvation allows Juansheng to ignore her particular quandary and shirk his responsibility towards her. Therefore, as a fictional rendition of his answer to the question "What Happens after Nora Leaves Home," "Regret for the Past" helped Lu Xun to fulfill his role as a truthful modern writer who relentlessly exposed social problems.

On the other hand, even as Lu Xun detected and disclosed the flaws of modern discourses and their ineffectuality in bringing about Chinese women's emancipation, he also repeated their practice of othering women. Lu Xun allegorized Zijun's tragedy to express his concerns about Chinese women's situation. If he was indeed examining the spiritual pathology of the nation and seeking its treatment, he did so with a sacrificial use of the female body. This move not only enabled his surreptitious identification with other radical male intellectuals, but also fed on their illusion of rebuilding the nationalistic male subject through such a narrative deployment of Chinese women. Furthermore, there is no denying that Lu Xun accentuated male emotions in "Regret for the Past." The first-person narrator, the genre of personal memoir, and the retrospective time frame all help to establish a lyrical mode that generated powerful affect, more so because of its univocalism. It can be argued that Lu Xun depended on the artistic representation of the artifice inherent in Juansheng's narrative in order to expose his duplicity. But even as Lu Xun sabotaged the narrator's performance, he simultaneously demonstrated the utility of an emotive, albeit artificial, narration for the formation of a coherent male subject.

Therefore, "Regret for the Past" is a mirror of many faces. Although Lu Xun both criticized a narrator who relies on the Other as a mirror image for his own subject formation and scrutinized the May Fourth discourses of women's emancipation through the lens of the heroine Zijun's tragedy, he also betrayed his own ambivalence towards the discursive practice of May Fourth intellectuals through his narrative execution. The effects of the narrative forms of "Regret for the Past" not only show Lu Xun's own mixed feelings about the male consciousness in the story due to his personal situation, but also prove that, despite his criticism of "excessive" feminine emotions, he both privileged male emotionality and utilized this practice to marginalize the new woman in the narrative, all for the reinforcement of his own extratextual subjectivity. His narrative manipulation of emotionality in "Regret for the Past" thus embodied the same problematic dichotomization of self-other, masculine-feminine, modern-traditional that he had also featured in his poetry and essays. Ultimately, the contradiction and tension created by Lu Xun's deployment of emotionality expose the suppressed link between the May Fourth project of modernization and the premodern cultural heritage of radical male intellectuals at one particular juncture: the male-centered gaze guiding their creation and utilization of women in literature for the articulation and fortification of male subjectivity.

THREE

From Girl Student to Proletarian Woman: Yu Dafu's Victimized Hero and His Female Other

Yu Dafu's narrative representation of women appeared to digress from the regular fares of May Fourth fiction. Not only did he privilege types of women, such as prostitutes and proletarian women, other than modern female intellectuals, but he also introduced into his fiction the figure of the Japanese woman, an Other alien in both gender and nationality. Yet Yu Dafu's fiction provided invaluable insights into the construction and deployment of the figure of the new woman in May Fourth fiction precisely because of these apparent differences. First, Yu Dafu's choice of different types of women for the constitution of male subjectivity more clearly pointed up the traditionality underlying the apparently modern fictional schema of many radical male intellectuals. Unabashedly resurrecting a premodern male-centered analogy—the loyal and ill-treated male minister with the suffering, more lowly woman—his narrative practice echoed that of his more radical comrades in the construction of women characters as foil for the central, culturally more important male intellectuals. Yu Dafu's use of the figure of Japan in his fiction and personal narratives also both alerts us to the tensions inherent in culture exchanges at a time of increasing nationalist sentiment and signals his own complex maneuver of dual othering—that of the woman and of the foreign—for the sake of male subject formation. Furthermore, his apparent shift from romantic individualism to collectivism in his fiction of the mid-1920s foreshadowed similar practices of his contemporaries a few years later. Indeed, it can be said that Yu Dafu's representation of new women illustrated the vicissitudes of the "translated modernity" (L. Liu 1995) of May Fourth era, not the least because he performed the typical May Fourth configuration of tradition and modernity, and Self and Other with more panache than most of his contemporaries.

Yu Dafu largely brought "notoriety" on himself through a claim of his fiction as self-exposure. In a diametric contrast to Lu Xun's reserve about personal affairs, he boldly declared: "All literary works are the author's autobiographies" ("Wuliu nian" 335). In practice, he apparently modeled all his fictive heroes after himself while assigning them the kind of behavior that caused an outcry of "depravity" at the time: auto-eroticism, voyeurism, fetishism, kleptomania, masochism, and many more. Not only did Yu frequently describe controversial sexual behavior in his fiction, but more importantly, his accentuation of individual psyche also distinguished his fiction from both traditional Chinese "pornographic" literature and the products of his contemporary Literary Research Association. Whereas the members of the Literary Research Association promoted "Art for life" and an objective representation of reality, Yu Dafu centralized the expression of individual male emotions, especially melancholy, to a degree that was almost peerless among his contemporary fiction writers.

We can attribute the distinct style of Yu Dafu's fiction partly to the general trend of the Creation Society, a literary group that apparently opposed the doctrines of Literary Research Association and advocated self-expression of the creative genius. Yet curiously, Yu Dafu was the only member of Creation Society that Lu Xun chose to befriend. Lu Xun described him as the one with the least "creative facade" (*chuangzao lian*) among all members of Creation Society (*Qianji* 3). Whether their friendship suggested that Lu Xun found his alter ego in Yu Dafu is open to discussion, but it will be shown in this chapter that despite the apparently different styles of their works, the two of them converged on at least one point; in the representation of new women, they adopted similar discursive patterns in the construction of this Other while deploying "emotions," both in fiction and extratextually, for a similar purpose of self-representation. But first, a brief sketch of Yu Dafu's fiction on new women is necessary to outline both its innovation and continuity with tradition.

The protagonist in Yu Dafu's early fiction is usually an emaciated male intellectual suffering from acute paranoia. Unlike the male intellectual in Lu Xun's "Regret for the Past," who at least claims to support women's liberation, Yu's victimized hero does not acknowledge any equality or solidarity between himself and the new woman. Even his self-proclaimed sympathy towards prostitutes is self-centered, for he frequently sees his visits to brothels as a form of self-punishment and self-purification. As this hero subconsciously insists on seeing only incompatibility between himself and the Other in order to protect himself against imagined assaults on the self, his attempts at integrating the Other into the formation of a coherent subjectivity are often manifested in a paradoxical way. The women whom the hero encounters intensify rather than alleviate his sense of paranoia and isolation. However, these negative emotions prove essential to his "modern" subjectivity not only because they signify his alienated state, and thus confirming his singularity, but also because they were deployed by Yu Dafu in his attempt at integrating the discourses of individualism and collectivism. For example, in "Sinking" ("Chenlun," 1921), one of Yu Dafu's earliest pieces, not only does the hero imagine himself to be an incarnation of the aloof Taoist recluse of the past, thus linking himself to the classical textual tradition, but he also manages to conjure up a vision of the collective victimization of the Chinese people in which he can take refuge, and thus disguising his personal failures through an invocation of nationalist discourses.

Yu Dafu's invocation of both individualism and collectivism without any noticeable sense of conflict in his early fiction partly explained his change of style in his later fiction on new women. In the mid-1920s, Yu apparently found another way to deploy the new woman for the articulation of male identity. Although he had started with portraying "distant" girl students and "encroaching" prostitutes, both menaces to the hero's fragile ego in the earlier period of his literary career, in 1924 he depicted a proletarian woman who reinforces the hero's subjectivity. Moreover, he changed from an exclusive featuring of the sentimental male psychology to adding more expressions of social concerns and depictions of realistic details. In the short story "Intoxicating Spring Nights" ("Chunfeng chenzui de wanshang," 1924), Yu Dafu described a friendship between the I-narrator, a male writer, and a female worker at a tobacco factory in Shanghai. Although the I-narrator is another incarnation of the quintessential neurotic and disenfranchised male that was the hallmark of Yu Dafu's literary endeavors, the story shows how the female factory worker's integrity and innocence despite all the hardship restore his self-confidence. The changes of theme and narrative style in Yu Dafu's "Intoxicating Spring Nights" testify to the turn towards leftist ideologies and collectivism among May Fourth intellectuals starting in the mid-1920s. But more importantly, a close look at the discursive practices of both his early and later works will reveal that Yu Dafu's advocacy of "individualism," just like his promotion of "collectivism," was from the very beginning an expedient enabling his contrastive positioning of the male intellectual and the new woman in the creation of a signifying configuration that constituted and reinforced the subjectivity of the male writer/character.

The Disenfranchised Hero in "Sinking"

In fiction Yu Dafu had privileged disenfranchised male intellectuals of melancholy disposition *ad nauseam* ever since the publication of his first stories in 1921, an anthology entitled *Sinking*, comprising three short pieces: "Chenlun" (Sinking), "Nanqian" (Migration to the South), and "Yinhuise de si" (Silver-Gray Death). His fiction, particularly the early *Sinking*, always stimulated passionate responses among his contemporaries for its purported autobiographical flavor. Some rhapsodized over Yu's audacious exposure of personal weaknesses and his frontal attack on the hypocrisy of Confucian morality (Guo 93), while others condemned his fiction as "literary prostitution" in which he flaunted his obsessive sexuality in order to attract sensation seekers (Su 386), but both sides based their assessment of Yu Dafu's fiction largely on its perceived autobiographical nature.

Compared to the relatively simplistic readings of Yu Dafu's fiction as autobiography in early years, recent scholars have been paying more attention to Yu's manipulation of narrative forms in the depiction of male psyche. In the particular case of "Sinking," some have noted an ironical dimension of the story, pointing out the discrepancy between the protagonist's self-perception and his true character as is presented to the reader (Egan). Others have remarked that in "Sinking," Yu Dafu self-consciously utilized both Western and Chinese texts in order to dramatize both the alienation of the protagonist and the general disintegration of the moral and religious framework of a Chinese society in transition (Feuerwerker, "Text, Intertext, and the Representation of the Writing Self"; Prusek 110-20). As further testimony to the psychological complexity of this story, still more scholars have sought to explain the troublesome relationship of the male individual to nationalism as portrayed in "Sinking." Kirk Denton interprets the protagonist's psychological turmoil as a reflection of the dilemma of the May Fourth self torn by such conflicting discourses as "iconoclasm, nationalism, universalist cosmopolitanism and a parochial nationalism" ("The Distant Shore" 123). Rey Chow, invoking the distinctive conceptualizations of masochism respectively by Freud and Gilles Deleuze, argues that the hero's submission to "China" is both a submission to a phallic mother and to his own "narcissism," and he is thus "at once active, passive, longing, and resentful—also at once masculine, feminized, and infantile" (*Woman and Chinese Modernity* 144). Also adopting a psychoanalytical framework but emphasizing the historical encounter between Freud and Chinese intellectuals, Jing Tsu points out that the particular kind of "love of the nation" espoused by Yu's hero in stories such as "Endless Night" ("Mangmang ye," 1922) and "Sinking" enabled a partial reconciliation of what a masculine subject must "renounce as a sexual nostalgia [homoeroticism] and what one must accept as its proper substitute [heterosexual love and nationalism]" (310). More recently, Janet Ng even suggests that Yu's fictional, as well as his autobiographical works, should be examined in light of the aesthetics of melodrama—a "gestural system of self-expression"—rather than psychoanalysis.

Taking into account both the narrative complexity of Yu's work and the historical ambiguities central to the collective identity of the May Fourth generation noted by Denton, I will adopt a approach other than the purely psychoanalytical to analyze "Sinking." Yu Dafu's representation of male sexuality was both subsumed under the rubric of vivifying unique individual psyche and deployed for the construction of a modern masculine subject that is both moral and nationalistic. As such, his narrative practice propagated a discourse that the originary Freud theory "neither does nor can authorize" (Tsu 276). Furthermore, in view of both the emotional reception of his fiction at his time and the general practice of othering the new woman among his fellow male intellectuals, Yu Dafu's particular way of incorporating emotions into the process of male subject formation demonstrated one of the most important strategies in the establishment of an authorial modern identity. In what follows I will first examine the way Yu Dafu promoted self-expression in his essays in order to solidify his modern status, and then focus on the narrative deployment of male emotions in his "Sinking." This story is particularly illuminating because through a complex use of the figure of Japan, it not only demonstrates the way male Chinese intellectuals constituted and consolidated a nationalist modern identity through the creation and deployment of a feminized Other, it also reveals the furious negotiations of discourses on different versions of "modernity," such as individualism and nationalism, as well as the negotiations of the contending forces of tradition and modernization at this particular moment of early twentieth-century Chinese history.

A scrutiny of his discursive essays reveals that Yu Dafu often portrayed himself as a "sincere" modern writer who was not only the quintessential Romantic artist but also one with strong moral commitment. In other words, even as he advocated the self-expression of the creative genius, he inevitably justified such an expression with both a proclamation of its faithfulness to "truth" and a tribute to its ethical social function. To be sure, he declared that the subjective nature of every literary work was an unavoidable and, indeed, desirable characteristic of artistic creation, in fact the *raison d'être* of writing ("Wuliu nian" 335). He also summoned up the principle of self-expression to refute criticism of his lack of literary skill (e.g., Su 386). Yet, in contrast to his Western models such as Oscar Wilde, he endorsed the subjective mode of representation on the grounds of its moral "usefulness." For instance, he favored the genre of diary fiction because he considered it particularly effective in not only producing plausible representations of individual emotions ("Riji wenxue" 255) but also in directing readers towards the goal of moral self-improvement by inducing in them powerful affective responses ("Wenyi yu daode" 545–46).

Yu Dafu's incorporation of individualism and collectivism, and subjective modes of representation and their utilization for social purposes was most clearly demonstrated in his comments on his own story "Sinking." One the one hand, he described himself as a veritable artist completely overcome by his own emotions when writing this story: "I just had to write. When somebody suffers, he is bound to call out. How can he mind whether his yelling is a high tune or low tune, or whether it harmonizes with the accompaniment?" ("Chanyu dubai" 466). On the other, he located the source of powerful individual emotions in his nationalist consciousness: "I have lived my lyrical period in a whimsical, cruel, militarist and despotic island empire [Japan], I have seen with my own eyes the drowning (*luchen*) of my own country, I have felt in myself the humiliation of my country [. . .] There was nothing else but sorrow" ("Chanyu dubai" 466). Yu Dafu's combination of individualist self-expression with nationalist impulse in fact constituted a key measure in the formulation of his own modern identity, for it helped him to proclaim his own moral conviction despite the risqué content of his fiction. As a result, not only did his more sympathetic contemporaries believe him to be "a make-believe reprobate but essentially a puritan (*qingjiaotu*)" (Guo 2), but later scholars have also remarked on the way he portrayed vices in order to fight against them and to attempt "a moral purification and an improvement of the character of modern Chinese men" (Galik, *The Genesis of Modern Chinese Literary Criticism* 109). If Yu Dafu's fiction indeed performed such services of self-purification and enlightenment of the people, they were also accomplished through the construction of a male-centered self-other dynamic between the victimized male intellectual and his female/feminized Other. This male gaze can be seen not only in the general arrangement of self and Other in his fiction but also in his unique use of the figure of Japan in "Sinking."

Yu Dafu apparently gloried in the multiplication of his own image in his fiction. His stories depicting a solitary hero away from home, such as "Sinking" and "Migration to the South," were allegedly based on his own experience, physical appearance, and disposition. In "Endless Night" and at least three other stories, he even dubbed the hero Yu Zhifu, a near homonym to his own name. Simultaneous with the apparent reproduction of the authorial self in his fiction, Yu Dafu transformed the female body into a site where an impressive variety of the male self's sexual and psychological "anomalies," most of them allegedly caused by or related to sexual frustration, are exhibited. Despite Yu Dafu's claim of "autobiography," it is unlikely that he himself had suffered from all the indispositions that he afflicted on his male protagonists. In fact, acquaintances often expressed surprise at his outgoing personality, which contrasted dramatically with his various alleged fictional incarnations (Chen X.). I argue that Yu Dafu accentuated the hero's sexual mishaps in order to not only bring about the display and voyeuristic consumption of the female body, but more importantly, also to repeatedly signify the victim status of the male intellectual. To condemn Yu Dafu for his exploitation of woman is both too convenient and too simplistic. A more productive approach by far is to examine how he narratively deployed women to provide a background, indeed a foil, for the action of his hero. Only in his case, the purpose of such a positioning of self and Other was to emphasize precisely the hero's lack of action and power.

Yu Dafu often constituted male subjectivity by assigning opposing roles to the girl student and the woman of "easy virtue" in order to illustrate the severity of the hero's victimization: the girl student to allegorize his spiritual crisis, and the prostitute to signify his material and physical deprivation. Furthermore, Yu Dafu emphasized the way the hero seeks to fortify himself when faced with these menacing female others through the performance of his emotions.

In contrast to his fellow radical intellectuals, Yu Dafu often had his heroes associate more closely with women from the pleasure quarters than with female intellectuals. When describing the hero's sexual failures with women of the night—waitresses, geishas, or prostitutes—Yu Dafu places his hero at the lowest rung of the social hierarchy by revealing both the economic and physical bases of his failure. As a poverty-stricken intellectual who nevertheless yearns for the luxury of life, the hero feels constrained by his less than ideal financial situation. But he harbors another, even more personal insecurity: his own physical strength, as he does not even possess the animal energy that he sees in his downtrodden Other. Some critics have noted Yu Dafu's penchant for reducing women's attraction to an animalistic sexual pull in his fiction (Xiao 396). His hero usually does not desire beauty or intellect, but "fleshiness" in prostitutes, thus transforming his own lacks into qualities desirable in the Other. However, this hero also seeks to fortify his subject position through more active means than transference. Although in some cases he justifies his deliberate choice of the most ugly prostitutes as an act of self-punishment that would allegedly lead to the moral purification of the self, he often emphasizes his "sincere" feelings towards his female Other. Yet, even as he expresses sympathy towards prostitutes, his tears are conjured up more by his imagination than a real understanding of their wretched life. Dismissing them as inarticulate and otherwise intellectually inferior creatures, he seldom bothers to really talk to the women in the brothel, choosing instead to project his imagination onto the female body. As such, not only does his apparent compassion for prostitutes always carry an objectifying or demeaning overtone, but it also proves to be another egocentric practice of corroborating his sensitivity, as self-serving as his frequent indulgence in self-pity.

Compared to his deployment of the figure of the prostitute, Yu Dafu utilized the figure of the girl student for the consolidation of male subject in a more complex way. Similar to his portrayal of prostitutes, the alienness of the girl student to the male self was often accentuated in order to illustrate the hero's acute identity crisis. However, Yu Dafu more emphasized the unattainability of this Other, thus signifying the intensification of the spiritual crisis of the male self by removing his false sense of superiority over the prostitute. Yet, Yu again privileged male emotions to enable the hero's self-reinforcement. This is particularly noticeable in his "Sinking." In this piece, by delineating and dramatizing the hero's psychological agony, Yu Dafu not only constructed a persecuted "individualist" hero but also passed him off as representative of the oppressed Chinese people for the purpose of reinforcing the vulnerable male self through a nationalist bonding with the collective.

Yu Dafu's complex treatment of male emotions—particularly revealed in his invocation of both the discourses of individualism and nationalism—was made possible through his deployment of the Japanese setting in "Sinking." Therefore, rather than regarding Japan only as a foreign background that accentuates the protagonist's alienation (Radtke 89) or symbolizes his multifaceted exile (Denton, "The Distant Shore" 110), I will look closely at the way it is configured both into the protagonist's attempts at self-invention through various literary transactions in the story and into the author's own narrative maneuvers.

The events narrated in "Sinking" unfold in Japan. The protagonist, a twenty-one-year-old Chinese exchange student, appearing only as a nameless "he" in the story, suffers from "hypochondria" (quoted in the original English within the story), a condition in this case brought on by compulsive masturbation that provokes extreme anxiety about the possible weakening of his physical and mental constitution. Moreover, he is also apparently afflicted with a persecution complex that alienates him from both his Japanese classmates and his fellow countrymen. Unable to bear the resulting isolation and misery, the protagonist is driven to visit a brothel in the city, gets drunk, and eventually goes to the seaside to contemplate suicide, where he utters a passionate prayer for national prosperity at the conclusion of the story.

One of the most striking features of "Sinking" lies in the alternation of description of the protagonist's external world with the portrayal of his ever-shifting psychological state that accompanies his quest for a stable identity that would alleviate his misery. Furthermore, these changes in his psychological state are marked and articulated by a series of literary citations and fabrications. "Sinking" begins with a description of the protagonist's solitary state: "Lately he had been feeling pitifully lonesome" ("Sinking" 125). Yet as the story progresses, the reader cannot help noticing that this "loneliness" is largely self-induced. For one so constantly beset by self-doubt, the protagonist demonstrates surprising resolution in his decisive isolation from others. He rejects the innocuous overtures of everyone around him: both those of his Japanese classmates and his Chinese compatriots, both those of mere acquaintances and even those of his own older brother. Finally, he moves into a remote cottage in a grove of plum trees, imagining this relocation will make him into "a sage or hermit," able to address any Japanese peasant he might happen to meet in the mountains with an eloquence worthy of Nietzsche's Zarathustra (127).

The protagonist's passionate, albeit rather spurious, renunciation of the world is caused to some extent by the paranoia and sense of alienation arising from his exile in a strange land, but, more importantly, it also exposes his efforts of reinventing himself. Unlike a romantic Western hero along the lines of Goethe's Werther, he possesses neither their driving ambition nor their strong will to defy society. And unlike the traditional Taoist recluse of premodern Chinese literature, he lacks an amused detachment from the world. What he can claim as his unique quality is "[his] emotional precocity [that] had placed him at constant odds with his fellow men" (125). In this light, the protagonist's addiction to the "infinite sweetness in chewing the cud of bitter sorrow" (136) exposes his particular brand of excessive self-regard, a view of himself that arises from his need to reaffirm and constantly perform an emotional refinement and sensitivity that places him apart from and above the vulgar, unfeeling external world that is Japan. Furthermore, such a self-image represents an attempt to realize the imaginary romantic world he has internalized through his reading of Western literature. As such, the proclamation of his solitude actually marks his attempt at portraying himself as an independent individual through the medium of his idiosyncratic understanding of literary models.

In "Sinking," the protagonist demonstrates his "sensitivity" in two related areas: his communion with nature and his literary sensibility. In the ideal scheme of things, the purportedly inseparable pair of nature and literature should nurture his inner spirit while elevating his experience of his external world to aesthetic or spiritual heights, thus proving him a true individualist, living self-sufficiently in a world of beauty and truth. However, his attempts at creating an individualistic identity through the preservation of solitude are repeatedly undermined. In "Sinking," the protagonist's aesthetic appreciation of nature and literature is constantly interrupted by the intrusion of his own sexuality. For instance, while reading a novel by George Gissing in the inn where he lodges, he hears the sound of splashing water, which he traces to the bathroom, where he finds (and watches in voyeuristic rapture) the landlord's daughter taking a bath. Although at certain point in the story human sexuality is construed as an integral part of the natural world (132), sexuality as "embodied" human nature often comes into direct conflict with a disembodied literature, and complicates the protagonist's attempts at forming a coherent image of himself through the blending of the two.

The most telling example of how this conflict between "nature" and literature erodes the hero's sense of self-worth occurs during one of his solitary strolls in the mountains. After quarreling bitterly with everybody, including his older brother, the protagonist is apparently finally able to find solace in a "textualized" nature: "The scene reminded him of a rural painting by Millet. Faced with the magnificence of Nature, he felt like an early Christian of Jesus' time" (137), and he magnanimously declares to the whole world his forgiveness of human folly. But, just when he is "contemplating — with a book of poems in hand and tears in eyes — the beauty of the autumnal scene and thus getting lost in thought" (137), he overhears two people making love in the tall grass beside him. This immediately makes him "prostrate himself on the ground, as stealthily as a dog with a stolen morsel in its mouth" in an effort to hear every sound (137). The protagonist's alarmingly swift transformation from a high-minded poet to slavering beast not only belies the thinness of his veneer of culture, but also reveals the ambiguous role played by nature in "Sinking." For, even as it inspires the protagonist's poetic imagination, it apparently also reduces him to a slave to his own sexual desires. These compulsions of "nature" perhaps represent a subtle form of self-justification on the part of the protagonist for his repeated failures, but they also confound his quest for a stable identity, and, consequently, spur his even more frantic literary imagination and invention of the self.

The defeat of Western literature by "natural" instincts, and the resultant collapse of his romanticized solitude, leads the protagonist on an increasingly frenzied search for other means to retrieve his sense of self-worth. It is at this point that the body of the Japanese woman, a fortuitous meeting ground for gender and nationalist politics, provides him with an opportunity to regain his lost sense of superiority through the invocation of nationalist discourse. Specifically, the protagonist places the female and Japanese

Other in an antagonistic opposition to his own self, a strategy that enables him to both gloss over his personal weaknesses and to play the role of literary talent that he continually asserts to be one of the anchors of his identity.

That the protagonist chooses literary means to incorporate a feminine Other into the enforcement of his subjectivity comes as no surprise to the reader. Earlier in the story we are told that he has a habit of seeking out literary precedents to justify his masturbation (132). He also has a history of inventing his own identity through fiction writing. For instance, as a teen-aged dropout, he often portrayed himself in his own fiction as a chivalrous knight who rescued damsels in distress and translated these stories into foreign languages for his own amusement (129). Such incidents reveal that in order to constitute a more desirable identity for himself, the protagonist often positions himself *vis-à-vis* a female Other in his writings that are inspired by the foreign literature in which he immersed himself. The objectifying use of female body for male subject formation takes on new literary forms when he goes to the lonely island of Japan. Living alone in his reclusive cottage in Japan, he would imagine hearing "a soft voice" speak to him from the sky, offering him both infinite comfort and the confirmation of his status as "indeed the most miserable of all men" (136). Yet, setting out to locate a corporeal manifestation of this imagined feminine voice of sympathy in the world of the "contemptuous" Japanese, he is repeatedly forced to take refuge in his literary imagination.

Indeed, the protagonist's fragile sense of self—more than his "metaphysical need" to end his isolation from the human community (Denton, "The Distant Shore" 113)—leads to his various imaginative and interpretive activities for the creation of a feminized "embodiment" of his desire for sympathy and recognition. His need for self-validation increases even more as he is often reduced to speechless agony on encountering an attractive, "respectable" Japanese woman. Such an episode occurs when he is a student in the city of N and meets two girl students by chance. His own painful silence at that chance meeting prompts his passionate prayer in diary for an understanding female companion, for "one beautiful woman who understands [his] suffering" (128). He claims: "O ye Heavens above, I want neither knowledge nor fame nor useless lucre. I shall be wholly content if you can grant me an Eve from the Garden of Eden, allowing me to possess her body and soul" (128). It is not surprising that the protagonist desires an understanding woman to be the anchor and reinforcement of the subjectivity he so obsessively desires to maintain. Moreover, he desires that his ideal woman be the "congruence of affection and sensuality" (Chow, *Woman and Chinese Modernity* 142), whom he can possess "body and soul." This proves to be an impossible dream. Rey Chow suggests that the hero's quest for such an ideal woman is doomed by what Freud described as the inevitable split of male libidinal investment: men divide women into either those that they revere or those that they feel excited about but degrade (*Woman and Chinese Modernity* 138). But even disregarding the limited heterosexist perspective underlying the Freudian scheme, I argue that a more obvious feature of the hero's failure is that he can find satisfaction with neither the more intellectual/respectable nor the more sensual/degraded women. In fact, not only does he fear the (imagined) mockery of the Japanese girl student, he is also *only* able to contrive the degradation of his more sensuous Japanese and female Other through the exercise of his literary imagination. As such, the hero's troubled relationships with women have their roots not so much in the irreconcilability of his affection and his erotic desire as in his sense of complete powerlessness. He seeks to overcome this sense of absolute abjection through the privileging of his own psyche, again citing literary precedents.

The hero's attempts at distinguishing himself from his fellow human beings by emphasizing his own unique emotional sensitivity sets up a telling contrast with his practice of reducing Japanese women to an anonymous, sexualized body. In this respect, perhaps most suggestive is his use of the biblical name Eve in his diary, a generic title for the quintessential female, as exotic as it is non-Japanese. Throughout "Sinking," the protagonist never deigns to give names to any of the Japanese women he meets. Even the landlord's daughter, whom he privately considers to be the only thing preventing him from committing suicide, is to remain nameless in the narrative. In fact, he mentally refers to her as "Eve" as well in the infamous voyeur passage. To be sure, the protagonist himself likewise remains unnamed in the narrative. However, it is the privileged status of his voice within the story that renders this absence of name a sign of power by conveying a subjectivity that the reader is invited or perhaps even compelled to take on as his or her own, if only for a short time.

In contrast to the dismissive attitude he displays towards the names of Japanese women, he shows an absorbing interest in their bodies. It is their body that provides him with a site for the constitution of his desired subjectivity through gender and political negotiations. In "Sinking," he is described as succumbing to the naked bodies of "the descendants of Eve" that materialize in his imagination, and he abandons himself to the resulting bouts of masturbation that he fears endanger his mental and physical health (132). Therefore, it would seem that the actual body of the Japanese woman could function as an object of desire, an Other that could not only divert him from his self-destructive desire for his own body but also expedite his quest for an (unattainable) subject position. In fact, the body of the female and Japanese Other, created and frequently invoked by his imagination, is more than sufficient for that task. It provokes both intense voyeuristic pleasure and an acute sense of shame, thus producing for the hero a mutually reinforcing interaction of heterosexual and moral consciousness. On the one hand, he confesses to become excited at the merest hint of the Japanese women's bodily presence: the scent they wear, the pink hem of their petticoats, a hazy shape in the foggy bathroom, a sound of lovemaking from somewhere in the grass. We are told that on these occasions he immediately metamorphoses into an "animal," at once titillated and frustrated almost to the brink of insanity. After each brief yet powerfully imagined encounter, the protagonist vehemently curses his own immorality and lack of shame in long monologues, sometimes even adding physical violence to verbal. In so doing, he is able to not only indulge his "baser nature" but also to maintain the illusion of his high sense of morality by performing his virtue and sincerity through repentance for his transgressions.

Not only does the figure of the Japanese woman provide a boost to the formation of his subjectivity by offering up a heady mixture of voyeuristic and masochistic pleasures, but it also equips the protagonist with a ready tool for the formation of modern male subjectivity in the invocation of nationalist discourse. According to him, "The Japanese look down upon Chinese just as we look down upon pigs and dogs. They call us *Shinajin*, 'Chinamen,' a term more derogatory than 'knave' in Chinese" (139). Although the reader sees little internal evidence to support this purportedly overwhelming racial hostility, the protagonist nevertheless uses it to justify his tongue-tied awkwardness in front of the Japanese waitress in the brothel (139). He even interprets the siren call of a Japanese prostitute as a challenge to his manhood and silently declares war on the simultaneously attractive and menacing presence of female temptation (139).

It can be seen that in addition to enabling him to blame his romantic failures on national conflicts, the imagined body of the Japanese woman also helps him to secure his own share in the collective victimization of the Chinese people and hence the (imagined) national solidarity that offers him another possible anchorage for his identity. His masochistic enjoyment of his own suffering derives, in no small part, from his creation of these imaginary slights by Japanese women, whom he believes to favor Japanese men above Chinese nationals like himself (128). Such paranoid and self-centered ideation produces enough emotional force for him to both disguise his sense of inadequacy as nationalist outrage and to distinguish himself yet again as the most wretched human being in the world. It provides him with a gratifying sense of power by elevating his personal experience to the level of a representation of national history and also renews his belief in his own sensitive nature and moral rectitude. His final call for national solidarity before his hinted suicide attempt must be construed in the same light. As we are told, he "stood still and uttered a long sigh. And then he said, between pauses: 'O China, my China, you are the cause of my death!...I wish you could become rich and strong soon!...Many, many of your children are still suffering'" (141). Rather than expressing a genuine appeal for China's prosperity, his last words more serve as a tool to both deflect attention from his own weakness and, more importantly, to give meaning to his life and anticipated death. The protagonist's practice of formulating male identity through literary performance is mirrored in Yu Dafu's narrative practices in "Sinking." This is particularly clear in the way the author organized allusions to various texts in an effort to articulate and reinforce his own male subjectivity extratextually.

Scholars have considered Yu Dafu's long, untranslated quotations of Western literature in "Sinking" to be either examples of the hero's affectation, faithful to the historical register of the transition period (Egan 320), or to be the reflection of a fragmented and incoherent subject (Radtke 95). But a more important dimension of Yu Dafu's citation of Western literary works in "Sinking," so far ignored by the scholars, is the way it enabled him to elide Japanese cultural influences. By Yu Dafu's own admission, while an exchange student in Japan he had been an avid reader of Japanese "I"-novels (*watakushi shosetsu*) and works by Japanese naturalist writers, the novelist Sato Haruo being his favorite of the contemporary Japanese writers ("Haishang tongxin" 185–86). Many critics have in fact noted the similarity between Yu Dafu's "Sinking" and Sato Haruo's *The Pastoral Melancholy* (*Den'en no yûutsu*, 1918) (Kumagaya, "Japanese Influences"; Kumagaya, "Quest for Truth"). Some even claim that the "relative closeness to the Japanese taste" of "Sinking" has made it quite well known in Japan (Radtke 88). Therefore, the omission of any references to or citations from Japanese literary works in "Sinking" more than illustrates what some describes as "the circuitous way of cultural transmission" (Radtke 94) demonstrated in the enthusiasm for Western literature of the Chinese exchange students of Yu Dafu's generation, who learned English and German in Japan in order to read European and American literatures in the original. It also reveals Yu Dafu's awareness of nationalist politics, which motivated his deployment of cited texts. Just as the protagonist utilizes the body of his female and Japanese Other to perform his modern identity, the author Yu Dafu also "others" Japan in "Sinking" through omission in order to enable his own performance as a modern nationalist male subject.

Yu Dafu's practice of consolidating his own modern status through the invocation of nationalism is perhaps more explicitly performed in his allegedly authentic autobiographical writings. In his "Xueye" (Snowy night, 1936), an essay he described as "one chapter of my autobiography," he again transformed the personal into the political through a performative accentuation of his emotions. In this essay, he implied that the hero's sudden outburst of nationalist sentiment at the end of "Sinking" arose from his own experience as a young student in Japan. Yu Dafu claimed that his experience in Japan had fostered his consciousness of a bifurcated identity: as a Chinese and as a young man. But he blamed his sexual frustrations not on any inadequacy of his masculinity, but solely on his Chinese nationality: "I felt most keenly and most unbearably the inequality between nations, and the humiliation and indignity of oppressed people from a weak nation, the moment Cupid's arrow struck" (58). He then elaborated on this by stating that he had traumatic experience while socializing with Japanese "girls from good families" at parks in Tokyo (59). According to him, the moment he admitted he was Chinese, Japanese women's attitude towards him immediately changed: "The word 'China' [*Zhina*] or 'Chinese' [*Zhina ren*], when uttered by young Japanese girls, aroused such feelings of humiliation, despair, indignation and pain, that Chinese compatriots who have never been to Japan cannot even imagine" (59–60). Whether racial hostility and prejudice from the Japanese can be held fully responsible for his personal problems is open to discussion, but Yu Dafu undoubtedly presented himself more as a victim of international politics than as a weak man with personal failings in his personal narratives. Furthermore, by a vivid representation of his emotions of humiliation on behalf of his nation, he simultaneously performed his "individualist" and "nationalist" identity and also sought to solicit equally passionate responses and a nationalist bonding from his readers.

From the above analysis of both his fiction and memoirs, we can see that Yu Dafu's various narrative maneuvers to isolate the woman as an alien force served to reconcile his promotions of individualist self-exposure and nationalist collectivism. He not only strategically aligned the girl student and the prostitute with different aspects of the hero's identity crisis—a device that was to be further developed in his later representation of women—but also attributed the hero's spiritual and physical lacking to the weakness of the nation, thus transforming individual male experience into a national allegory. The creation of a persecuted hero served a double purpose. On the one hand, as representative of the wronged Chinese people, this figure can be deployed to protest national humiliation and prick the reader's social conscience. On the other hand, the author found release and a sense of security in placing this solitary hero among the legions of the abused Chinese people. Indeed, Yu Dafu flouted social conventions to expose the hero's weakness, but he also invoked nationalist slogan to justify such a transgression. As such, he pivoted the construction of both his fictional and autobiographical self on the representation of the "topologies" of a trouble-ridden nation.

Yu Dafu's narrative strategy of connecting an individualistic hero with the collective national fate reveals the fusion of the individual and the collective in May Fourth fiction. His deployment of new women in the service of male subject formation also echoes the scheme of othering the new woman prevalent in this body of literature. At first sight, Yu Dafu's depiction of woman seemed to produce a somewhat ironic twist on the typical May Fourth fare. May Fourth writers generally did not privilege the figure of the prostitute in fiction (though prostitutes are the oldest kind of footloose women) mostly because they wished to construct more positive role models in new types such as students and revolutionaries to promote their project of Chinese modernization. The distinctive treatments of the prostitute and the girl student in Yu Dafu's early fiction hint at his ambivalence towards modernity and tradition, for his hero often finds traditions reassuring and modernity terrifying. One the one hand, this hero is often depicted as feeling more at ease with prostitutes, who are less threatening to him because of the familiarity and conventionality of their trade as well as their lower social status. By contrast, he becomes speechless when confronted by the girl student, who is not only a new social phenomenon, but also presumably possesses the kind of knowledge and social status more on a par with those of the male intellectual.

However, Yu Dafu's fiction and essays also reaffirm the self-other relationship typical in May Fourth literature. The less congenial attitude towards the girl student displayed by Yu's hero merely originates from a male subject even weaker than Juansheng from Lu Xun's "Regret for the Past," who at least smugly entertains the knowledge of his own mastery of Western discourses. Yu's hero, on the other hand, experiences more acute insecurity when his superiority is threatened by his perception, rightly or wrongly, of a new Other on equal footing with him or even superior in social status (in the case of the Japanese girl student). This mindset not only explains the hero's paranoia, but also illuminates his efforts to isolate, and thus to contain, this imagined menace to his subjectivity by vivifying the male subject's emotions while denying similar representations of his female Other. Therefore, it can be said that the hero's increasing sense of crisis dictates a changed strategy for integrating the Other into his subjectivity. Of course, this sense of crisis was also cultivated and dramatized by Yu Dafu to reinforce the male subjectivity. Juxtaposed with Yu Dafu's critical essays, the "autobiographical" exposure of male paranoia in his fiction proves to be a painstakingly contrived tale about the emotive male self the construction of which aims to unite the hero with his national group and the author with his comrades in the May Fourth New Culture Movement. In identifying the hero as representative of the persecuted Chinese people, Yu Dafu eventually turned his gaze towards the national fate. As such, Yu's seemingly daring portrayal of male sexuality was belied by his invocation of nationalism as well as the Western theory of Romanticism in order to justify his iconoclasm.

Yu Dafu's tendency to "collectivize" the individual and to exploit the representation of women for purposes of male subject formation in narratives partly anticipated his short story "Intoxicating Spring Nights" written in 1924, a piece that, at first glance, may seem very different from his early fictional works.

Venture into "Revolutionary Literature": "Intoxicating Spring Nights"

In view of Yu Dafu's earlier literary endeavors that invoked the discourse of nationalism for the construction of male subjectivity, it should perhaps come as no surprise that he made even more conspicuous moves to collectivism amidst the increasing radicalization of intellectuals starting in the mid-1920s (Galik, *The Genesis of Modern Chinese Literary Criticism* 104–28). Published in 1924, his "Intoxicating Spring Nights" is one of the earliest representations of the Chinese urban proletariat in May Fourth fiction. It is also one of the few pieces in Yu Dafu's oeuvre that he acknowledged as "having a little socialist color" ("*Dafu zixuan ji* xu" 836). Yu Dafu devoted the majority of his attention and literary skill to the portrayal of the male intellectual's interactions with prostitutes, actresses, and to a lesser extent, girl students, in the early years of the May Fourth period. Therefore, "Intoxicating Spring Nights" enjoys a unique status in Yu Dafu's works, since in this story, Yu Dafu has apparently switched his focus to a different type of new woman. Moreover, the proletarian woman in the story was created with different narrative devices, and the story was narrated in a more constrained tone. Seen in a historical perspective, Yu Dafu's alterations of narrative forms in this story heralded a crucial turn towards leftist ideologies made by many May Fourth writers, such as Ding Ling, in the late 1920s and early 1930s.

Although the debate on "Revolutionary Literature" per se occurred only after the split between the Nationalists and the Communists in 1927, calls for class-conscious literature had emerged earlier, first coming, perhaps rather unexpectedly, from Yu Dafu's fellow Romantic Creationists such as Guo Moruo and Cheng Fangwu. In fact, the title of Cheng Fangwu's essay "From Literary Revolution to Revolutionary Literature" became something of a banner slogan around which young radicals rallied, purportedly to overcome the "limits" of the May Fourth literature of early years. For instance, Qian Xingcun, a young member of the radical Sun Society, openly attacked Lu Xun, declaring, "The present age is not one that can be represented by a writer without political ideology. The age of Ah Q died long ago!" ("The Bygone Age of Ah Q" 287). His colleague Jiang Guangci more definitively outlined the characteristics of Revolutionary Literature: "Revolutionary Literature must be an anti-individualist literature, its heroes must be the masses, not individuals; it must be directed not toward individualism, but toward collectivism. The duty of revolutionary literature is to show in this life struggle the power of the masses, to instill into people collective tendencies" (qtd. in Galik, *The Genesis of Modern Chinese Literary Criticism* 157). Probably an indication of their early subscription to Romanticism, they also promoted the utility of affective narratives for the inducement of revolutionary zeal in the readers.

"Intoxicating Spring Nights" not only indicates such changes of ideological trends starting in the mid-1920s, it also presents a compelling example of May Fourth authors' adaptations to political pressure through narrative strategy. Precisely because Yu Dafu had made a name for himself as a confirmed "individualist" committed to writing autobiographical fiction, this story provides a perfect opportunity for us to explore the logic and problematic of May Fourth intellectuals' mass exodus from "literature of the self" in later years. Like his Creationist colleagues, Yu Dafu participated in the promotion of proletarian literature. He even wrote an essay entitled "Class Struggle in Literature" ("Wenxue shang de jieji douzheng") in 1923. Denton has characterized this essay as revealing Yu's "highly romantic understanding of class literature" (Introduction 258), since Yu apparently expected to bridge the gap between the Realists of the Literary Research Association and the Romanticists of the Creation Society with little more than the force of rhetoric. Yu Dafu declared, "In my view, the French literary critics who first invented those terms ["Art for life's sake" and "Art for Art's sake"] should have died a thousand deaths. Art is life, and life is art, and nothing is served by making them antagonistic!" ("Class Struggle in Literature" 264). He further advocated that Literary Research Association and Creation Society, the two most prominent literary societies in modern China, should join forces in order to emulate the "magnificent Russians" and produce a proletarian literature: "So in the spirit of Marx and Engels, let me proclaim: all writers warring against the running dogs of the bourgeois and ruling classes, we must unite" (267–68).

Nevertheless, revolutionary rhetoric aside, Yu Dafu also appeared highly self-conscious about the radical changes he made in "Intoxicating Spring Nights." In 1932 on including it in a self-selected anthology of fiction and essays, he half defensively and half mockingly remarked on the deficiencies of "Intoxicating Spring Nights" as compared to other pieces of Revolutionary Literature. In the preface to that anthology, Yu Dafu stated that, because he had written this story a long time before, it possessed only "a murky ideology" and "meager force" without "promoting any slogans" ("*Dafu zixuan ji* xu" 836). He would have removed it from *Yu Dafu's Self-Selected Anthology* to "avoid doing harm to later writers," he added, had he not been concerned that, since this story had already been translated into various foreign languages, its deletion would surely "hurt the feelings of comrades (*tongzhi*) in Russia, Japan, Britain, Germany and elsewhere" (836).

Yu Dafu was, of course, not above being sarcastic about contemporary political fashions, as demonstrated both by his parodic use of the then popular term "comrade" and by his subtle expression of pride on the wide international circulation of his story. However, the fact that he, a self-styled individualist and Romanticist, portrayed a proletarian woman in this story in 1924 and commented on the story's social effects in 1932 not only illustrated the distinct "turn to the left" among modern Chinese writers, but also demonstrated the pervasiveness of Marxist ideology in modern Chinese literature. Commenting on his "Intoxicating Spring Nights," Yu Dafu evidently felt the need to address the issue of ideology in literature in general and to defend the lack of forceful revolutionary propaganda in his fiction in particular. More tellingly, critics at the time expressed enthusiasm over his apparent conversion to Marxism, oblivious to the ambivalence towards Revolutionary Literature Yu expressed in the preface mentioned above. Some commended the sympathy the author expressed towards working class people, regarding it as a sign of his growing "humanitarian tendency" that set this story apart from the self-absorption of his earlier works such as "Sinking" (Zheng 326). Others even compared it to Dostoyevsky's *Crime and Punishment*, claiming that the depiction of the female tobacco factory worker helped to awaken people whose spirits were "drugged by modern life" (Jin M. 334). Yet, despite the apparent Marxist flavor of this story, Yu Dafu ironically betrayed his link to premodern literary tradition in a more revealing way through his resurrection of the traditional representation of male emotions.

The story in "Intoxicating Spring Nights" takes place in Shanghai, the foremost metropolis of China in the 1920s. The "I"-narrator of the story, an unemployed male writer, moves into a small dilapidated attic in a ghetto, sharing living space with a female tobacco factory worker by the name of Chen Ermei. Living in what was previously a larger room divided into two parts, the two of them gradually develop a friendship due to their shared poverty and loneliness. When spring comes, the writer suffers from insomnia and a nervous anxiety, and therefore has to go out every evening for a stroll in order to be able to write. Chen Ermei, knowing nothing of his illness and understanding his writing career even less, suspects that he is taking part in illicit activities such as theft or robbery. One day the writer receives five dollars for some translation work he did and buys food to treat her. Unable to contain her worries anymore, she confronts him and pleads with him to mend his ways. The writer is greatly moved by her genuine kindness, and explains the reason for his evening outings. The end of the story sees the writer's brief internal struggle and final decision against expressing his gratitude-induced love for her, reminding himself "you are in no position to love anybody" ("Intoxicating Spring Nights" 243).

At first glance, this story contrasts sharply with Yu Dafu's earlier works such as "Sinking" and "Endless Night" in the delineation of the woman. Not only is the woman in this story an urban factory worker, the "I"-narrator and the woman also interact with each other in very different ways. For the first time in one of Yu Dafu's stories, the "I" and a woman live closely with each other for a sustained period of time, and become virtually family to each other, as they share daily living quarters and an occasional simple meal together. They have no other close relatives or friends in their lives. Whereas women in Yu Dafu's earlier stories such as "Sinking" stand for both a temptation and a threat to the male self, in "Intoxicating Spring Nights," Yu Dafu apparently created a bond between Chen Ermei and the writer. The feelings the writer harbors towards her are also depicted as primarily nonsexual in nature, characterized rather more by sympathy and understanding. The male writer also shows genuine interest in the woman's life and often asks about her life story.

However, in "Intoxicating Spring Nights," the woman provides more uncomplicated reinforcement for male subjectivity than in any of Yu Dafu's earlier works precisely because of these differences. In contrast to the seduction and menace women represented in Yu Dafu's early fiction, the woman in this story is securely contained through the creation of a clear-cut Self-Other boundary. At the thematic level, it is revealing how Yu emphasized Chen Ermei's inarticulateness, a characteristic of lower-class women Yu also hinted at in his earlier fiction. In the story, Chen Ermei constantly appears to have difficulty understanding the writer: his books, his works, and his real status in life. She misreads the writer's habits and profession to the point of accusing him of committing felonies. When informed that he earns the money from translation, she cannot even repeat the term, and naïvely suggests to him: "That thing you just mentioned that sold for five dollars, wouldn't it be great if you can make one every day?" (248). In contrast, the writer is depicted as able to interpret her accurately. At their first meeting he "at once knew this must be the female factory worker the landlord mentioned," and "felt she was a pitiful woman for no reason at all" (237-38). At each stage of their relationship, the writer invariably reads her expressions and draws his own conclusions, which later circumstances prove correct, without even talking to her. In addition, their communication is not completely reciprocal, as she offers far more information about her life and family, while he usually withholds his personal data, apparently thinking that she would not understand his problems.

Furthermore, "Intoxicating Spring Nights" resurrects the classical *topos* of a male literatus empathizing with a socially underprivileged female Other, in order not only to prove the elite male's social conscience and his capacity for compassion, but also to affirm his own status as an unjustly persecuted, and hence both notable and noble, personage. In so doing, Yu Dafu also featured the familiar May Fourth motif of a silent victimized woman represented by a male intellectual narrator with superior understanding of not only this particular woman but also of the larger sociopolitical context (Feuerwerker, *Ideology, Power, Text* 84–89). Demonstrative of what Feuerwerker has termed "the writer/intellectual as martyr syndrome" (*Ideology, Power, Text* 19), the I-narrator represents the quandary of the female worker only to create an allegory for his own wretched fate. In a move reminiscent of the Tang poet Bai Juyi's (772-846) famous poem "Pipa xing," (Song of *Pipa* [a Chinese musical instrument]), the story ends with his, rather than her, tragedy. With the lament that "even though I want to find jobs, I still cannot" (249) because of physical weakness, the "I"-narrator wanders off again into the intoxicating spring night, for the moment conveniently forgetting the fragile physique of Chen Ermei and the lethal work environment in the tobacco factory.

Simply put, Yu Dafu again used the female worker as a foil to establish the male "I"-narrator's identity. She not only provides a surface for the narrator to probe in search of *her* underlying truth, an interpretive activity in which he frequently engages; she also functions as a catalyst for the expression of his own emotions and self-analysis. On one occasion they start talking to each other about their own lives. When Chen Ermei asks about the narrator's employment status and his friends and family, he is depicted as being visited by a sudden realization of his own gradual deterioration. "From last year I just started to crumble daily. I almost forgot to ask myself questions such as 'Who am I?', 'What is my current situation?', and 'Am I feeling happy or sad?'" (241). Contrasted with his profound philosophical pondering related in a typical melancholy tone, she only accepts his silence as confirmation of a similarly miserable life and readily offers sympathy based on ignorance. As such, even though they experience the same feeling of sorrow, it is shown that the sources of such emotions vary. He is shown to be superior since he alone can transcend instinctive emotions to arrive at a profound understanding of the real tragedy of life while she is seen as only motivated by emotions. Therefore, the male intellectual is endowed with the kind of knowledge denied to the illiterate female worker, and his accurate and constant assessment of his environment is contrasted with her more instinctive, emotional responses to the external world.

Not only did Yu Dafu differentiate the male I-narrator from Chen Ermei by the degree of their self-awareness, as has been mentioned above, but he also contrived to deal the narrator a nervous affliction, a mental frailness due to high sensitivity, as opposed to Chen Ermei's less glamorous physical fatigue. Thus, the distinction between the two characters, one is tempted to conclude, is between culture and nature, and between psyche and physique. But more importantly, this hierarchical positioning of Self and Other was achieved again through Yu Dafu's adroit deployment of emotions. Just like the "he" in "Sinking," the "I"-narrator in this story also craves affective sympathy rather than rational understanding from his female Other. The "I"-narrator hungers for such indiscriminating sympathy from the female worker to the point of intentionally misinterpreting her behavior towards him: "I knew her tears were shed out of resentment against the tobacco factory, but my heart did not allow me to think so. I would rather think that she shed those tears to caution me" (247–48). As such, the centralization of male emotions in effect resulted in the willful exclusion and denial of the woman's subject position.

The ultimate privileging and sublimation of his emotions take place in the final scene, in which the male intellectual resists the impulse to embrace the female worker, claiming that he does not want to taint "this pure virgin" with his love (243). This scene signifies another case of narrative othering of the female Other by the male intellectual; first he presumes knowledge of her, and then he voluntarily distances himself from her in order to maintain the integrity of the self. Although some claim that the "I"-narrator's voluntary withdrawal suggests his realization "he was no longer the strong one who should pass out sympathy" (Chan W. 116) and hence the hint of role change between the intellectual and the masses, it can be seen that Yu Dafu paradoxically depended on such an apparent limitation of the male intellectual's power to confirm his superiority. This is because, not only is the male self made unique yet again by an accentuation of his realization of the full wretchedness of his life situation, a mark of his superiority in a Socratic sense (i.e., awareness of one's own ignorance is a sign of wisdom), but he also demonstrates heroic self-control in overcoming his passions through a recollection of his responsibility.

Yu's emphasis of the male intellectual's self-awareness and emotional control proved to be different strategies of consolidating male subjectivity. In parallel, he also deployed the new women in this story differently from what he did in his early "Sinking." To characterize the male intellectual's "sinking" or "sublimation" as a case of divergent male responses towards the stereotypes of women as whore/angel (as the Freudian division of women seems to suggest) would be to oversimplify the issue, even though Chen Ermei, the woman in this case, is represented as the diametric opposite of the licensed temptress who claims center stage in "Sinking." More importantly, Chen Ermei is designed not as an unattainable bourgeois girl student to expose the hero's failure, but as a sympathetic female worker who provides a sense of security for the male self. In the story, Chen Ermei's physical attributes do not possess the power to dazzle and threaten the male writer. As has been mentioned above, her thoughts are also transparent to him. Without either sexual allure or a sense of mystery to titillate him, she can neither jeopardize his self-control nor challenge his sense of superiority. Similarly, the narrator's emphasis on the female worker's virginity is motivated by the intention of self-reification. Perhaps the most significant aspect of his self-restraint does not consist in his marking her off as a "sacred" object. Rather, the narrator ultimately redeems his masculinity through this gesture of self-denial. The female worker's virginity is a symbol of her innocence and vulnerability, an affirmation of her status as victim of society, as both traits were frequently attributed to this category of people within the discourse of Revolutionary Literature. Thus by stopping short at expressing his love for the woman, the writer not only demonstrates admirable self-discipline when faced with female temptation, but also proves himself to be the preserver and savior, not the spoiler, of the oppressed class.

The story ends with the writer roaming the street once more on a spring night. Significantly, he is the only person awake in the slum, gazing at the lights and listening to the music from the high-rise modern buildings on the opposite side of the street. The ending thus symbolizes the writer's position in society envisioned by Yu Dafu in the mid-1920s. As a departure from the neurotic hero in "Sinking," the writer acquires a sense of purpose and mission, albeit understated in "Intoxicating Spring Nights," through his interaction with the new Other. That is to say, having been evicted from more affluent residences and ending up in the ghetto, he proves himself to be a perceptive eye and a speaking voice in the dark of the night, a representative more *for* the people than *of* the people. But in portraying an Other who shares with the male Self the material hardship but not the intellectual understanding of such a situation, "Intoxicating Spring Nights" reverts to the same male-centered power structure inherent in Yu Dafu's "Sinking."

Therefore, although Yu Dafu gestured towards collectivism in "Intoxicating Spring Nights," his positioning of Self and Other remained essentially the same. On the one hand, he acknowledged the revolutionary discourse of the time by portraying a male writer sensitive to the suffering of the proletarian woman. On the other, by privileging the pro-found introspection of the male intellectual over the unenlightened living of the female worker, he also ensured the redemption of the hero's masculinity through his recognition and preservation of the status of the proletarian woman as innocent victim of society. In other words, the hero in "Intoxicating Spring Nights" finds reinforcement for his subjectivity in the woman precisely because he consciously delineates her difference to mark the boundary between an intellectually superior Self and an unaware, albeit sympathetic, Other. Interestingly, Yu Dafu also resorted to "Realism" in his narration in "Intoxicating Spring Nights." This story includes various realistic details of the shabby lodging, the meager food, and Chen Ermei's family and work. With these trappings, the narrative acquires a verisimilitude that serves to arrest any potential emotional upheaval and stabilize the encounter between the male writer and the female worker, thus assisting to maintain the status quo of intellect triumphing over instinct.

Yu Dafu's "realistic" depiction of the proletarian woman in his fiction, and perhaps more importantly, the establishment of a modern male identity through the traditional alignment of control and masculinity, was by no means an exception in the May Fourth literature of the 1920s and 1930s. In fact, Yu's attempt at demonstrating socialist consciousness in "Intoxicating Spring Nights" was declared insufficient by some of his contemporaries because they considered Yu still privileged self-expression too much and did not try hard enough to arouse moral indignation among his readers. For example, Zheng Boqi, a fellow member of the Creation Society, urged him to "move one step forward, to depict [Chen Ermei's] life in a more objective and realistic style [. . .] If he described Chen Ermei as falling ill from overwork, or going blind from the tobacco-infused steam, or becoming an unlicensed prostitute due to poverty, or being seduced by her supervisor, pregnant and abandoned," he speculated, "we as readers would feel more sympathy towards the miserable fate of the people. And we would feel more anger towards the social institutions" (322). But, Zheng Boqi concluded, "the story did not achieve such a forceful effect, because the author's initial intention was to express his own sorrow instead of delineating the sufferings of people in reality" (322). In view of the self-other relationship depicted in the story, Zheng Boqi was right in pointing out the way Yu Dafu deployed the woman only for the purpose of representing the male intellectual. However, in his own fashion Yu Dafu also responded to the increasing accentuation of the collective by his fellow modern intellectuals; he deployed emotions differently, even though his construction of self-other power relationship remained essentially unchanged.

Given that Yu Dafu attempted to bond the male intellectual with the oppressed Chinese people through alleging a shared victimization in his early fiction such as "Sinking," it is perhaps not surprising that he had the male intellectual identify with his new, oppressed Other, a proletarian woman, in "Intoxicating Spring Nights" in 1924. Only in this case, he secured for the Self a position that is related to but higher than that of the Other, who was perceived as a specific representative of the previously amorphous group of the oppressed Chinese people. But Yu Dafu's change of style manifested in "Intoxicating Spring Nights" also indicated the shift in the sociopolitical milieu of the 1920s. As Marston Anderson observed, at that time "Creationists simply generalized their individual emotions and, overriding the obvious class distinction, pronounced themselves spokesperson for the masses" ("The Specular Self" 77). The interesting question raised by Yu Dafu's work is how much an author is able to deviate from his previous narrative practice even with (self-proclaimed) changed political conviction. Yu Dafu's fiction suggests that he did not, after all, alter his structural positioning of the male Self and the female Other despite his alleged new fealty to Revolutionary Literature. Taking a step further, we could conceivably question the equally convenient, if only more convincing, iconoclasm avowed by May Fourth intellectuals. Did they succeed in translating their self-proclaimed radical ideological differences from premodern literati into fundamental changes in the new literature? Furthermore, were there really irreconcilable differences between "conservative" Confucianism, May Fourth antitraditionalism, and Marxist radicalism in its Chinese incarnate, with regard to the treatment of Chinese women in male literature?

Since the turn from "individualism" to "collectivism" was a pervasive trend in May Fourth fiction starting in the mid-1920s, an examination of fiction representing new women by other May Fourth writers will provide an even more rounded picture of not only the configuration of literature and politics in specific works but also the kind of "modernization" of Chinese literature that May Fourth intellectuals were promoting. As I will show in the following chapters, male May Fourth intellectuals could not address the questions of Chinese modernization without the intricate integration of "emotionality" into their construction of new women.

FOUR

En/gendering the *Bildungsroman* of the Radical Male: Ba Jin's Girl Students and Women Revolutionaries

If for Lu Xun, in order to be modern one had to be masculine while for Yu Dafu, in order to seem masculine one had to appear modern, then what happened when women writers also wanted to claim a share of modernity? Did they have to become more "like men" in order to be considered modern? Or did there exist an alternative modernity that would not only authorize women's participation in the project of Chinese modernization but also enable them to produce their own discourses of modernity? After examining the configuration of gender and modernity in the representation of new women by Lu Xun and Yu Dafu—two of the first generation of radical May Fourth fiction writers—by whose labor Chinese women were often excluded implicitly or explicitly from modernity, the remainder of this book will explore in what way, if any, Chinese women were able to contribute to the discourses of Chinese modernity and create a modern identity for themselves. This will be fulfilled in the next five chapters through a juxtaposition of both male writers' representations of increased female agency and the May Fourth women writers' own literary and political efforts of (re)defining the relationship between gender and Chinese modernity.

As many intellectuals turned from the promotion of individualism to Marxist collectivism starting in the mid-1920s, new women seemed to gain more mobility and access to modernity in May Fourth literature. In fiction, not only did the girl student become more involved in radical politics, the woman revolutionary—a more forceful and active female figure who appears as political activist, union organizer, or even enlisted soldier in this literature—also gradually replaced the girl student as the most prominent type of new women. At first sight, women revolutionaries seem to embody the most radical departure from tradition up to their time. Unlike the female cross-dresser in vernacular stories, the woman revolutionary "flaunts" her femininity in public and does not rejoin her family after serving the people, since a break from the family is always defined as the point of embarkation on her revolutionary path. She also appears to be more radical than the girl student, for she more often rebels against rather than unquestioningly follows the more socially acceptable path for women of her time and class: seeking independence through modern education.

Ironically, despite the increasingly radical stance of new women, their narrative construction by male authors embodied a more forceful return of the (repressed) male-centered tradition. That is, radical male intellectuals more explicitly betrayed their suppressed ties with the patriarchal tradition in their attempts at subjugating radical women under their twin projects of self-representation and Chinese modernization. This can be seen in the case of Ba Jin, whose mode of representation in fiction not only earned him loyal readers but also brought the author precariously close to the writers of "Butterfly Fiction," whom May Fourth intellectuals had sternly criticized for their purported traditional outlook.

Ba Jin's surreptitious resurrection of what had been denounced as "traditional" exposes the inner contradictions of his iconoclasm. These contradictions can be seen not so much in the commercial success of his most popular fictional work, the novel *Jia* (*Family*, 1931–32) — the sales figure of which arguably blurred the boundary between serious and popular literature at the time (L. Liu, *Translingual Practice* 216) — as in the precise nature of the power of his fiction. I argue that the capacity of his fiction to inspire affective identification among his readers resulted from a combination of revolutionary passion and an easily recognizable and consumable narrative form that drew on premodern vernacular narratives. Because of the uneasiness of this alliance of tradition and modernity, Ba Jin also struggled to demarcate tradition and modernity through his artful differentiation and repeated performance of masculinity and femininity in his fiction. In representing the new woman, he often portrayed a temporary solidarity between male and female intellectuals only to expedite the displacement of male emotional weakness onto his female Other. As such, the male intellectual is shown to be superior to his female counterpart because he is able to sever his emotional ties to the traditional family while she remains a slave to her emotions. Thus, the modernity of male intellectuals was accomplished through his masculine control while her "feminine emotions" apparently domesticate her and obstruct her break from tradition. Furthermore, although Lu Xun's works also embody similar alignment of the feminine and the traditional, it was Ba Jin who depicted new women who wish to emulate modern men in order to become independent modern individuals themselves. In that aspect, his works set up a useful comparison with apparently similar conceptualization of female agency by the woman writer Ding Ling, to be discussed later.

Ba Jin's way of integrating tradition into his depiction of modernity, and femininity into the construction of masculinity, reflected the general sociopolitical milieu of the time, though his narrative practice warrants a closer scrutiny at a later point in this chapter. It is my contention that in addition to his own upbringing as son of a gentry family and his knowledge of classical literature, Ba Jin's paradoxical resurrection of the traditional for the conveyance of radical messages suggested an increasing anxiety that May Fourth intellectuals felt about their identity amidst the further radicalization of the 1930s. This can be seen in that, like Ba Jin, they invoked traditional discursive patterns in more explicit ways than before in order to formulate a coherent identity for themselves, even as they fervently promoted Marxism, anarchism, or various other brands of radicalism. The representation of radical women in their fiction encapsulated such tensions between a radical surface text and a more traditional subtext.

Some may argue that the girl student's decreased prominence in May Fourth fiction only reflected real life situations. After all, by the late 1920s many female intellectuals who came of age during the May Fourth Movement would have grown from girl students into professional women, and would presumably be applying what they had learned at school to their careers. In fact, women writers of the May Fourth group provided real life proof to this projection. However, it is also significant that radical male writers privileged revolutionary women rather than the more common and more "realistic" types such as female teachers or writers. To be sure, their penchant for privileging radical women in fiction signaled the general turn towards leftist radicalism among Chinese intellectuals that was caused by various sociopolitical factors (see Yü, Apter and Saich, and Lin, *The Crisis of Chinese Consciousness*). For example, the full-scale Japanese invasion of China in the 1930s sensitized intellectuals to nationalist struggle, while the persecution of leftist activists by the Nationalist government drove more intellectuals to join forces with the Communist Party. As a result, the promotion of Revolutionary Literature endorsing Marxist ideology and class consciousness gained so much momentum that it even overruled some of the most representative doctrines of the May Fourth Movement. For instance, individualism was deemed to conflict with the fundamental Marxist principle of solidarity among the oppressed classes and summarily denounced by radical intellectuals of the time. As has been mentioned in chapter three, Lu Xun was dismissed by the revolutionary critic Qian Xingcun as a relic of a dead age and an unfit role model for modern writers because of his perspicacious portrayal of the spiritual ailment of the Chinese people. Yu Dafu, the renowned "individualist," also had to modify the theme and style of his depiction of the new woman in order to adapt to the rise of Revolutionary Literature.

But the radical sociopolitical environment of the late 1920s and early 1930s alone cannot fully explicate the representation of the woman revolutionary in May Fourth fiction. For an examination of the narrative permutations in the portrayal of radical women reveals that the politics embedded in narrative forms often contradict the authors' explicitly stated ideologies. As I have mentioned earlier, although Lu Xun and Yu Dafu promoted the modernization of Chinese literature and the demolition of traditions, they also resurrected premodern allegorical strategy in deploying the representation of new women to make social commentaries and construct male subjectivity. Similarly, in the increasingly radical late 1920s and 1930s, male intellectuals often betrayed their traditional assumptions about and attitudes towards women in their narrative practice despite their fervent invocation of revolutionary agendas. This is because in writing fiction, May Fourth writers often had to grapple with the complication of their own emotions that can be more conveniently elided when espousing abstract ideologies in their essays, and their surreptitious attachment to their cultural past resurfaced in their representation of new women. However, at that time radical male intellectuals severely reprimanded "emotional" bourgeois women writers through the invocation of gender stereotypes while privileging the revolutionary woman in their fiction. In view of both radical male intellectuals' own contradictory narrative practice and their didactic habit, their criticism of "feminine emotionalism" marked a self-conscious pedagogical effort. This move signaled their attempt at not only educating and guiding their female "disciples" but also demonstrating their own commitment to Chinese modernization precisely through their discipline of the "unruly" literary endeavors by female and male authors alike. Yet, when they deployed representation of emotions to signify their modern identity in fiction, the tensions caused by their conflicted loyalties to tradition and modernity became all the more volatile and striking. This can be particularly seen in an author like Ba Jin, whose writing style at this point of his career was generally acknowledged as "evocative" and "emotive."

The New Woman to Facilitate Male Growth

Ba Jin started to write fiction in the late 1920s. His works reflected the ideological trend of his time in privileging the more radical types of new women, including revolutionary-minded girl students as well as women revolutionaries proper. Furthermore, demonstrative of his penchant for both the genre of novel and for coming-of-age narratives, Ba Jin brought these women to bear on male psychological growth in order to produce the *Bildungsroman* of radical male intellectuals. In light of his long-standing devotion to narratives of youth, it should perhaps come as no surprise that Ba Jin's depiction of modern Chinese women began with, and centered on, the image of the girl student. One of his first and most popular novels, *Family*, provided an unforgettable role model for young women of his time in the girl student Qin. By contrast, woman revolutionary in his other fiction never managed to make the same lasting impact as did Qin, not the least because Ba Jin did not assign the same degree of psychological complexity, and particularly not the same amount of passion, to his professional revolutionary women as to revolutionary girl students.

As such, emotionality apparently played a more positive role both in Ba Jin's depiction of new women and in his self-representation (for the two were always interrelated in May Fourth fiction) compared to either Lu Xun or Yu Dafu. Unlike Lu Xun's Zijun, a victim of circumstances, girl students in Ba Jin's fiction are depicted as able to change their fates, for the May Fourth Movement not only equipped them with a modern consciousness but also liberated their youthful passion and thus enabled them to rebel against traditions in a more effective way. Ba Jin's girl students are empowered rather than cheated and crushed by modern ideologies. They purposefully seek a modern education away from home, join forces with male intellectuals to disseminate revolutionary ideologies, and bravely stand up for the freedom of choice in marriage partners. Although Ba Jin also depicted obstacles to the emancipation of Chinese women, he more often emphasized modern women's valiant battles against patriarchal restrictions. Largely devoid of the ambivalence towards modernity palpable in Lu Xun's representation of the girl student, Ba Jin's fiction features girl students who forthrightly represent the May Fourth ideals of the modern Chinese woman; they are intelligent, courageous, and perhaps most importantly, successful according to standards set by the May Fourth discourses.

Resonant with Ba Jin's more positive portrayal of the girl student, his equally passionate hero usually enthusiastically praises girl students for their courage to challenge social norms, as opposed to the perpetually lamenting hero in Yu Dafu's fiction who feels threatened by the girl student. Ba Jin portrayed heroes who appreciate and admire the girl student's modern and revolutionary qualities, thus linking male and female intellectuals together through their shared ideals of modernization and revolution. Ba Jin's unique pairing of the female and male intellectual not only testified to the increasing tendency toward radical collectivism in May Fourth fiction, it also presented a new form of utilizing and integrating girl students for the representation of male growth in fiction. In an arrangement reminiscent of the relationship between Juansheng and Zijun, Ba Jin's hero often seeks from the girl student the encouragement necessary for his own breakaway from the family as he struggles to overcome both external and internal impediments. But in contrast to Juansheng's increasing dissatisfaction with Zijun's "weakness," in Ba Jin's fiction the girl student usually stands side by side with the hero and faithfully mirrors each stage of his growth. However, she is also shown to feel passionately about her own inadequacy and eventually fall short of the hero's accomplishments. In many cases in Bai Jin's fiction, the girl student is made to acknowledge that her inner emotional weakness, more than the external constraint imposed by society on her gender, prevents her from achieving a complete liberation such as that enjoyed by the hero. As such, Ba Jin's representation of the girl student reveals the woman to be an inferior copy of the man: an almost-but-not-quite modern man. Furthermore, in highlighting the character flaws of the new woman, he in effect declared the "essential" weakness of the female gender even as he expressed sympathy toward the plight of his women characters. He thus also affirmed the inherent merit of the hero's gender and his role as peerless individual by placing him side by side with his imperfect simulacrum, the girl student. Therefore, as Ba Jin appropriated the woman's agency to represent male subjectivity, his scheme of othering the new woman resulted in at best a qualified endorsement of this figure for the purpose of accentuating the male hero's revolutionary credentials.

In his most famous work, *Family*, Ba Jin configured the girl student, Qin, and the hero Juehui in just such a way for the sake of vivifying male subject formation. Nevertheless, the remarkable success of *Family* suggests that despite (or, precisely because of) such a treatment of women in this novel, the author was able to construct for his audience a widely acceptable and eagerly received narrative. I argue that the popularity of *Family* was secured, to no small part, through the author's deft blending of "traditional" sentiment and revolutionary zeal for the depiction of what he alleged was the inner truth of the characters. The importance of this formula to the success of Ba Jin's works can also be contrastively illustrated by the lesser popularity of his other works written around the same time, particularly his *Love Trilogy*, including "Wu" (Fog, 1931), "Yu" (Rain, 1932), and "Dian" (Lightning, 1933). *Love Trilogy* more explicitly demonstrates Ba Jin's scheme of building up the hero by juxtaposing him with the similarly-yet-less revolutionary new woman, not the least because the author in this case eliminated the traditional family structure that has generated ambiguous emotions in *Family*. The sentimental and romantic atmosphere surrounding the representation of the family thus gives way to more confrontational and volatile interactions in the young people's revolutionary activities in *Love Trilogy*. As such, Ba Jin's more subtle narrative manipulation of women made possible through a deft mixture of "traditional" and "modern" sensibilities in *Family* becomes decidedly manifest and even simplistic in *Love Trilogy*. In what follows I first focus on Ba Jin's representation of the girl student in *Family*, and then use the observations derived from this novel to comment on his later *Love Trilogy*.

Ba Jin's "Instrumental" Girl Student in *Family*

Ba Jin's *Family* has enjoyed immense popularity since its first appearance in 1931. Originally entitled *Jiliu* (The Torrent), it was serialized in *Shanghai Times* (*Shanghai shibao*) between April 18, 1931, and May 22, 1932. In May 1933 it was first published as a single edition under its current title by Kaiming Bookstore in Shanghai. From then to 1937, it went through ten printings. This novel is striking for its ready acceptance by the readers of its time as an accurate representation of the traditional Confucian family. In fact, it has immortalized the May Fourth representation of the traditional family and has in time become a cultural index in its own right. In order to effectively delve into Ba Jin's representation of the girl student in this novel, we must do so through an examination of his depiction of her relationships with other family members, especially her male counterpart, the boy student and her cousin, Juehui. This approach is useful not only for assessing the typical May Fourth representation of new women whose revolutionary character must find affirmation in a complete break from the traditional family but also for gauging the particular conflict in this novel: the younger generation's complex relationships with the older generation, who, to the younger generation, embodies traditional mores and moralities. Ultimately, Ba Jin portrayed the girl student not so much to praise her revolutionary qualities as to represent the growth of the male protagonist Juehui.

In *Family*, the girl student Qin is ensconced, somewhat ironically, in extensive and complex familial relationships to the extent that her life outside the family is rarely mentioned. Such a "domestication" of the girl student is necessary because she is assigned by the author to be the feminine and inferior counterpart to her cousin Juehui — who is also the center of consciousness in the novel — a girl student to his boy student. At first glance, in *Family* the girl student and the male protagonist seem to be more similar than different. Indeed, *Family* embodies an intersubjective duplication, or a "figural density," to borrow Andrew Plaks's term (*The Four Masterworks of the Ming Novel*), in that both young people are portrayed as modern intellectuals possessed of social conscience and sincere emotions. However, the symmetrical and parallel placement of the characters Juehui and Qin also serves to both segregate the domains of their activities by gender and to differentiate the degree of their radicalism. In the novel Juehui usually displays an antagonistic attitude towards the older males in his family, while Qin not only never comes into direct conflict with any men in either her immediate or extended family but also acts as a dutiful and loving daughter to her widowed mother. Moreover, Juehui alone makes the ultimate revolutionary gesture of leaving home, an ending that implies his conflicts with the traditional family system are more fundamental and irreconcilable than those in Qin's case. Even Juehui's ambivalence towards the family appears to be less debilitating than Qin's dilemma, for Ba Jin has located the source of Qin's weakness in her gender and thus reaffirmed Juehui's superiority. We will see that it is precisely by emphasizing the differences in their respective relationships and emotional responses to the traditional family that Ba Jin deployed Qin to magnify Juehui's revolutionary zeal.

Ba Jin attempted such a Self and Other positioning between Juehui and Qin particularly through a differential treatment of "sincere emotions" in the portrayal of their character. That is, although sincerity is used as *the* criterion to evaluate every character's morality in the novel, Juehui's realization and confession of his own contradictions are shown to facilitate his maturation and rejection of the traditional family while Qin's only confirm her weakness and bind her more securely to her family. As such, Ba Jin suggested that the different outcomes of their rebellion can be attributed to their different ability to transform negative emotions into positive actions, a distinction that he also aligned with mutually exclusive gender categories.

However, Ba Jin's narration of difference-within-solidarity between self and Other proved to be an arduous and risky undertaking. For his essentialization of sincerity also threatened to reveal both the inner contradictions of the character Juehui and the subversion of his revolutionary commitment by his emotional attachment to tradition. Although *Family* built its success among young readers on demonstrations of idealism and passion, it is perhaps inevitable that Juehui's break from his family can never be absolute, for his discontent is described as largely rooted in his instinctive emotional outrage against, instead of rational critiques of, the family. Indeed, Juehui betrays the most pronounced contradictions through his interaction with his family. Although apparently the most fearless and rebellious of the three brothers, he is by no means the heroic role model that he has read about in new books and journals—the sources of all his new ideas. Within his family, he often finds himself helplessly entangled in ambivalent feelings. For instance, Juehui regards his oldest brother Juexin—a character used as a foil to impress upon the reader Juehui's revolutionary courage as compared to people of his own generation and gender—as a coward who makes "unnecessary sacrifices" of himself and the women he loves. Yet he cannot help but sympathize with Juexin's dilemma, and in fact often depends on him as a buffer against abuses by their grandfather and uncles.

Although it can be argued that a modern/ist consciousness manifests itself precisely in an individual's contradictory feelings and heightened self-awareness, the author's uneasiness with this notion of modernity is evident. In fact, since emotional ambivalence also led to moral ambivalence within the novel, Ba Jin employed various narrative strategies to justify Juehui's conflicted loyalties. Particularly, Ba Jin introduced the figure of the girl student for the reinforcement of male subjectivity. He accentuated the difference-within-similarity between the boy and girl student in order to not only make the revolutionary commitment of the male protagonist appear all the more distinct but also convert his emotional "weakness" to motivation for revolution.

To be sure, Ba Jin also utilized other strategies to accentuate Juehui's psychological growth as a modern individual, such as describing Juehui's volatile relationship with his grandfather, the Venerable Master Gao (Gao Lao Taiye), the despotic patriarch of the family. Juehui at first regards his grandfather as a dictator who casts an ominous shadow over the lives of other family members. He holds his grandfather directly or indirectly responsible for the miserable lives of several people within the family. Mingfeng, a bondmaid promised to one of the grandfather's elderly friends as a concubine, commits suicide in despair. Master Gao is also blamed by Juehui for causing his brother Juemin to flee home by arranging Juemin's marriage. Personally, Juehui bears the brunt of the stern patriarch's discipline because of his involvement in political rallies and the publication of radical journals. In response, Juehui demonstrates his heroic mettle by being the most vocal of all family members in venting anger at his grandfather's autocracy. When being grounded by Master Gao for his participation in student demonstrations against soldiers of the warlord government, Juehui laments the tyranny that permeates his family in his diary, "I'm so lonely! Our home is like a desert, a narrow cage. I want activity. I want life. In our family, I can't even find anyone I can talk to" (85).

Ba Jin not only highlighted Juehui's revolutionary spirit by pitting him against the corrupt older males in the household, but also added to Juehui's psychological complexity by depicting his changing feelings towards his grandfather. It is shown in the novel that Juehui has no difficulty siding with the oppressed and raging against his grandfather's behavior when belaboring Master Gao as the symbol of patriarchal rule. The moment he starts to think of Master Gao as a human being, however, his emotions become less clear-cut. Significantly, Juehui's change of heart happens when his grandfather is on his deathbed, no longer a tyrannical power to be reckoned with. In his final audience with his grandfather, Juehui sees that

> He [Master Gao] lay with his bald head propped against high-piled pillows, his face bloodless and thinner than ever, his mouth slackly open. Above high cheekbones, his large eyes were sunken; from time to time he closes them wearily. To Juehui, his grandfather looked weak and pitiful; he no longer resembled the awesome and frightening Venerable Master Gao. (288)

The realization of his grandfather's impending death disarms Juehui. He finds himself no longer "awed" or "frightened" by the old man, because his grandfather's physical condition reminds him of human mortality in a very concrete way. Boundaries between abstract categories such as "tradition" and "modernity," "dictatorship" and "rebellion" also become blurred for him, as he feels a new bond with his grandfather as a fellow human being. Moreover, this is also a moment of self-awareness for Juehui. On this occasion Master Gao expresses his wish to make amends before he dies; he praises Juehui as "a good boy" and promises to call off Juemin's arranged marriage. Master Gao's gesture of repentance not only convinces Juehui of his sincerity, and thus in Juehui's eyes, partly redeems his moral character, it also reminds Juehui of his own contradictions.

He has just failed Mingfeng, the bondmaid he loved, who did not even dare to beseech him to rescue her from concubinage. Hearing from Juemin of her impending marriage and not knowing of Mingfeng's planned suicide, Juehui privately convinces himself on the absurdity of the idea of a marriage between himself and Mingfeng, since they come from different classes. Mingfeng ends up committing suicide in despair but also as a sacrifice, in order not to burden Juehui with her difficult situation. Her death forcefully confirms both Juehui's lack of power in his own family and the superficiality of his "humanitarian" sympathy towards the servants of the family. In the final meeting with Master Gao, Juehui finds it easier to forgive his grandfather, because he recognizes his own complicity in the destruction of the weak and the oppressed. After all, he just tacitly allowed Mingfeng to be devoured by the old family. Juehui admits to his second brother Juemin after Mingfeng's death, "I used to blame you and Big Brother for being spineless. Now I know I'm not any different. We're all sons of the same parents, raised in the same family. None of us have any courage. I hate everyone. I hate myself" (229).

Juehui's recognition of the similarity between himself and the other male family members is devastating for him, because up to that point he has launched all his attacks on the patriarchal family from the vintage point of his own moral superiority. By admitting to his own sin, Juehui can no longer draw a clear boundary between himself and the older male family members he previously despised. Although Ba Jin hinted that Juehui's gesture of self-confession was essential for the birth of his modern identity, Juehui's emotional ambivalence also created the kind of moral ambiguity that Ba Jin was anxious to clarify and dispel.

Although it is shown in the novel that only after his acknowledgment of his ties to the morally bankrupt older generation is he able to leave the traditional family to join in revolution, Juehui's ultimate renunciation of the family can also be construed as an escape after all his attempts at rebelling against and reforming the traditional family from within have failed. Despite the grand gesture of giving up his family for the sake of revolution, he also leaves behind the very real suffering of the people confined within that family. Furthermore, the timing of his departure is very telling. Neither Mingfeng's death nor the recognition of his guilt directly drives Juehui from home. Rather, Ba Jin arranged that Juehui leave home only after his grandfather's death, when the patriarch's emotional hold over him is irrevocably severed. Master Gao holds such tremendous emotional power over Juehui because Juehui always harbors an emotional rather than analytical view of the family. Although regarding himself as a defector (*pantu*) of the family, Juehui has never consciously questioned the premise of the Confucian family structure: the moral authority allocated to the position of patriarch. In impugning the immorality of the older males of the family, he is actually venting his disappointment with his male relatives, who turn out to be unsuitable moral leaders for the younger generation, rather than issuing a clear-sighted denunciation of the principle of moral hierarchy that organizes the patriarchal family. Given the profound and all too plausible ambiguity inherent in Juehui's revolutionary commitment, Ba Jin had to take some steps to salvage his hero's failed mission of demarcating a revolutionary self from antirevolutionary others within the family.

Ba Jin ingeniously planted Juehui's cousin, the girl student Qin, into the story as his female counterpart in order to verify the hero's devotion to the causes of Chinese modernization and revolution. In the novel, Qin appears as a new woman who challenges stifling traditional norms. She fights, though without success, for an opportunity to go to a co-educational school, supports and sustains her lover Juemin in his rebellion against an arranged marriage, and generally acts as a model modern woman for both her female and male cousins. Just as Juehui is the most radical of his brothers and male cousins, Qin's modern education and revolutionary courage distinguish her from her less outspoken and less fortunate female cousins. Nevertheless, it is her male cousin Juehui who eventually breaks away from the family, while she falls in love with Juehui's brother Juemin and stays home at the end of the novel. Thus, despite all her impressive feat, in failing to deliver the ultimately revolutionary gesture of rejecting her family, Qin becomes both an exceptional woman and an almost-but-not-quite man, thus providing a contrast to set off the more thorough iconoclasm of the hero, Juehui. As Juehui's kindred spirit, Qin echoes his concerns and social conscience. Apparently not resolute enough to leave the family, Qin also makes Juehui's intrepidity look all the more outstanding. This respective central and peripheral positioning of Juehui and Qin is illustrated most obviously by the space given to representations of not only Juehui's rebellious action but also his psychological development in the novel, such as the intense inner conflicts he experiences over the behavior of his family mentioned above.

To be sure, Qin is granted certain degree of psychological complexity as well, but the depiction of her inner thoughts was used to endorse the male-centered May Fourth discourses of modernity rather than to represent her individuality. Rey Chow has already remarked on the narrative voice that "levels class and gender differences" in *Family* (*Woman and Chinese Modernity* 99). She observes that Mingfeng's status as an uneducated bondmaid within the family contrasts glaringly with the author's bestowment on her psyche a "uniform meditative complexity" (*Woman and Chinese Modernity* 99). Compared to Mingfeng, Qin, as an educated modern woman, provides a more facile tool for the author to conceal his gendered narrative practice. This can be seen particularly in Ba Jin's portrayal of the negative role that emotionality plays in Qin's quest for a modern identity. In contrast to the representation of Juehui, whose fierce inner battle eventually frees him from his attachment to the family, her emotions are depicted as more crippling than liberating. For instance, Qin is shown to be enslaved by her devotion to her mother. Faced with the typical May Fourth conflict between filial love and revolutionary commitment, Qin declares, "I love my future, but I love my mother too. I love light, but for the sake of my mother, I would remain in darkness to keep her company" (197). She even refuses to cut her hair, a widely recognized sign of modernity at the time, lest it upset her mother. Moreover, Qin's internal conflicts always seem to root in her awareness of the disadvantages of being a woman, of the inherent inferiority of the feminine position as compared to the masculine. Bombarded by her mother's repeated attempts at matchmaking on her behalf, the only escape route Qin can think of is to become a man: "I will not take that road [arranged marriage]. I want to be a human being, *a human being just like a man* [. . .] I don't want to go that way, I want to take a new road, I will take a new road" (203, emphasis mine). As indicated in the above quote, Qin considers "being a man" the equivalent of not only being free and modern, but also being human. Whereas her expression of resistance to arranged marriage offers the reader a glimpse into her yearning for a masculine position, her internal turmoil when faced with the danger of rape by looting soldiers even more dramatically reveals Qin's dissatisfaction with a feminine one. In this scene, she is depicted as associating masculinity with strength, and femininity with weakness.

When fighting breaks out in the city, amidst the widespread panic among family members and her womenfolk's avowals to kill themselves if cornered by soldiers, Qin is beset by self-doubt:

> "You could never do it [commit suicide]," a voice inside her said. Although she could think of no other alternative, she felt there must be one. All her new ideas, her new books and periodicals, Ibsen's social dramas, the writings of the Japanese author Akiko Yosano—had vanished from her mind. She could see only outrage and humiliation, leering at her, mocking her. The shame would be something she could not live with. She had her pride. It was hopeless; none of them [her extended family] could save her. Yet they all were infinitely precious to her; she couldn't bear to leave them. Weary, despondent, for the first time Qin began to think she was no different from women like Mei and Ruijue. She was just as weak, after all. (177)

Qin's thoughts when she is faced with the threat of violation expose the problematic in the construction of her modern identity. The novel tells us that she has had access to Western ideas mainly through texts: books, journals, and newspapers. She has in fact built her aspirations on what she has read about women's liberation, freedom of the younger generation, and modernization of the nation. As such, she is actually depending on the gendered interpretation of what means to be a modern Chinese woman provided by male intellectuals for the construction of her own identity. Therefore, Qin's gendered self-image also calls into question the validity and applicability of a male-centered modernization scheme to women's true development.

In the above passage, Qin laments that she is no different from other women because she is just as weak as they are, mirroring Juehui's acknowledgement of his similarity to corrupt male family members. But, unlike Juehui, Qin's disappointment with herself is shown to only increase her sense of helplessness rather than spur her to leave the family. This is because, while Juehui's awareness of his complicity in patriarchal corruption induces in him a strong desire to separate himself from the source of contamination, Qin's refusal to identify with other, even more oppressed, women only further traps her in her gender. In other words, she aspires for the kind of modern identity that is actually a copy of (constructed) modern masculinity, and, as a result, finds herself frustrated in her pursuit precisely because the construction of such a masculinity necessarily depends on repeated protestation of unalterable and mutually exclusive gender positions. Furthermore, in her eagerness to embrace the May Fourth gender discourses, she also internalizes their underlying traditional male-centered consciousness that further impedes her liberation.

In the looting scene, Qin's paralyzing misery is partially caused by her unquestioning acceptance of the absolute importance of female "chastity," a distinct echo of the neo-Confucian cult of women's virtue, which claimed that even the loss of chastity under duress was grounds enough for women to commit suicide. But more tellingly, she regards her female relatives such as Mei and Ruijue, two women whose lives are destroyed by the family, as symbols of weakness and failure. The two women Qin pities, and whom she perhaps subconsciously holds in contempt, actually show far more poise and determination than she in the face of death or "a fate worse than death." Yet Qin dismisses as insignificant both their strength of character and their struggle, despite arranged marriages and unconsummated loves, to build a life within the patriarchal restrictions. Qin's ideal of female autonomy is the one and only version of women's emancipation handed down by male intellectuals: A liberated woman should receive a modern education, choose her own husband, and join in revolutionary work. Having convinced herself that she can never transcend the weakness of her gender to attain such a personal autonomy, she in effect suspends herself between the reality of women's struggle and her vision of (masculine) power. Supposedly a pioneer of modern Chinese women, Qin is actually caught in a position of isolation and powerlessness.

Nevertheless, rather than acknowledging that Qin's subscription to the May Fourth modernization discourses is one reason for her captivity, Ba Jin blamed her quandary on her "soft-hearted" emotions. Although Qin's "feminine" traits such as compassion and gentleness are described as highly desirable to the young men in the novel, she is also shown to allow herself to be overwhelmed by her own emotions in the looting scene just mentioned. As a result, Qin appears inferior to the more radical Juehui, whose righteous indignation prompts him to leave the family after the death of his grandfather. By contrast, Qin has to play the role of filial daughter, supportive lover, and generally speaking, the nurturing woman within the family. In this light, her betrothal to Juemin, although signaling a victory gained through her revolutionary protest against arranged marriages, indicates both her domestication and her symbolic contingency with masculinity, if only by becoming a man's extension: a wife. Not coincidentally, Qin plays a relatively static role in the two other novels that, along with *Family*, make up Ba Jin's *Torrent Trilogy*, *Spring* (*Chun*, 1938) and *Autumn* (*Qiu*, 1940). Although her cousin Shuying, another girl student, leaves home in *Spring*, Qin stays home until the end of *Autumn*, when the reader is told that she finally cuts her hair, and plans to get married to Juemin and accompany him to his teaching position. In these two sequels to *Family*, Qin in fact becomes the revolutionary man's link with the old family by maintaining regular correspondence with those who have left home. She is portrayed as being blessed with the best of both worlds by staying home: She is the rebel within the family, and the nurturing female for (male) radicals outside the family.

Both the praise of Qin's merits and the exposure of her emotional weakness are thus brought to bear on the development of the male protagonist's revolutionary qualities. Significantly, the novel ends with Juehui's departure for Shanghai:

> A new emotion gradually possessed Juehui. He didn't know whether it was joy or sorrow, but one thing was clear—he was leaving his family. Before him was an endless stretch of water sweeping steadily forward, bearing him to an unfamiliar city. There, all that was new was developing—new activities, new people, new friends. This river, this blessed river, was taking him away from the home he had lived in for eighteen years to a city and people he had never seen. The prospect dazzled him; he had no time to regret the life that he had cast behind. For the last time, he looked back. "Goodbye," Juehui said softly. He turned to watch the on-rushing river, the green water that never for an instant halted its rapidly advancing flow. (329)

The image of the flowing river, a conventional metaphor for development and progress, forms a sharp contrast with the imagery at the start of the novel. Whereas the novel begins with the two brothers Juehui and Juemin walking home one winter evening through a heavy snowfall, it ends on a spring morning when Juehui embarks on a new journey, closing on a self-consciously optimistic tone. But Juehui's emotions are as turbulent as the rushing waters. On a more mundane yet practical level, he still has to rely on family subsidies, especially money contributed by his big brother, in order to survive in a strange city away from home. Just like the rushing river, he is moving towards an unknown future whose only discernible characteristic to him is its "newness." Even though the future promises excitement, it also induces feelings of bedazzlement, of uncertainty, and maybe even of suppressed terror. As described in the passage above, Juehui's determined gaze towards the future can only follow his last look backward.

Such a double vision also characterizes Ba Jin's own narrative practice in *Family*. That is, Ba Jin's modern, progressive, and revolutionary messages are nonetheless juxtaposed with a lingering attachment to premodern literary traditions, manifested in both the traditional male-centered consciousness inherent in his deployment of the girl student for the representation of the male subject, and in his adoption of premodern narrative devices. Indeed, in addition to Ba Jin's molding of Qin for the reinforcement of Juehui's subjectivity, other aspects of the narrative modes of *Family* also reveal Ba Jin's conflicted loyalties towards both tradition and modernity. In the novel two types of narratives evolve synchronically. Ba Jin delivered the ideological message of the novel by exposing the older males within the family through the agency of the center of consciousness, Juehui, thus making the family into an allegory of the morally bank-corrupt Confucian tradition. However, Ba Jin's loving depiction of the domestic space betrayed his emotional ties to the old family as a "presence," an aesthetic entity so deeply rooted in his cultural and psychological makeup that it escaped the censorship of his ideological conviction. Such a subconscious perception of the family was more difficult to dismiss on moral and rational grounds because it had been formed prior to and outside of the author's cognizance of modern knowledge and revolutionary ideologies. It follows that although Ba Jin considered himself to be one of the most relentlessly antitraditional modern Chinese authors and the one who had been most influenced by foreign models ("Da Faguo *Shijie bao* jizhe wen" 326), he adopted a significant number of plot structures and literary devices from *Dream of the Red Chamber* for his most popular modern novel (Gu), pointing up yet again the inconsistency in May Fourth intellectuals' cultural iconoclasm.

Ba Jin's poetic delineation of the family gardens in particular reveals his own paradoxical move of both affiliation with and dissociation from the family as a cultural icon. Similar to the Grand Prospect Garden (Daguan yuan) in *Dream of the Red Chamber*, the Gao family garden serves as the stage for various human dramas, especially those of a romantic nature. For example, after many years of separation Juexin encounters his old lover in this garden, where his wife then happens upon the grief-stricken couple. Here Juehui also expresses his love for Mingfeng, who later commits suicide in the lake inside the same garden. However, it is in the depiction of the garden as a site of seasonal changes and wistful dreams, with a descriptive rather than dramatic mode of presentation, that the author's deepest ambivalence is revealed.

Significantly, the family garden is frequently a location of reunion and revelry in *Family*. Chapters twelve to nineteen are devoted to the Gao family's celebration of Chinese New Year in the garden, a section that makes up almost a quarter of the entire novel. The narrative tempo slows down in these eight chapters, constituting a prolonged narrative arrest, i.e., a non-linear, descriptive interlude inserted between major action units. Before the description of the New Year's celebration in chapter twelve, chapter eleven treats Juehui's interview with his grand-father who then grounds him. After the long section on the New Year's celebration, chapter twenty begins with the startling news of the riot and looting in the city. We can see that before this narrative arrest, various conflicts and Juehui's rebelliousness have been gradually building up; and after the elaborate celebration and sacrificial ceremony of the New Year's Festival, the fortunes of the Gao family then take a turn for the worse. Chapters twelve to nineteen thus embody a peak that both summarizes the previous developments and prepares for the deterioration of the family and the dispersal of its members. In so doing, the novel adopts a convention often featured in premodern vernacular novels such as *Outlaws of the Water Marsh* (*Shuihu zhuan*, c. 1573–1620), *Plum in the Gold Vase* (*Jin Ping Mei*, c. 1580) as well as *Dream of the Red Chamber*. Furthermore, Ba Jin betrayed his emotional attachment to the family through the extensive, almost caressing description featured in these chapters. Although the remainder of the novel witnesses the death of family members, the disintegration of the clan, and the departure of various characters, the deliberately lingering pace of these eight chapters facilitates a leisurely savoring of the merriment of the festive occasion even as it, as Rey Chow argues, exposes the hypocrisy of traditional rituals (Woman and Chinese Modernity 100).

Ba Jin's revival of narrative conventions in premodern vernacular novels suggests his subconscious attachment to tradition. Yet, while admitting to using *Family* as a way to exorcise his nostalgia about his own family, he also emphasized that rather than debilitated him, this lingering attachment spurred him to launch even more vigorous attack on the traditional system. As he claimed, "it is this attachment [to the family] that incited in me greater anger, encouraging me to write a history of an old family, 'a complete history of the vicissitudes of a feudal family coming undone.' I wanted to call out '*J'accuse*' against a dying system" ("*Jia*" 375). It can be seen that in a move echoing his depiction of Juehui, Ba Jin rationalized his emotional ties to the traditional family by describing them as the motivating force for his rebellion against tradition. However, Ba Jin also took pains to distance himself from Juehui, whose ambivalence towards the traditional family rendered him a potential hazard for Ba Jin's construction of his own modernity. Ba Jin claimed that *Family* was not autobiographical even though he based it on the life stories of several people he knew. He emphatically declared that he was not Juehui ("*Jia*" 378). With those assertions, Ba Jin was not only attempting to make readers accept the truthfulness of his account and hence the legitimacy of his "indictment" of the traditional family, but also to prove that he was an objective "historian" and a fearless warrior who successfully purged nostalgic feelings towards the old family through his fiction writing. Indeed, just as in his narrative practice in *Family*, in his essays Ba Jin also depended on the performance of exorcising debilitating emotions for the solidification of a modern masculinity.

The Woman Revolutionary in *Love Trilogy*

In light of the success Ba Jin obtained through an ingenious blending of traditional and modern sensibilities and discursive practices in *Family*, it perhaps should come as no surprise that his *Love Trilogy*, made up by the novellas "Fog," "Rain," and "Lightning," did not fare as well. The most obvious "failing" of these novellas is that Ba Jin hardly invoked any premodern vernacular novel, thus unable to draw on the readership's previous experience with vernacular narratives to promote the trilogy. However, Ba Jin's unsubtle use of women characters solely for the sake of facilitating male subject formation was more at fault. Although the more radical new women in this trilogy also aid the male intellectual's rebellion against tradition, just as Qin does in *Family*, Ba Jin's oversimplification of human emotions and relationships in the trilogy proved detrimental to its success among readers of the time.

The three novellas in this trilogy share some characters, though the first two of them unfold in the urban setting of Shanghai while the third takes place in an unspecified small town. Ba Jin's penchant for tripartite structure manifests itself again in the grouping of characters in *Love Trilogy*. In his *Family*, three brothers, Juexin, Juemin, and Juehui were made to represent values that range from the most conservative to the most radical. In "Fog," three male characters contrast with each other in the degree of their dedication to the anarchist cause: Chen Zhen, the most committed and steadfast; Wu Renmin, passionate yet rash; and Zhou Rushui, the most indifferent to the revolution and the weakest in character. They also contrast with each other in their relationships with women. In "Fog," Chen Zhen devotes himself completely to the revolutionary cause, and displays a misogynist attitude towards women. In the same story, Zhou Rushui pursues a modern girl student, only to back out at the last minute because he is already married. Another failed romance pushes him to commit suicide in "Rain." Wu Renmin forms a contrast with these two in that he proves to be the most interested and persistent in romance. He is also the male character who links the three novellas together. While in "Fog" he appears as a happily married family man and hot-tempered revolutionary, he enters "Rain" a recent widower and gets involved with another woman, a former student of his. In "Lightning" he emerges as a mature revolutionary leader and winner of the heart of Li Peizhu, former girl student and now woman revolutionary *extraordinaire*.

In fact, Wu Renmin's growth is facilitated and marked by his associations with three different women in his life: his wife ("Fog"), his first lover Xiong Zhijun ("Rain"), and his second lover Li Peizhu ("Lightning"). His degree of revolutionary commitment is shown to be proportionate to the amount of revolutionary zeal possessed by the woman involved with him. While his wife always stays home to take care of him and their household, Xiong Zhijun is a young widow and former student of his who comes to Shanghai to eke out a living on her own. However, like Wu's wife, she also sacrifices herself for him. When an officer in the warlord army threatens to execute Wu, she consents to marry the officer in order to save Wu, and eventually dies of tuberculosis. In comparison, Li Peizhu is the most radical of the three women. She leaves her old father, and goes to the countryside to organize revolutionary activities. She is also the most independent of the three women, and seems to get involved with Wu not so much out of romantic love as because they are comrades fighting for the same cause. Yet, even though by far the most positive and aggressive new woman in Ba Jin's fiction, Li Peizhu is still placed as a link in a sequence to best display Wu Renmin's growth. For it can be seen that Wu Renmin's development into a mature revolutionary leader and a strong man is illustrated in the trajectory of his love life: from being devoted to his sickly wife, to manifesting a savior complex in his relationship with Xiong Zhijun, and finally, to accepting a partnership in revolution with Li Peizhu.

Ba Jin readily admitted that he was not very familiar with revolutionary women when he wrote these three novellas, but explained that he portrayal their relationships with male intellectuals in order to "bring romantic relationships to bear on the character of the hero" ("*Aiqing de sanbu qu zongxu*" 317). Although he had adopted similar narrative strategies of bringing an idealized new woman to bear on the *Bildungsroman* of the hero in Family, in Love Trilogy he even more explicitly and simplistically appropriated the agency of new women to reinforce male subjectivity. For instance, the novellas feature a male center of consciousness that actively categorizes all the new women the man encounters. Chen Zhen groups his female acquaintances into three types: demure and innocent bourgeois girl students such as Zhang Ruolan, aggressive seductresses such as Qin Yunyu, and revolutionary women such as Li Peizhu. In so far as the new women facilitate and testify to the growth of the male characters, they play roles similar to that of Qin in *Family*. However, as these women are assigned the single task of providing a convincing testimony to male growth, their characters are also portrayed with less emotional depth and appear more one-dimensional than Qin. Revealingly, the characterization of the male characters that structurally correspond to these women also suffers a loss of psychological complexity as a result.

In conclusion, Ba Jin's deployment of emotionality in his representation of new women both reaffirmed the typical discursive pattern privileged by radical male intellectuals and signaled changes. On the one hand, both his displacement of male weakness onto his female Other in *Family* and his continuous utility of new women to signify male growth in *Love Trilogy* echo similar efforts by Yu Dafu and Lu Xun, and thus demonstrating the traditional male-centered consciousness in fiction by these male writers. However, he differed from those two authors in his accentuation of difference-in-affinity rather than antagonism between modern men and women. By thus displaying more optimism about both the future of the emancipation of Chinese women and of male intellectuals' growth, Ba Jin's fiction illustrates the gradual replacement of individualism by collectivism as dominant discourse in the 1930s. Furthermore, his symmetrical placement of male and female radical intellectuals made possible by his essentialization of emotions also signals a new strategy of self-representation for radical male intellectuals. That is, in the age of revolution, passionate promotion of revolutionary causes in fiction not only obtained moral authority for the writer but also endorsed a masculinized modern femininity that ostensibly supported women's emancipation but actually enabled the male writer to more effectively elide and appropriate female agency for the reinforcement of male subjectivity. The ambiguous position of the male writer between tradition and modernity will come into view once again in Mao Dun's fiction, generating new ways yet of deploying new women for the construction of male identity, the topic of next chapter.

FIVE

The Temptation and Salvation of the Male Intellectual: Mao Dun's Women Revolutionaries

The differences between the two writers, Ba Jin and Mao Dun, are obvious. Ba Jin, a relatively obscure young author in 1931, bombarded his audience with a series of emotionally explosive novels and novellas that indicted the traditional system. By contrast, Mao Dun belonged to an earlier generation of May Fourth intellectuals that also included Lu Xun and Yu Dafu, and had established his literary reputation as editor, literary theorist, and translator of foreign literature even before he started writing fiction in the late 1920s. Furthermore, in contrast to Ba Jin's claim that his personal experiences within the Confucian family triggered off his vehement denunciation of tradition, Mao Dun characterized his promotion of modernity and revolution as the result of rational self-reflection. Even as Mao Dun assigned the woman revolutionary, a figure known for her passion and radicalism in his work, to the role of representative of modern Chinese women, he did so through a deliberate invocation of "objectivity" and "realism." However, a close scrutiny of both his fiction and essays reveals that just like Ba Jin, Mao Dun created and managed his own modern identity through the deployment of emotions. Only in his case, Mao Dun performed the withholding and controlling of his private emotions under the rubric of promoting the doctrines of the Western theory of "Realism."

Because of his already prominent status in literary circles by the late 1920s, Mao Dun certainly had more at stake than Ba Jin when faced with harsh criticism from radical intellectuals. His most important strategy to deflect criticism of "pessimism" and "sensuality" was to represent himself as a true "Realist." This motive prompted him to vigorously advertise more his political experiences than his literary expertise. By all accounts, Mao Dun was one of the chief disseminators of Western literary theories and arbiters of modern Chinese literature who enjoyed widespread influence at the time. Mao Dun began his literary career in 1916 as an editor and translator for the then largest commercial publisher in China, the Commercial Press (Shangwu yinshu guan) in Shanghai. During his tenure as editor at the Commercial Press, the May Fourth Movement broke out in 1919. Subsequently, he translated into Chinese a large amount of Western literature from English translations, such as works by Anton Tchekhov, Guy de Maupassant, Arthur Schnitzler, Maurice Maeterlinck, Gorky, Nietzsche, and many more. He was also a well-known editor of modern magazines. In addition to having spearheaded the publication of *Xuesheng zazhi* (Student magazine), he reformed one of the most prestigious literary magazines of the May Fourth period, *Short Story Monthly* (*Xiaoshuo yuebao*), transforming it from the hub of "Mandarin Duck and Butterfly Fiction" to that of May Fourth fiction. In addition, he cofounded one of the two most influential literary societies, the Literary Research Association, and promoted "Realist" fiction with both his extensive critiques of almost all the major authors of modern Chinese literature and his numerous theoretical essays.

Although Mao Dun was also one of the earliest May Fourth intellectuals to join the Chinese Communist Party (CCP), his literary accomplishments far outshone his political feat. However, Mao Dun emphasized the fact that he was first a political activist and secondly a fiction writer in order to establish his credibility as a writer. He claimed that his skirmishes with politics had made him a better fiction writer, since they had afforded him the opportunity to live in the real world first. According to his account, the breakup of the alliance between the CCP and the Nationalist Party in 1927, and the Nationalist government's subsequent massacre of CCP members and leftist radicals forced him to flee China and take refuge in Japan for over a year. During the perilous time of September 1927, he began to write his first novella, "Disillusionment" ("Huanmie"):

> I had lived truly first. I experienced one of the most complex scenes in China's chaotic modern history; as a result I came to feel disillusioned with the contradictions of human life. Feeling profoundly depressed and alone—to say nothing of the external circumstances that constrained me—I determined to light a spark in this confused, gray life from the remnant of the life force in me. Therefore I began to write. ("Cong Guli dao Dongjing" 2, translation partly adapted from M. Anderson, *The Limits of Realism* 121)

The above personal narrative epitomizes Mao Dun's attempts at establishing his status as a modern writer by representing himself as a "Realist." For Mao Dun, being "modern" essentially meant being "realistic." He accentuated his political experiences because the image of an author who already had the raw material of real life for fiction writing fit well with his idea of "Realism." However, Mao Dun also surprisingly cited his own emotional responses to traumatic political events as a powerful motive for writing. As such, we can see that even though his version of "Realism" purportedly entailed the objective observation and unflinching representation of reality (M. Anderson, *The Limits of Realism* 119-51), it differed from the representation of "objective reality" exemplified by Western fiction written by Zola or Flaubert. As we can see from his personal narrative, Mao Dun actually attempted to mesh the Western model of Realism with his premodern literary heritage by demanding that Realist literature be rooted in the author's subjective experience of the world and that it be utilized as a tool to improve the overall morale of the revolutionary intellectuals. As Marston Anderson has convincingly argued, Mao Dun, like many of his fellow Chinese promoters of Realism, actually shied away from the hard objectivism implicit in the doctrine of Western Realism but chose to reassert the experiencing self into the creative process (The Limits of Realism 43-44).

However, neither Mao Dun's emphasis of his political experience nor his unique definition of Realist literature managed to fend off accusations of "false realism" leveled against him by radical intellectuals in the late 1920s. The leftist critics, conceptualizing the "Real" very differently, repeatedly challenged Mao Dun's defense of his works as "realistic." They declared that his first three novellas, "Disillusionment," "Vacillation" (Dongyao, 1928), and "Pursuit" (Zhuiqiu, 1929), later collectively called the *Eclipse Trilogy* (*Shi sanbuqu*), had failed to capture the essence of an historical period of profound changes in China. For instance, in 1928 Qian Xingcun labeled *Eclipse* as "detailed expressions of bourgeois pathological psychology" in the historical context of the ebb of revolutionary causes ("Mao Dun yu xianshi" 106). Qian based his judgment of Mao Dun's fiction on his observation that "Mao Dun only exposed the darkness; he stopped at depicting decadence and reminiscing about the past. He forgot to look to the future" (129), a comment uncannily echoed by critics on mainland China twenty years later (Fan J. 151-52). The radical critics of Mao Dun's works, although apparently expressing dissatisfaction with his failure to capture the truth of reality, actually more concerned themselves with the lack of "revolutionary optimism" in his fiction. "Pessimism" in this case was a charge more serious than it had first appeared, for it connoted the author's unrevolutionary and unmodern position by describing him as clinging to the old mode of "realistic" representation while refusing to embrace the new revolutionary ideology. As a result, although a long-time enthusiastic promoter of Realist fiction, Mao Dun faced the unusual task of having to convince his readers and critics of the legitimacy of his version of Realism in the late 1920s. He proceeded, somewhat paradoxically, by attempting to objectify his personal emotions.

As mentioned above, in his reminiscence about his early fiction writing, Mao Dun accentuated the personal, emotional experience that had compelled him to write. Mao Dun called *Eclipse* his "honest confessions," for, he explained, it had captured his disillusionment, pessimism, and depression at the time ("Cong Guli dao Dongjing" 5). However, even if such invocations of his psychological and emotional experiences had succeeded in convincing his readers of the realistic basis of his fiction, he still needed to defend its objectivity, as he was allegedly describing highly personal emotions in his works. Consequently, Mao Dun at times tried to distance his fiction from his source materials, i.e., his personal experiences. He declared, "There are no thoughts from me in 'Disillusionment' and 'Vacillation.' There are only *objective* descriptions. 'Pursuit' does reflect my most recent thoughts and emotions, but the young characters' discontent, depression, and search for new routes are all *objectively* observed realities" ("Cong Guli dao Dongjing" 5–6; emphases mine). He also declared himself to be on moral high ground in representing these objective and truthful realities. In response to criticism of his backwardness, he thus defended the pessimistic portrayals in his works: "I could not point out a new path for people in my fiction, because I did not want to utter anything against my conscience [. . .] If this is called 'vacillation,' then I do not want to defend myself" ("Cong Guli dao Dongjing" 6).

Most importantly, Mao Dun conceived of the notion of "the true spirit of the times" (*shidaixing*), a kind of collective psychology of the people in a particular historical context, in order to prove the representation of his personal feelings to be true reflections of the reality. In his essays, Mao Dun had always insisted that the grasp of "the true spirit of the times" was vital for achieving "Realism" in fiction. In order to objectify his fiction in works such as *Eclipse*, the writing of which was admittedly motivated by personal emotions, Mao Dun had to establish an accord between "the true spirit of the times" and his emotions. As Marston Anderson observes, "In defense of his work he [Mao Dun] seems to say that if his own frustrations were discovered in the psychology of his compatriots as well, they could be identified as objective facts and were therefore acceptable for fictional representation" (*The Limits of Realism* 126). Mao Dun's idea of "the true spirit of the times" thus ironically boils down to a collective psychological realism, the genuineness of which can be easily confirmed by his own emotions. But more importantly, the notion of "the true spirit of the times" enabled Mao Dun to demonstrate through his fiction his courageous penetration into historical truth against the odds of his overpowering despair.

For the revelation of "the spirit of the times," Mao Dun used his narrative practice in fiction to perform "penetrating observation, sober analysis, and meticulous composition" ("Du *Ni Huanzhi*" 207), all core requirements of fictional realism by his standard, and thus to establish himself as a Realist writer with moral courage and the strength of character. Particularly, in all his fiction written in the late 1920s and early 1930s, he self-consciously represented strong-willed and over-sexualized women revolutionaries who often overwhelm their male counterpart, weaker modern male intellectuals, in their joint search for meanings in the chaotic Chinese revolution. Such a gender configuration in Mao Dun's fiction served two purposes. For one thing, Mao Dun sought to objectify subjective emotions by erecting boundaries of gender and genre while studiously avoiding first-person narration. After all, he was apparently writing about female "others" with objective modes of narration. More importantly, it was precisely through the exposure of male weakness by comparing him to the woman revolutionary that the author displayed his own mastery of personal despair and his ability to move beyond pessimism in search of painful yet liberating historical truth.

However, Mao Dun's representation of the woman revolutionary simultaneously betrayed the nonrealistic and nonmodern aspects of his fiction. By appropriating the figure of the woman for the construction of male subjectivity, Mao Dun manifested a male-centered consciousness also apparent in such works as Ba Jin's *Family*. But unlike Ba Jin, Mao Dun did not advocate the kind of gender equality that required women's emulation of men, and hence the eradication of gender differences, but instead accentuated male delectation of both the female body and female emotions. Mao Dun's infusion of a heavy dose of eroticism in the representation of new women not only linked him to Yu Dafu's less-than-revolutionary objectification of the female body but also exposed his ambiguous relationship to popular fiction of his time, which had previously provoked his wrath for allegedly degrading women and poisoning Chinese people's spirit. Furthermore, Mao Dun proved to be a connoisseur of female emotions as well as the female body. Resurrecting the traditional discourse of female virtue and bringing it into conjunction with the equally male-centered revolutionary discourses, he contrasted the constrained expression of decorous, gentle, maternal feelings by the more traditional type of women with the vivacity and uninhibited display of sexuality of revolutionary women, and revealingly allocated more male affection to the traditional type. As such, Mao Dun's representation of the woman revolutionary reveals the complex relationships both between the canons of classical Chinese literature and May Fourth literature, and between May Fourth literature and its contemporary popular fiction.

Below I first examine Mao Dun's earliest representation of the two types of women he claimed to have produced repeatedly in his fiction, the hesitant, bourgeois and the destructive, rebellious heroine. I will then explore the developments of these two types of women in his later fiction in order to illustrate Mao Dun's surreptitious bartering and trafficking of modern and traditional discourses even as he promoted "true" Realism.

Miss Jing and Miss Hui: The Paradox of Tradition and Modernity in *Eclipse*

Mao Dun had made a name for himself with his adroit fictional representation of women ever since the publication of his *Eclipse Trilogy*. As Mao Dun's earliest fictional work, the three novellas included in this trilogy encapsulated his "othering" strategy in the representation of women that would recur in his later works. As I have mentioned above, depicting women afforded Mao Dun a chance to objectify subjective emotions through the invocation of the conventions of Realism (Martin 65–71), for he was ostensibly merely portraying fictional women characters, the Other marked off by boundaries of gender and genre. The figure of the woman revolutionary particularly provided him with a convenient trope both to release personal anxiety and to convey revolutionary messages. In this respect, Mao Dun resurrected the allegorical tradition of classical Chinese poetry, in which literati created a literary persona through the figure of the abandoned woman to vent their own political frustrations.

Yet Mao Dun's fiction also carries a particular narrative tension of its own as he sought to establish his status as a *bona fide* Realist. Mao Dun's desire to appear realistic motivated his accentuation of the universality of the psychological state that he depicted while attempting at self-effacement: "It was not my intention to portray either the conflict between love and revolution or the vacillation of the bourgeois class in this novella ["Disillusionment"] [. . .] My focus was the topic 'disillusionment,' as if I was writing an assigned composition in high school" ("Cong Guli dao Dongjing" 5–6). Similarly, he declared: "'Vacillation' only describes vacillation, the vacillation of the revolutionaries when political struggle intensifies" (8). He even went so far as to claim that he had designated the characters in his fiction as manifestations of certain collective psychological traits rather than as "protagonists" (*zhuren gong*) in their own right (8). Whether that claim proved that some kind of conceptual framework had really preceded Mao Dun's characterization is open to discussion. But it undoubtedly revealed Mao Dun's anxiety to present himself as a self-possessed historian of a tumultuous age, one who carried out detached and keen observation of the collective psychology rather than being overcome by personal emotions when writing fiction. He asserted, "I have taken pains not to mix my 'subjectivity' [*zhuguan*] into 'Disillusionment' and 'Vacillation.' I have also made the characters' reactions towards the [1920s] revolution correspond to the objective [*keguan*] circumstances of the time" (5).

The intent to appear objective and masterful also explains Mao Dun's penchant for categorizing his women characters. He claimed that he had only portrayed two types of women in *Eclipse*: "Miss Jing [from "Disillusionment"] and Mrs. Fang [from "Vacillation"] belong together, and Miss Hui [from "Disillusionment"], Sun Wuyang [from "Vacillation"], and Zhang Qiuliu [from "Pursuit"] belong together" ("Cong Guli dao Dongjing" 5). He further endeavored to differentiate the two types of women by means of his own projection of what his readers' affective responses might be: "Miss Jing and Mrs. Fang will naturally draw sympathy from the public, or some might scold them as not being 'thorough' [in revolution]. But Miss Hui, Sun Wuyang, and Zhang Qiuliu, although not [completely] women revolutionaries, are not just superficial romantic women either. If readers do not find them lovable and pitiable, then it is the author's failure" (6). Yet, just as Mao Dun's abstract distinction between psychological states such as "disillusionment" and "vacillation" usually collapses at the levels of plot and characterization, his categorization of women characters also proves far from absolute. By examining the relationship between the author, the narrator, and the characters, we will find that Mao Dun assigned female characters to different roles only to accommodate the diverse needs of male subject formation more effectively.

Mao Dun originally planned to write a novel of over two hundred thousand words to depict the "three phases of modern young people's involvement in revolution" ("Cong Guli dao Dongjing" 4). These are: their excitement before the revolution occurs, their disappointment and vacillation when faced with the increasingly intense conflict between the revolutionary and antirevolutionary groups, and finally, their pursuit for a new meaningful goal to purge their disillusionment and vacillation. He eventually condensed this master plan into the three novellas as they stand now, though he claimed that he intended for "Disillusionment," "Vacillation," and "Pursuit" to constitute a cohesive unit. These three novellas share the same historical background and occasionally the same characters. Furthermore, Mao Dun wished for the combination of the three novellas not only to provide a complete picture of the psychological developments of the young people who took part in revolutionary activities but also to discover a way of regeneration for the dispirited revolutionaries of his time, and thus fending off criticism of "pessimism" and establishing his credit as a "Realist." Nevertheless, the plot of the three novels seems to illustrate the escalation of the revolutionary young people's pessimism without providing the characters or the readers with any feasible deliverance.

"Disillusionment" depicts the quest of Miss Jing, a girl student living alone in Shanghai, during the historical turmoil of the late 1920s. Like many young women of her time, Miss Jing leaves her home in the countryside, and goes to school in a big city. She is soon surrounded by unwelcome male suitors who enjoy nothing better than gossiping about women and passing around libelous sexual anecdotes. Her friend Miss Hui, who recently returned from Paris, lives with her for a short time, and meets one of her suitors, a male student named Baosu. Hui flirts with Baosu but then suddenly leaves Shanghai. Miss Jing feels great sympathy towards the lovelorn Baosu and spends the night with him, only to discover in the morning that she has been seduced by an immoral scoundrel who is not only a seasoned womanizer but also a paid informer for the government who has been spying on student activities. Jing falls ill and takes refuge in a hospital. Upon hearing the news of the Northern Expedition led by the Nationalist party and with her friends' encouragement, she goes to Wuhan to devote herself to the revolutionary cause. But she is once again disillusioned by the corruption and ineffectuality of the so-called revolutionary organizations. She then goes to a hospital to work as a nurse, where she meets a wounded lieutenant from the Northern Expedition Army by the name of Qiang Weili. The two of them fall in love and get married. But Qiang Weili is soon summoned back into the army and has to return to combat. At the end of the story Jing decides to wait for him with one of her old friends whose husband has also gone to battle. "It is as if I only had a dream, a happy dream," she sobs after Qiang Weili leaves her ("Huanmie" 99).

In contrast to the constant change of setting in "Disillusionment," the story in "Vacillation" takes place in one geographical location, a small county in the throes of revolution. Instead of following the life of one particular character, it incorporates multiple perspectives into the narration. Mao Dun especially privileged the viewpoints of two male characters: an opportunistic local squire who had recently renamed himself Hu Guoguang (meaning "nation's light"), and a weak political leader with unspecified party allegiance by the name of Fang Luolan (a transliteration of the name of the French Realist novelist Roman Roland). The power struggle between the two men climaxes in a bitter conflict between leftist activists on the one side and the antirevolutionary merchants and members of the local gentry on the other. Hu manages to take advantage of the union members' violent antagonism towards their employers and stirs up trouble in order to gain power. In contrast, Fang finds himself torn between the radicalism of his more revolutionary comrades on the one hand, and his sympathy towards shop owners as human beings on the other. To further complicate matters, Fang similarly wavers in his personal affairs. Although a happily married man with a small child, he finds himself fascinated by the dazzling woman revolutionary Sun Wuyang. This ill-fated attraction sparks rumors among the revolutionary community and jeopardizes the marital harmony of his own household. The triangle between Fang Luolan, his wife Meili, and the woman revolutionary Sun Wunyang constitutes a second story line. The end of the novella sees the collapse of these two storylines and failure in both Fang Luolan's public and private lives. Because of the mishandling of political affairs by political leaders such as Fang Luolan, the county government comes under a full-scale armed attack by the united forces of a warlord army and local antirevolutionary landlords and merchants led by Hu Guoguang. Fang Luolan, his wife, and Sun Wuyang coincidentally retreat to the refuge of the same old temple on the fringe of the town. Mrs. Fang breaks down after hearing about her good friend Miss Zhang's brutal death at the hands of the antirevolutionary forces and seeing Fang Luolan and Sun Wuyang talk together. In a hallucination, she sees a spider web in the dilapidated temple that seems to devour the whole universe and pitch everything into complete darkness.

Compared to the other two novellas in the trilogy, "Pursuit" represents the nadir of the revolutionaries' morale. The title is, to a large extent, a diametric contrast to the content of the story, for the characters in the novella all fail in their various pursuits, not to mention the fact that they are not very clear about what they wish to pursue in the first place. Mao Dun claimed that there are no protagonists in this novella. The story moves from one center of consciousness to another, representing the lives and psyches of a group of young people stumbling along in the aftermath of a failed revolution. Zhang Manqing wishes to reform education, but fails miserably even to reform his wife, a fellow teacher whom he previously regarded as a comrade with similar educational ideals. Wang Zhongzhao works as a journalist, and plans to make a name for himself in journalism in order to win the admiration of his attractive and ambitious fiancée. Yet at the end of the novella he receives a telegram informing him that she has been in an accident and been disfigured. Zhang Qiuliu, the only woman within this group, at first plunges herself into a ceaseless pursuit of amusement. She later decides to marry in order to take care of the very sick Shi Xun, only to see the death of her intended shortly after getting engaged. The same Shi Xun, the confirmed "skeptic" of the group and Zhang Qiuliu's sometime fiancé, likewise cannot achieve what he pursues: voluntary self-term-ination. His suicide attempt fails, and he dies instead from an acute illness just when he is planning to change his lifestyle and live with Zhang Qiuliu.

Mao Dun's objective of depicting the development of the collective psychology through the narrative progression of these three novellas falls short. For by repeatedly producing the same types of characters who react to their environment in predictable ways, the distinctive psychological stages (e.g., disillusionment, vacillation) that they purportedly embody also share recurrent traits that form a repetition rather than evolution between the novellas. Furthermore, through the description of the repeated setbacks faced by these characters, all three novellas exude an acute sense of despair rather than convey any optimistic messages. As I mentioned earlier, faced with criticism of "pessimism" and "false realism" from radical intellectuals, Mao Dun cited a truthful representation of the collective psychology as sufficient evidence of his revolutionary commitment, particularly emphasizing his depiction of women in order to establish his modern and revolutionary credentials. Therefore, it is all the more necessary for us to bring a close scrutiny to his narrative representation of the two "archetypal" female characters in these three novellas for the evaluation of his claim to a revolutionary and modern identity.

In "Disillusionment" Mao Dun established these two types of women in the characters Miss Jing and Miss Hui. He characterized Miss Jing as "ceaselessly pursuing something, and ceaselessly disillusioned" ("Cong Guling dao Dongjing" 6). In contrast, Miss Hui is bolder, more experienced, and hardened by her past sexual debacles. As the heroine of "Disillusionment," Miss Jing presumably should occupy the focus of the narration, since her life was meant to represent the universal "disillusionment people felt between the summer and fall of 1927, a feeling shared not only by the petit bourgeois class, but also by the proletariat and peasantry" ("Cong Guling dao Dongjing" 7). However, the omniscient narrator's gaze constantly strays to Miss Hui whenever she appears on the scene. For instance, in Chapter Three of the novella, Hui, Jing, and Baosu go to a movie together. The narrative shifts to the description of the appearance of Miss Hui and Miss Jing:

> When half of the movie had been shown, there was a ten-minute intermission. The lights went on inside the theatre. We could see the three of them sitting on the same row of chairs, with Jing in the

middle. It was quite warm in May. Hui was wearing a purple silk *qipao*. The soft silk fit her body tightly, one hundred and ten percent snug, outlining every detail of its round protrusions in a most uninhibited fashion. She had a pair of limpid, lively eyes under curvy eyebrows, small flowery lips wrapping around even and small white teeth. Miss Hui was really enchanting! ("Huanmie" 20)

The women are sitting in a movie theatre. As they watch the movie, they themselves are simultaneously on display. It is the omniscient narrator who examines and savors their beauty. He also compares the two of them and makes suitable evaluations:

> But you couldn't say that Miss Jing wasn't beautiful as well. Hui's beauty could be described, while Jing's could not; you could not point to any feature of Jing's face or body and say how it conformed to the Grecian standard of beauty, and you also couldn't point out what the special features of her body were, its sensual attractions. You could go so far as to say that Miss Jing's eyes, nose, and mouth were an ordinary set of eyes, nose, and mouth, but when all these ordinary features were gathered together as "Miss Jing," they immediately took on a magical quality, as though there were something that could be neither seen nor described integrating her limbs and bones, permeating her every cell; and the result was a complete beauty that couldn't be analyzed. (20, trans. in Lieberman 129)

The most interesting aspect of the above portrayal of Miss Jing and Miss Hui lies not so much in the fact that the narrator offers "two very different erotic objects" (Lieberman 129) as in the different narrative devices he adopts to describe the two women. To be sure, the narrator invokes the storyteller manner of premodern vernacular fiction to depict both women. He especially simulates the interaction between the traditional storyteller and his audience. When depicting the two women, he adopts the comradely "we" and "you" to encourage his audience's participation. He delivers his words of wisdom, asks for confirmation, and implicitly invites his audience to join in a collective fantasy: "If, such a time, there were a thousand beauties available for your choosing [. . .]" (20). The male-centered tone is unmistakable.

However, it is even more striking to note the way different narrative models are invoked in the depiction of the two types of women. The narrator's lingering, almost tactile gaze seeks out a variety of details of Hui's facial features, her bodily contours, and her dress. Jing, on the other hand, is described with minimal detail, as the narrator ingeniously resorts to nondescription as description, appealing to the reader's imagination through the use of words such as "magic." Apparently modeling himself on the realistic style of authors like Zola, the narrator goes into meticulous detail in the depiction of Hui's physical appearance, but when describing Jing's external beauty, which defies "the Grecian standard of beauty" (20), he immediately applies the classical Chinese literary aesthetic that emphasizes conciseness, brevity, and the use of allusions and implications.

The intentional inventory or omission of details in the description of the two women's appearances suggests that the narrator identifies with the womanizer Baosu's gaze, who is at that point more enamored of the obvious and aggressive sensuality of Miss Hui than of the subtle beauty of Miss Jing. Yet, despite the erotic fascination suggested by the space given to the depiction of Miss Hui's appearance, the narrator claims to favor the quieter and more decorous beauty of Jing, as if wishing to distance himself from the womanizing Baosu. Miss Hui's beauty is evaluated as more eye-catching. But the narrator is quick to point out its flaws, "Hui gets you excited; she has a mysterious power of attraction that irresistibly draws one close to her; but excitement soon gives way to weariness and numbness, and you then yearn to escape from Hui's feminine provocation" (20). Conversely, he rhapsodizes over the ineffable beauty of Jing: "Her serene beauty can stabilize your nerves; she intoxicates you, as though her body exudes some delicate fragrance or shoots forth some electrical current that flows stronger over time, until you are finally besieged and must 'surrender your weapons and quietly await your punishment'" (20). Whether the narrator approves of Jing because she is more "motherly" than Hui (Lieberman 129) is open to debate, but she undeniably appears to be a more traditional, decorous type of Chinese beauty who soothes and nurtures with her subtler charms. As such, it is all the more significant that the narrator endows her with "a magical quality," describing her as possessing "something that could be neither seen nor described integrating her limbs and bones, permeating her every cell; and the result was a complete beauty that couldn't be analyzed" (20). Furthermore, Mao Dun seemed to suggest that this "something" that made the more traditional woman superior to the modern type was the psychological depth possessed by the former.

As a significant contrast to the allocation of space for the description of the two women's external appearances, the more traditional Jing is portrayed as psychologically more complex than the bolder Hui in the story. Therefore, we can see that while Mao Dun utilized a replica of the traditional male storyteller to express his nostalgia for the imagined serenity of tradition embodied in the more traditional woman, his deep involvement in the production of modern discourses also ironically equipped him with modern devices for the resurrection of tradition. In other words, Mao Dun's conceptualization of Realism prompted him to claim that he developed Jing's psyche in depth only for the illustration of collective disillusionment, but at the same time, his detailed description of her psyche also enabled him to surreptitiously cast tradition in a more positive and appealing light.

Mao Dun's relationships to both tradition and modernity were both complex and ambiguous. At first glance, his differential treatment of the two women's physical and psychological traits in "Disillusionment," and of male sexual and emotive responses towards them, would seem to bear out the division of male libidinal energies into "the two strains of tenderness and sensuality" suggested by Freud: "the man almost always feels his sexual activity hampered by his respect for the woman and only develops full sexual potency when he finds himself in the presence of a lower type of sexual object" (64). But as I will demonstrate in the following analysis of "Vacillation"—which features the same divide of women's sexual versus spiritual attraction, and men's sexual versus emotional bonding with them—the revolutionary male intellectual experiences impotency and harbors feelings of confusion and trepidation when faced with the sexually uninhibited woman revolutionary, whereas the more "respectable" traditional woman helps to restore his self-confidence in his masculine prowess as well as secures his affection.

Like "Disillusionment," "Vacillation" also betrays the contradictions within Mao Dun's "modernity," particularly in his delineation of the relationships between Fang Luolan, his wife Meili, and the woman revolutionary Sun Wuyang, a triangular arrangement that would resurface in various forms in Mao Dun's other stories. As was the case in "Disillusionment," in "Vacillation" Mao Dun not only invoked the allegorical tradition of classical Chinese poetry but also eroticized the female body (see also Lieberman 124–33 and D. Wang, *Fictional Realism* 77–89), thus using the female body as a "mediating place" (D. Wang, *Fictional Realism* 77–79) to represent the abstract categories of tradition and modernity and resurrecting the traditional patriarchal gaze that objectifies women. But "Vacillation" also more explicitly reveals Mao Dun's ambivalence towards popular fiction of his time in his construction of the romantic triangle.

According to Perry Link, the triangle in "Mandarin Duck and Butterfly Fiction"—popular love stories that flourished in large cities in China in the early twentieth century—typically involves one man as the pinnacle of a pyramid arrangement and two women respectively representing traditional and modern values who are subject to his often voyeuristic gaze (196–235). Comprised of a man and two women—Fang Luolan, his wife Meili, and the woman revolutionary Sun Wuyang—the romantic triangle in "Vacillation" seems dangerously akin to those prevalent in the "Butterfly Fiction." Since Mao Dun had persistently attacked "Butterfly Fiction," which he accused of "poisoning Chinese people" with "a worldview of playing with life and indulging in one's desires" (qtd. in Mao D., "Zhenyou daibiao" 311), he was naturally eager to emphasize that his triangular arrangement was different from that of "Butterfly Fiction." He declared that he had intended the romantic triangle in the novella to reveal the character Fang Luolan's political vacillation and impotency in the public arena, stating, "Currently we can still write about characters' political allegiance directly, unlike Turgenev, who had to resort to romance to depict politics. But Fang Luolan's romance with Sun Wuyang is not just an idle episode (*xianbi*) either, because it proves that he vacillates on all fronts, including in romance" ("Cong Guli dao Dongjing" 9).

In addition to his claim to have deployed romance as an allegory for politics, in narrative execution Mao Dun apparently reversed the power structure of the old romantic triangle of "Butterfly Fiction," intent as he seemed on exposing the hero's weakness rather than upholding his control of the triangle. In the novella Fang Luolan is portrayed as lacking initiative both in romance and in politics. He is very attracted to Sun Wuyang, who confuses even as she dazzles him; yet he refuses to divorce his wife Meili, even though Meili insists on it. Whenever rebuffed by one woman, he always gravitates towards the other. Thus trapped in "a romantic double bind" (M. Anderson, *The Limits of Realism* 138), Fang Luolan's personal life appears to be completely dominated by two opposite forces of attraction. In a similar vein, in his public life Fang does not demonstrate any political conviction in his dealings with party leaders, fellow political workers, or the town residents. He sympathizes with shop owners who claim that they are going bankrupt because of the sales clerks' strike, but he also feels alarmed when the antirevolutionary forces assemble to attack union members. Consequently, his efforts to mitigate the more radical demands of his colleagues or to placate the disgruntled gentry class both fail miserably.

Furthermore, Mao Dun unwittingly invoked what René Girard has described as the triangle of circular desires to reveal Fang's weakness. Girard suggests that in certain romantic triangles it is not the courted object that sparks competition. Rather, the two suitors compete with each other precisely because each believes that the other desires the object (Girard 7). Therefore, it is the desire to be the other suitor rather than the desire for the allegedly coveted object that sustains the triangle. In "Vacillation," Fang Luolan is described as voluntarily turning himself into the object of desire. On the one hand, he entertains fantasies that the two women compete for his affection. It gratifies him and provides him with a sense of security to imagine two women vying for his attention and affection, particularly when he is experiencing agonizing uncertainty caused by political chaos. On the other hand, his desire for both women also only reflects what he perceives as their desire for him. For instance, he is drawn to Sun Wuyang because he believes she "understands" him. Conversely, he resents his wife Meili when she treats him coldly. In turning himself into the object of desire, Fang Luolan not only surrenders his personal agency, but also consigns himself to the position of the superfluous factor in the triangle. This is because, as the Girardian triangle suggests, the two suitors actually compete with each other out of a desire for the other's position in the triangle rather than for the purported object of desire. Utterly passive in his pursuit of romance, Fang Luolan appears as a diametric contrast to the suitor in "Butterfly Fiction" who energetically pursues two women. By thus conjuring up an ostensibly different triangle to expose Fang Luolan's flaws, Mao Dun fulfilled his mission of representing intellectuals' "vacillation."

Indeed, in revealing Fang Luolan's weakness, Mao Dun changed the dynamics in the romantic triangle of "Butterfly Fiction" and established himself as a Realist novelist who unflinchingly exposed the character flaws and flagging spirits of revolutionaries in spite of his own personal emotional chaos. However, as he exploited the images of the two women and accentuated their sexuality in order to construct an apparently new triangle, he ironically made a centripetal move to "Butterfly Fiction." This is because, in contrast to the plot of "Vacillation," where the male protagonist is denied the control of the triangle, on the narrative level Mao Dun installed a male-identified omniscient narrator who deftly deploys the two female characters and allegorizes the rivalry between them as the competition between more conservative and more radical attitudes towards revolutions, thus resurrecting the power relationship characteristic of the original triangle in "Butterfly Fiction." Just like the popular authors whom he had denounced as antirevolutionary and poisoning Chinese people's spirit, Mao Dun positioned two women against each other as symbols of mutually exclusive ideological tendencies.

Not only did Mao Dun base his own modern identity on the construction of this traditional male-centered triangle, he also partly redeemed Fang Luolan's masculinity and modernity through the strategy of deploying women to accentuate the uniqueness and centrality of Fang's psyche. In "Vacillation" the two women never directly confront each other. Meili accuses Fang Luolan of infidelity only behind closed doors at home. Sun Wuyang declares that she does not want Fang Luolan for a lover, and instead advises Fang to make amends to his wife and reconcile with her. But the author devised their battles in Fang Luolan's psyche, and consigned the two women as ideological types to be fixed in antagonistic locations through his deployment of the omniscient narrator. As such, even though portraying Fang as a weak male, Mao Dun still credited him with a psychological complexity less noticeable in the women characters. Furthermore, Mao Dun seemed to suggest that the hesitancy and weakness Fang demonstrates in his sexual encounters with the woman revolutionary signifies an innate moral core, for only depraved antirevolutionary males such as Baosu (in "Disillusionment") and Hu Guoguang were portrayed as having no qualms about trampling moral code for the gratification of their sexual appetites. This moralistic coloring of Mao Dun conception of modern masculinity is echoed by his male-centered moralistic treatment of female sexuality.

Mao Dun displayed an objectifying attitude towards modern women in basing his judgment of a woman's degree of commitment to modern or revolutionary principles on their sexual behaviors. He seemed to define modernity in women mostly as the kind of uninhibited female sexuality or even promiscuity demonstrated in the character Sun Wuyang, who claims to be "toying with men" rather than loving them. Moreover, Mao Dun contrived to have the hero, Fang Luolan, emotionally more attached to the more traditional woman of the pair. Sun Wuyang is a source of bafflement and intimidation for Fang Luolan. On one occasion, he even mistakes Sun's contraceptive medicine for cosmetics. By contrast, his wife Meili provides him with a more secure anchor not only because they have been married for more than five years, but also because Fang Luolan shares with her similar feelings of confusion and disorientation at a chaotic time. To be sure, he at first expresses discontent or even exasperation towards Meili's "backwardness," but that is precisely because he cannot stand seeing his own weakness revealed to him in the image of the Other. Even though easily captivated by character traits that complement his own shortcomings and repulsed by weakness similar to his own, Fang Luolan is more emotionally engaged with the traditional woman than with the modern woman. To put it simplistically, he cannot help experiencing more complex and more deeply felt reactions to the traditional woman, for it is she, rather than the modern woman, who provides a faithful mirror to himself. Not surprisingly, Mao Dun had Fang eventually return to his wife's side like the proverbial strayed and repent husband. Fang Luolan is described as reviving both his affection *and* sexual desires for his wife faced with his wife's devotion to the family, her gentle caring of their son, and her dignified demand for a divorce after finding out about Fang's attraction by Sun Wuyang—she declares, "The education I received was not modern, of course, but it did teach me not to play the fool" ("Dongyao" 206).

Just like the case with "Disillusionment," in depicting Fang Luolan's relationships with the two types of women, Mao Dun allocated more space to the description of the psyche of the traditional woman than that of the modern woman. In this way, he came up with a more nuanced picture of Meili, rather than Sun Wuyang, through the eyes of Fang Luolan. Since Meili's psychology provides a more faithful copy of that of Fang Luolan, Mao Dun's depiction of Fang's impotency towards the revolutionary woman, rather than the more respectable traditional woman (as suggested by Freud), signifies not only the character's moral inhibition but also a profound male narcissism. Fang's love for himself apparently rechannels his erotic passions, diverting them from the revolutionary woman, a morally "lower" sexual object by Freudian standards, towards the more respectable traditional woman.

However, Mao Dun also showed that male self-love subsists on the man's "loving" of both types of women, albeit in different ways. The traditional woman, with her psychological similarity to the man, confirms the core "spiritual" values cherished by the male intellectual. In contrast, the sexually uninhibited revolutionary woman, by flaunting her exotic attraction, induces in him not only the sense of his own moral righteousness but also erotic titillation. Mao Dun frequently betrayed in "Vacillation" a motivating force similar to that featured in popular fiction: male erotic fantasy. Contrary to Mao Dun's claim that he had designed Fang Luolan's romantic failures as a metaphor for his political foibles, eroticism actually overrules political concerns in "Vacillation." The narrator constantly highlights sexual tensions in various political activities, such as by describing how Sun Wuyang flirts with the party leader, Shi Jun. He also implicitly measures the male characters' strength or weakness by their sexual conquests. Hu Guoguang, "the old fox of long standing," for instance, cleverly manipulates the political movement of liberating the country women from arranged marriages to satisfy his own lust, and emerges as the real leader in the community. Fang's romantic debacles, rather than playing second fiddle to politics, as Mao Dun would have us believe, at times disconcert him so much that he cannot concentrate on his political work. His negligence of work due to romantic distractions also plays a part in the complete collapse of the county government at the end of the novella.

From the above analysis of the complex triangular configuration in "Vacillation," we can see that by privileging the male voice and male gaze, Mao Dun deployed women as convenient tools to demarcate either male emotional sensitivity and moral superiority or his sexual prowess and political wiliness. The woman in effect becomes a double signifier that serves as both a political allegory and as a barometer of masculine prowess, be it more "spiritual" or "corporeal." As such, Mao Dun's effort of distancing himself from popular fiction and tradition met with only a dubious success.

The problematic in Mao Dun's deployment of women in his fiction takes on new forms in "Pursuit." In this novella, the woman Zhang Qiuliu appears as another incarnation of the Miss Hui-type character. She is a former revolutionary disheartened by the 1927 Nationalist massacre of the Communist Party members. In addition to the uninhibited exhibition of sexuality also characteristic of Miss Hui and Sun Wuyang, Zhang Qiuliu embarks on a restless pursuit, moving from one project to another. When the novella begins, she participates in the launch of a society with the vaguely phrased purpose of "criticizing the current state of the nation" ("Zhuiqiu" 271). Yet she seems to devote most of her time to playing around: dancing, drinking, and going to movies. She finally decides to have a relationship with Shi Xun, the cynical and very ill "doubter" of the group. But he dies before very long and leaves her groping for a purpose in life again.

Zhang Qiuliu is depicted as masculine in temperament: "Friends always say that she is a woman in flesh but a man in disposition. She has indeed proven herself a daring person without fear in a lot of things. She has a strong personality, sometimes akin to being egotistical and individualistic" (320). Significantly, this more masculine woman fares even worse than Miss Hui and Sun Wuyang, as if her more explicitly masculinized strength has to be punished and contained. After the death of her lover Shi Xun, she discovers that she has contracted syphilis from him. Not only is her health threatened, she could also become a pariah due to the stigma traditionally attached to sexually transmitted diseases in Chinese culture. Furthermore, Zhang Qiuliu is narratively assigned to play a limited role. She constitutes neither the center (e.g., Miss Jing) nor one of the two wings (e.g., Meili and Sun Wuyang) of the narrative. She is only one example of a group of young people who pursue different goals in life, contributing to the large picture of "the sorrow of disillusionment, the anxiety about self-improvement, and the impulse towards decadence" (Mao D., *Wo zouguo de daolu* 265). The end of the novella sees her declare her *carpe diem* philosophy to friends in the hospital, while the downpour of rain outside the window sounds "like the bullets fired outside Jinan city on May the Third" ("Zhuiqiu" 420). The image of bullets echoes Zhang Qiuliu's avowal to enjoy life to the fullest, even if she should meet with a violent death that would suddenly cut it short. Although some of Mao Dun's contemporaries read in this ending Zhang Qiuliu's eventual return to the revolutionary path because of her passionate pursuit for an "explosive, unusual death" (Xing 107), the image of bullets also causes the narrative to shift from her fate to a historical event, thus further assimilating Zhang's life into the sociopolitical environment of the time.

Another narrative strategy to diminish Zhang Qiuliu consists in the alteration of the triangle existing in Mao Dun's two previous novellas. In "Pursuit" Mao Dun not only re-assembled the dyadic arrangement of women characters as symbols of tradition and modernity, but also replaced the man in the original triangle with children as a new definitive point. Wang Shitao, a female character who first appears in "Disillusionment," presents a sharp contrast to Zhang Qiuliu. Wang is pregnant with the child of a revolutionary who has died in battle and left her quite destitute. However, she decides to carry the child to its full term despite Zhang's skepticism. Wang understands that "in an era full of intense conflicts, women suffer the most, especially those women with children" (372). But she wants to have the baby, because, she explains, "I always feel that children are necessary. They are the hope of future. Our lives are limited, but our struggle is long. Children can carry on our torches into the future" (372). Commenting on Zhang Qiuliu's disapproval of her friend's decision, the narrator adds, "A woman cannot understand a mother's feelings until she is taught by the mystery of pregnancy" (372). This brings into sharp relief Mao Dun's tendency to associate revolutionary women with infertility and lack of proper "feminine" feelings including maternal instincts, and more traditional women with the role of mother. For instance, Sun Wuyang uses contraceptives while Meili has a son. Compared to Zhang Qiuliu's barrenness and sexual impairment caused by disease, Wang is portrayed as a courageous and high-minded mother who sees in her offspring the promise of victory of the revolutionary cause. In this way, Zhang Qiuliu is further reduced in stature and character. The narrator's sympathy decidedly inclines toward the more tradition-bound Wang Shitao rather than towards Zhang Qiuliu. In the end, while Zhang's life is damaged by venereal disease, Wang can still entertain hope for the future. Once again, Mao Dun produced a dazzling modern woman only to have her morally eclipsed by a more traditional rival. Thus, we can see that Mao Dun's apparent enchantment with revolutionary women proved no match for his more profound attachment to the traditional discourses of female virtue. This deep-rooted traditionality in him would cause him to adopt new strategies to channel the new woman's passions from sex to revolution in his novel *Hong* (*Rainbow*), and thus to simultaneously mold her into a better mirror for the extratextual authorial psychological development.

Mao Dun ascribed the changes in his representation of new women to his own psychological needs. He reminisced that he wrote the three novellas of *Eclipse* while he was a blacklisted political refugee in hiding from the Nationalist government. He claimed that "Pursuit" particularly registered his internal turmoil, and that it took him twice as much time to finish as did either "Disillusionment" or "Vacillation," stating: "I was experiencing spiritual agony at the time [of writing "Pursuit"]" ("Cong Guli dao Dongjing" 10). But he vowed to shake himself free of the shadow that his works such as *Eclipse* had cast upon his mood: "I do not want to feel depressed anymore. I believe I really can bestir myself. I can see the goddess Verdandi [of the three goddesses of fate from Nordic myths; Verdandi, the middle one, represents the present] beckoning to me, urging me to march forward" ("Cong Guli dao Dongjing" 10). These words of self-encouragement reappear in Mao Dun's preface to his anthology of short stories entitled *Wild Roses* (*Ye qiangwei*, 1928), signaling an altered strategy in his deployment of emotions for the consolidation of his modern identity. That is, in addition to the realistic depiction of the collective emotional and psychological state, he was also to demonstrate his own masculine and heroic forbearance through his attempts at generating "revolutionary optimism" regardless of his personal feelings. Interestingly, he also toned down description of female sexuality and accentuated the psychological complexity of the woman revolutionary in his later *Rainbow*. This fact reveals the close connection of his representation of woman's psychological depth, his proclamation of moral rectitude (often associated by him with revolutionary commitment), and the extratextual performance of his modern masculinity.

From *Wild Roses* to *Rainbow*

When Mao Dun published the short stories later anthologized as *Wild Roses*, he encountered criticisms of "sensuality" (*rougan*) or even "pornography" for his depiction of women. Seen in hindsight, the criticism of "sensuality" of Mao Dun's fiction in the 1920s and 1930s revealed the gender politics in play at the time. A significant difference between the criticisms of Mao Dun's early fiction by his contemporaries and by more recent scholars consists in that it was mostly criticized as "unrevolutionary" by the former while characterized as "feminine" by the latter. For instance, C. T. Hsia claims that Mao Dun's fiction was typical of "the more feminine South, romantic, sensuous, and melancholic" (*A History of Modern Chinese Fiction* 165). David Wang also observes that Mao Dun wrote "like a woman" (*Fictional Realism* 79). Most recently, Chinese scholar Yan Jiayan even ascribes Mao Dun's supposed feminine style to the topography of his hometown in western Zhejiang province (261–67). Mao Dun had criticized the fiction by his contemporary women writers such as Bing Xin and Lu Yin for their alleged feminine emotionalism, and arguably contributed to the marginalization of modern Chinese women writers (D. Wang, *Fictional Realism* 77–89; Lieberman 124–25). In this light, his contemporary male critics' refraining from dealing him the epithet of "feminine writer" seems to indicate a kind of male solidarity performed in critical literature, which further excluded women from Chinese modernity. Despite this possible male support, however, Mao Dun's fervent and repeated self-justification also suggests his awareness of his precarious position as a modern and masculine intellectual and of his urgent need to perform his modernity and masculinity.

Just as he had in his defense against the charge of "pessimism" against his *Eclipse*, Mao Dun invoked the concept of "Realism" as well as revolutionary rhetoric to defend his *Wild Roses*. He claimed to have "exposed the characters' class ideologies through their romantic behavior" in this anthology ("Xie zai *Ye qiangwei* de qianmian" 13). He also argued that the sexual liberation of the female characters demonstrated their break from "traditional thought," and thus signaled their revolutionary potential ("Xie zai *Ye qiangwei* de qianmian" 13). Moreover, Mao Dun again summoned "Realism" to his aid. In the preface to *Wild Roses*, he implied that he regarded it his mission to reveal defects in life for the betterment of society. Mao Dun described himself as one with the courage and selflessness to sacrifice personal reputation for the collective good. Alluding to the Norwegian novelist Johan Bojer's fable about wild roses, he declared: "Life is just like wild roses [. . .] We ought to identify where the thorns are and pluck them. If my works can serve the purpose of plucking thorns, I will be happy even with hurting my own hands [in the process]" ("Xie zai *Ye qiangwei* de qianmian" 14). Yet his narrative practice in *Wild Roses* jeopardizes his claim to revolutionary Realism, and thus thwarts his performance of his modern identity.

Wild Roses consists of five stories, all featuring women, but only three of them concentrate on the images of modern women: "Creation" ("Chuangzao," 1928), "Poetry and Prose" ("Shi yu sanwen," 1928), and "Haze" ("Tan," 1929). In these three stories Mao Dun poked fun at male characters who are self-styled mentors and creators of modern Chinese women. By representing these male intellectuals as invariably routed or frustrated by the women of their "creation," Mao Dun established the superiority of a narrator/author who presents ironic or satirical pictures of the unenlightened male who cannot appreciate the modern qualities in women. Yet, at the same time, Mao Dun's narrative practice also betrays his own ties to a patriarchal tradition. This can be illustrated particularly through an examination of his short story "Creation."

In this Chinese *Pygmalion*, a male intellectual named Junshi is dismayed by the fruits of his intellectual labor in shaping an example of the new woman. He has reeducated his wife, Xianxian, disabusing her of traditional ideals and instilling in her modern values. However, he succeeds beyond his wildest dreams. Previously shy, she becomes sexually aggressive. Previously indifferent to politics, now she actively participates in political meetings and takes a radical stand on the issues of the day. In the past she was content with a simple life, but now she demands material gratification. Junshi laments that his creation is a destruction of Xianxian's appealing old qualities, for he thinks Xianxian became corrupted by the volatile social environment immediately after he had broken her of her old habits. Xianxian, on the other hand, proceeds to go out to one of her political meetings, leaving him a note stating: "I am going out. Please catch up with me, otherwise I will not be waiting for you" ("Chuangzao" 31).

This story reveals Junshi's male narcissism as manifested in his attempt to create an image of the Self in the Other. It also questions the usual methods that May Fourth intellectuals had employed to modernize Chinese women by showing that the alleged "modernizers" themselves fell woefully short in the face of modernization. As is revealed in the story, after a traditional woman is convinced to adopt modern values, her mentor, the purportedly modern man, immediately turns into a conservative husband, for he discovers that his authority has slipped away from him as a result of his creation of a modern woman. Despite Mao Dun's valid social criticism, however, "Creation" illustrates once again that the author's male-centered consciousness has organized the entire narration. Even though ostensibly extolled for her liberation, the modern woman is still subjugated by the author's male gaze. Not only is she classified as "modern" mostly due to her brash sexuality, but the author also adopted certain narrative devices to curtail her autonomy. A telling detail in this regard is the different modes of representation before and after Xianxian's "transformation." When she is a more reserved traditional woman, the narrator relays all her conversations with her husband Junshi, giving a painstaking inventory of the various topics of their dialogues and the husband's contemplation of counter measures to reform Xianxian's traditional worldview. Although marking each stage of the creation of Xianxian only from Junshi's point of view, Mao Dun at least described Junshi's mental and emotional engagement with his wife at this stage. However, once she becomes a new woman, Xianxian's clothes, her physical beauty, and aggressive sexuality become the descriptive focus, implying that physical attributes alone make the modern woman. Of course, Xianxian's modernity is purportedly also demonstrated by her political activism. However, Xianxian's life outside the home is only vaguely touched upon, and to Junshi's mind, presents only a minor annoyance compared to her aggressive sexuality. Xianxian is represented first and foremost as a truant wife, not as a revolutionary woman. Mao Dun's narrative execution in "Creation" reveals that although mocking the hapless Junshi in the story in order to demonstrate his own modern consciousness, he secretly joined in the hero's labors to contain the modern woman through narrative devices. By accentuating the modern woman's alluring physical appearance but not her psychological individuality, Mao Dun not only allowed his voyeuristic fascination to contradict his self-proclaimed political intention, but also betrayed once again the way that the traditional discourses of female virtue determined the scope of his literary modernization.

We can see that Mao Dun's performance of his masculine modern identity was not entirely successful in *Wild Roses*. By privileging erotic images of modern women, he not only failed to create a heroine resembling the goddess Verdandi who would point him to a bright future, but also betrayed his own absorption with "sensual, indulgent" (Qian X., "Mao Dun yu xianshi" 124), and, allegedly, feminine pleasures. Small wonder Mao Dun next produced the novel *Rainbow* (*Hong*, 1929), in which he strove to delineate the making of a woman revolutionary with more masculine austerity.

Rainbow stands as the first climax in Mao Dun's fiction writing career, since for the first time he featured a full-length *Bildungsroman* of a modern Chinese woman, by the name Mei Xingsu. In that Mei plays different roles at different stages of her life, the representation of this heroine provides an apt vehicle for the reader to revisit Mao Dun's previous literary endeavors. She is a girl student when the May Fourth Movement breaks out. She then fights her way out of a confining arranged marriage and becomes a professional woman living in the city. Last, she joins in the revolutionary cause in Shanghai in the 1920s. Mei Xingsu also encounters different types of women in her struggle, who variously recall Miss Hui, Miss Jing, Sun Wuyang, Meili, and Zhang Qiuliu. Moreover, not only did Mao Dun integrate the previously dyadic paring of women characters (i.e., conservative vs. revolutionary) into Mei's complex psyche, he also had her alternate between masculine and feminine positions in her consciousness. Therefore, the reader can find in Mei's psychological development versions of the attacks of weakness suffered by Fang Luolan and Meili, the aggressive sexuality of Miss Hui, and the kind of revolutionary zeal demonstrated by Sun Wuyang. Additionally, Mao Dun portrayed Mei's transformation from a bourgeois individualist into a woman revolutionary devoted to collective causes, thus promoting the radical ideology of his time by presenting Mei's metamorphosis as the ideal model for modern intellectuals. He himself explicitly stated the "positive significance" of having Mei joining in the revolution in the novel, claiming that he produced through this novel a "bridge of rainbow and hope" ("Mao Dun huiyi lu" 418) not only for the reader but also for himself. This is because, he elaborated, although his "complicated thoughts and feelings" added to the ambivalence of the novel, the end product could steer him in a new direction ("Mao Dun huiyi lu" 418). It is therefore all the more important to examine to what extent his self-conscious construction and deployment of the new woman Mei succeeded in generating such revolutionary optimism.

Mao Dun's attempts at creating a more positive role model in Mei Xingsu are apparent from the very beginning. The heroine's name alone signals the adaptation of traditional values into a modern context. Her family name is Mei, homophone of plum blossom, which traditionally symbolizes aloofness and integrity in classical Chinese aesthetics. Her personal name "Xingsu" is taken from the idiom *wo xing wo su*, denoting the characteristic of following one's own chosen path and ignoring the constraint of social norms. Living up to her significant name, Mei Xingsu demonstrates in the earlier part of the novel a personality that illustrates not only a fusion of traditional elitist sensibility and modern individualistic ideals but also masculine courage and resolution. The narrator summarizes her temperament in the very first chapter, "She was no ordinary girl. She was like a rainbow [...] She simply charged forward with the spirit of a warrior, doing what circumstances dictated. Indeed, her special talent was 'charging forward.' Her only ambition was to overcome her environment, overcome her fate" (4).

In a similar effort to commend Mei's character, Mao Dun described Mei's transformation from being merely a courageous individualist to a revolutionary woman warrior, casting her in a more positive light than her predecessors, such as Sun Wuyang and Zhang Qiuliu, through the emphasis of not only her individualist courage but also her revolutionary moral fiber. Mei is portrayed as having a strong personality, but as being less egoistic than Miss Hui or Zhang Qiuliu. She is never as promiscuous as Sun Wuyang and, in the end, devotes herself to the collective revolutionary cause because of her love for one man. But Mao Dun's teleological narrative of the making of a woman revolutionary was not always successful. At times he manifested some uncertainty in his account of her transformation, leaving the novel unfinished and disjointed.

Mao Dun originally planned to "trace the great drama in China that has happened over the past ten years" through the writing of *Rainbow* ("*Hong* ba" 15). Yet the novel turned out to cover only the first five years after the May Fourth Movement, abruptly ending with the May 30 rally in Shanghai in 1925. This is, of course, yet another example of Mao Dun's tendency to truncate his original plans, as demonstrated in his scaling down of *Eclipse* and *Midnight* (*Ziye*, 1933). Marston Anderson attributed this to Mao Dun's failure to discover "a structural framework that would both envelop the particulars of his social observations and place those particulars in just proportion to one another" (*The Limits of Realism* 129). In the particular case of *Rainbow*, however, Mao Dun's uneasiness about the heroine's fortuitous turn towards collectivism also contributed to the unfinished state of the novel.

As I have mentioned earlier, Mao Dun had intended to make a fresh start after writing *Eclipse* in the grip of deep despair, both to raise his own morale and to justify himself in the eyes of his more radical comrades. Yet the solution he outlined for modern intellectuals in *Rainbow* was neither new nor convincing. Chronologically speaking, the story in this novel takes place before the disillusionment caused by the 1927 political turmoil represented in *Eclipse*. Therefore, the validity of political work, promoted as it is in the latter half of *Rainbow* as the only meaningful way for modern intellectuals to realize themselves, was already called into question by Mao Dun's earlier *Eclipse*. Mao Dun was also a political activist himself who had actually experienced the carnage and despair of 1927. It seems that Mao Dun would have to both purposely deviate from the practice in his earlier fiction and ignore his real life experiences in order to inject a more optimistic tone into *Rainbow*. This also means that Mao Dun had to not only relinquish his cherished theoretical construct, "the true spirit of the times," but also engineer a conversion to collectivism for his heroine despite his own penchant for and success in delineating recalcitrant individualistic heroines in his earlier works.

The tension between Mao Dun's authorial intention and his narrative capability manifests itself first in the temporal arrangement of the novel. *Rainbow* demonstrates an imbalance between the narrative pace and Mao Dun's avowed intention. It begins in the middle of the story, when Mei Xingsu leaves her home province Sichuan to travel to Shanghai by boat. Chapter one provides a stage for her entrance, symbolizing the beginning of her new life with the image of the boat sailing into open waters after passing the treacherous terrain of the Three Gorges. Chapters two to seven then switch back to her life from the May Fourth Movement to her departure from Sichuan. But only three chapters—eight, nine, and ten—are allocated to her life in Shanghai, the purported turning point in her life. Furthermore, Mei's life as an individualist is presented in greater detail and with more dramatic flair than is her time as a revolutionary political worker in Shanghai. As an individualist heroine, she moves from place to place in Sichuan, dodging an unwelcome husband while seeking to make a living by teaching in several schools. In contrast, her life as a woman revolutionary in Shanghai proves more static. Although she apparently takes part in political work and is constantly involved in personal conflicts, the circle of her life has shrunk and the nature of her quarrels with her colleagues uniformly petty. Therefore, despite his avowed intention to demonstrate more optimism about the Chinese revolution, Mao Dun actually painted a rather unappealing picture of Mei's life after her conversion from an individualist to a Marxist revolutionary.

In addition to the problematic temporal arrangement of the novel, Mao Dun's utility of the romantic triangle in *Rainbow* also revealed his ambiguous position on tradition and modernity. In this novel, he deliberately staged a reversal of Mei's role in the romantic triangle in the course of the narrative, presumably for the purpose of demonstrating her revolutionary consciousness but actually depriving her of personal agency. In the first half of the novel about her life in Sichuan, Mei occupies the center of male attention. Before leaving her hometown Chengdu, she is involved with her two cousins, Liu Yuchun and Wei Yu. She is repulsed by the former but attracted to the latter, not just because of the contrast between the upstart Liu's vulgar mien and Wei's more refined sensibilities, but also because Wei Yu is weaker and she can take control in their relationship. When teaching at schools in other parts of Sichuan, Mei becomes a high profile personage and feeds the fantasies of her male colleagues. This time a triangle forms between her, her fellow Chinese literature teacher Li Wuji, and a warlord, the district commander Hui. The novel offers little detail concerning Mei's life as a governess in Hui's household. Yet her long talks with Li Wuji are not only represented in detail, but also used to illustrate her personality. In those scenes Mei's internal struggles are also detailed to illustrate again her tendency to favor weaker men.

This kind of triangular dynamics changes abruptly after she arrives in Shanghai. For the first time in her life, Mei is slighted by a man, a revolutionary named Liang Gangfu, and, inexplicably, loves him all the more for it to the point that she joins in revolutionary activities for his sake. Liang's personal name means "strong man" in Chinese, echoing the name of Miss Jing's lover, Qiang Weili, or "strong, all power." Mei is depicted as eager to be friends with Liang than with her more friendly yet weaker former colleague Li Wuji, who has also moved to Shanghai by this point. Not only is Mei more attracted to the stronger, more masculine Liang, she is also shown willing to give up her independence for his love. Mei concedes: "It was in trying to deal with his [Liang's] stronger personality that she herself had become weak" (167). Apparently, this weaker Mei is more feminine: "This was a new, second self that had emerged since her arrival in Shanghai: a self stripped of self-confidence, an irresolute and hesitant self, a more feminine self" (163). Since this weaker Mei is also a more revolutionary Mei, her loss of power in the love triangle apparently represents a necessary step on the way to becoming a true revolutionary. The author juxtaposed her personal life with her revolutionary activities in Shanghai, implying that not only is the increase in her "feminine" weakness only proper in her transformation, but her move towards collectivism is enough to redeem any personal failure and salvage her *Bildungsroman*. What is proposed as an empowerment of the intellectual woman boils down to her submission to the revolutionary man who personifies the revolutionary cause.

True to form, Mao Dun also utilized female sexuality and psychology to promote the revolutionary cause. The novel abruptly ends at the May 30 rally in Shanghai. Mei takes part in the demonstration but is soon separated from her comrades by police fire hoses. She runs into an old acquaintance, a cousin of her best friend who had helped her to escape her husband in the past. The young man, now an officer in the Nationalist army, invites her to his hotel room to change clothes, with the ulterior motive of staging a seduction. But Mei resolutely rejects his advances and returns to the street, after putting on the new *qipao* that he gave her. The reader witnesses the exhibition of the female body also seen in *Eclipse* and *Wild Roses*. Only this time Mei is the moral woman revolutionary who firmly rejects the antirevolutionary lecher. Thus, her female sexuality is appropriated to serve the cause of revolution, even as its display would gratify the voyeuristic fantasies of the narrator and (presumed) reader alike. Furthermore, by moving from the portrayal of the male revolutionary Fang Luolan's impotency towards the over-sexed revolutionary woman to Mei's firm refusal of sexual temptation presented by the enemy, Mao Dun suggested that the "right" political conviction can elevate the woman revolutionary's moral character and, as a result, supply her with more strength of character. Since Mei's commitment to revolutionary causes is both spurred and supported by her love for a revolutionary man, the woman's psyche was again appropriated for the idealization and adulation of a form of politicized modern masculinity.

Despite, or, precisely because of Mao Dun's best intentions and efforts of adopting a more optimistic tone, *Rainbow* leaves many questions unanswered concerning the growth of the woman revolutionary Mei Xingsu. In this novel Mao Dun depicted all the revolutionaries Mei encountered as deeply flawed characters, Liang Gangfu included. Yet, in contrast to his usual practice, in this novel Mao Dun also self-consciously provides only titillating hints of the sexual relationships between the revolutionaries instead of explicit descriptions, though demonstrating no such self-restraint when describing the rowdy nonrevolutionaries. The author obviously performed an act of self-censorship in order to correct his old "sensual" style. But this move, echoing the moral elevation of the woman revolutionary in the novel, also reaffirmed his acceptance of the traditional discourse on female virtue, which also contributed to the incoherent feel of the novel.

Through the above study of Mao Dun's fictional representation of the woman revolutionary, I have illustrated that in response to the increasing radicalization starting in the late 1920s, he deliberately invoked the theory of "Realism" and performed a control of his private pessimism through fiction writing in order to establish his modernity. In representing and criticizing the weakness of modern intellectuals who participated in the revolution, Mao Dun sought to represent himself as a revolutionary Realist writer who unflinchingly exposed collective psychological reality. However, Mao Dun's allegedly realistic representation of radical women was also organized by a male-centered consciousness. He echoed "Mandarin Duck and Butterfly Fiction" in the construction of male-dominated triangles, where women are always deployed as ideological types to facilitate male subject formation. His surreptitious invocation of patriarchal moralistic discourses and his detour into eroticism also objectified women through the adoption of a voyeuristic narrative gaze. Ultimately, Mao Dun's promotion of Realism proved to be a strategy of self-representation that nevertheless failed to eliminate all traditional traces from his fiction, for his narrative practice reaffirmed some of the traditional values and praxes shared by both premodern literature and contemporary popular fiction.

SIX

"Sentimental Autobiographies": Feng Yuanjun, Lu Yin and the New Woman

The first generation of May Fourth women writers such as Feng Yuanjun (1900-74) and Lu Yin (1898-1934) had to grapple with the complications of occupying a position defined as both the subject and object of the project of Chinese modernization. On the one hand, the emergence of women writers in the early decades of the twentieth century marked a significant stage in the emancipation of Chinese women. As Wendy Larson points out, the classical Chinese literary tradition had always sought to contain women's literary creation through the claim of an antagonistic relationship between women and writing, and hence the dichotomization of female virtue versus male literary talent (*Women and Writing* 44-63). By contrast, the opportunity of becoming a writer in the May Fourth era seemed to have provided Chinese women a hitherto denied location from which to speak and be heard. Utilizing their own "liberated" state to let loose their creative voice, the women writers not only challenged social norms by bringing attention to hitherto underrepresented female experiences, such as romantic relationships between women; they also established women as I-narrators in fiction for the first time in Chinese literary history, thus taking important steps in their creation of their own version of an independent modern identity through ingenious and versatile use of first-person narration.

However, even as women writers used their writings to claim for themselves the position as the subject of Chinese modernization, they also encountered formidable forces of devoicing and objectification. Not surprisingly, the conservative social forces presented many obstacles in their writing career. Not only did writing fail to provide them with sufficient financial security because of the limited audience for May Fourth "new literature," but women writers' serious literary endeavors were also more easily dismissed by the general public at the time, due to both the male-centered tradition of premodern literary production and the fact that popular writers and commercial booksellers promoted salacious tales of women's "secret" lives by alleging female authorship for them (see chapter one). In addition to the deeply entrenched social conventions that demanded women's silent submission, women writers also had to contend with barriers ironically set by modern male intellectuals who had promoted the liberation of Chinese women. As I mentioned in chapter one, the emancipation of Chinese women had long been subsumed under the May Fourth nation-building project. In a self-proclaimed effort to advance the May Fourth agenda of national salvation, male intellectuals used literary criticism and other pedagogical tools to censure fictional works that they claimed to have wandered off onto subjects and emotions detrimental to the project of nation building. Their vigilant police of modern literature was by no means gender-blind. The epithets forced on the women writers alone indicate that the conventional gender codes predetermined the reception of women's fiction. For instance, in the early 1930s, a critic categorically grouped his contemporary Chinese women writers into "Lady Writers" (*guixiu pai*), "New Lady Writers" (*xin guixiu pai*), and "New Woman Writers" (*xin nüxing pai*) (Yi, "Jiwei dangdai zhongguo nü xiaoshuojia" 1). Furthermore, women writers were more often subject to criticism for the weaknesses of their gender than their male counterparts.

Male intellectuals asserted their authority over women writers particularly by criticizing the "emotional" and "autobiographical" nature of their fiction. Like many of their male peers, most of the May Fourth women writers had come from socially privileged families, where the classical education of the daughters of the family enjoyed more tolerance and attention, and they went on to receive a "modern" education away from home. However, more than their male peers, their family backgrounds and personal lives provided fodder for criticisms of their works. Central to the male criticism of "autobiographical" female fiction was the charge of feminine emotionalism. That is, women writers were especially criticized for being "obsessed" with the emotional experiences of the self, as male critics interpreted this as evidence for both their complete divorce from social reality and their ambivalence towards tradition. In fact, women writers were often accused of resurrecting the image of *cainü*, the talented women of the traditional society, who allegedly embodied such emotional and ideological deficiencies.

The depiction of emotions in fiction had not always been deemed incompatible with the May Fourth discourses of modernity. Along with Chinese intellectuals' violent attack on Confucianism in the early decades of the twentieth century, (male) expression of emotions in literature was celebrated as the liberation of intrinsic humanity and the embracing of the doctrine of individualism. Women writers, particularly those who had kept emotions within the "proper" boundaries, were also initially praised for their delineation of female emotions. A case in point is Bing Xin (1900–1999). She self-consciously claimed: " I am not romantic at all. Some people say I am too rational" (qtd. in Zi 106), as if to hold off any criticism of excessive emotionalism. In her early fiction, she not only promoted positive female role models in the characters of modern wife and mother (e.g., her first story, "Two Families" ["Liangge jiating"]), but also, according to male critics, produced a "feminine" (*"nüxing"*) depiction of moderate emotions: "gentle (*wenrou*), exquisite (*xini*), warm (*nuanhuo*), plain (*pingdan*), and loving" (Zhang T. 194). Whereas the favor-able initial reception of Bing Xin's fiction already hints at an undercurrent of male uneasiness about excessive emotions, the practice of identifying emotionalism as an exclusively feminine weakness derived more momentum from the increasing radicalization of modern intellectuals starting in the mid- to the late 1920s.

With the rise of Marxism, modern intellectuals felt compelled to promote writing about others instead of the self, for the accentuation of personal emotions seemed to not only unduly privilege the individual over the collective but also threat the masculine image of self-control. Therefore, male intellectuals isolated "emotionalism" as an attribute of their female Other in order to forestall charges of either "emasculation" or "ultra-individualism" against themselves. Despite the fact that women writers' sensitive representations of the plight of Chinese women revealed social problems otherwise overlooked by many men, male critics alleged that the narrowness of the scope of women's fiction was a result of their fixation on the self and their *feminine* emotions. Women writers became convenient targets of radical criticism, for the general perception had always been that they tended to be preoccupied with their personal emotions rather than the suffering of the proletariat or the peasantry. As such, the criticism of feminine emotionalism not only indicated the further radicalization of modern Chinese intellectuals, it also revealed a persistent conventional gender profile underlying the revolutionary rhetoric of the time.

A telling example is Mao Dun's inconsistent position on emotionality in fiction. In 1922, Mao Dun highly praised Yu Dafu's sentimental work "Sinking" for its "realistic" depiction of the hero's psychological development ("Tongxin" 304). But in 1934 he criticized the woman writer Lu Yin's similar "sentimentality" ("Lu Yin lun" 139–40). In the essay "Lu Yin lun" (On Lu Yin), Mao Dun declared Lu Yin's seven earliest short stories to be the only redeeming part of her anthology *Seaside Friends* (*Haibin guren*, 1934), simply because they delineated the tragic lives of peasants and the proletariat instead of the bourgeois class (136). During the intervening twelve years between Mao Dun's critiques of Yu Dafu and Lu Yin, modern China's political landscape had undergone significant changes. In the 1930s writers were expected to renounce individualism; they were required to demonstrate their nationalist and class-consciousness in response to both the impending war between China and Japan and the increasing influence of Marxist ideology. As one anonymous critic pointed out in 1932, "The kind of romanticism that is only concerned with personal emotions has come to an end at this age. For romantic qualities to exist in literature, the best way is for authors to expand individual, particular emotions to the collective state of mankind" ("Yijiu saner nian" 6). However, Mao Dun's criticism of female authors did not merely indicate the changing ideological orientation among May Fourth intellectuals in the 1930s, it also revealed a stereotypical imagining of the weakness of the female gender. After all, in the same period the male writer Ba Jin was praised for writing about emotions: "It was Ba Jin who made the first successful experiment of this kind [of expanding individual emotions to the collective psyche]. We can say that Romanticism survived in literature after 1932 entirely thanks to Ba Jin" ("Yijiu saner nian" 6). In contrast to the accolade bestowed on Ba Jin, women writers such as Feng Yuanjun and Lu Yin were accused of "emotionalism" by male critics such as Mao Dun, and, as a result, had to retreat into scholarly research (i.e., Feng Yuanjun) or change their writing styles (i.e., Lu Yin).

Needless to say, the male disapprobation of the "autobiographical" and "emotional" female fiction was not merely a disapproval of its style or even its ideology. Just like their deployment of emotions in their own fiction and essays, this kind of criticism reveals male intellectuals' need to mask their own ambiguous relationships to tradition. In a move reminiscent of the heroes in male authors' fiction, who often project their own weakness onto their female Other, male intellectuals identified the flaws of women writers' fiction as a feminine obsession with the authors' limited individual *and* emotional experiences. Ultimately, the male criticism of both the "autobiographical" and "emotional" excessiveness of women's fiction can be seen as a gender-inflected practice aimed to masquerade the inadequacy of the Self as the failings of the Other.

In spite of the stern criticism of their male counterparts, women writers of the May Fourth era contributed to the definitions and meanings of Chinese modernity through both their life and their work. The women writers' delimited position as a female Other to male intellectuals did not lead to a complete deprivation of female agency. Although apparently accepting the austere canons of literary composition dictated by their male colleagues, these women writers also formed a complex relationship to the male-dominated May Fourth discourses of Chinese modernity. To some extent, that relationship can be construed in the light of Antonio Gramsci's notion of hegemony—namely, the predominance of certain cultural forms over others not through domination but through "consent"—but in practice its complexity even exceeded Gramsci's conceptualization. First of all, women writers' enthusiasm about the May Fourth discourses of modernity was not devoid of personal motives; for, even as the dominant discourse sought its own articulation in the subjugation of women's voice, it also earned support from radical female intellectuals by promising an appealing future of women's liberation and national prosperity. As such, women writers participated in Chinese modernization not only for collective attainment but also for the sake of self-enhancement through such a collective enterprise. As mentioned above, under the auspices of the May Fourth Movement, they not only enjoyed increasing freedom and mobility as professional women, but were also able to invoke their experiential authority to speak out about their individualist emotions from the location of "I." Furthermore, as I will demonstrate through the analysis of Feng Yuanjun and Lu Yin's fiction in this chapter, their fictional narratives often subverted the dominant discourses of modernity even though apparently promoting them, particularly by proposing alternative models of representing basic human experiences such as time and place.

Women writers' relationship to the May Fourth discourses of modernity had never been one of unconditional cooperation, but neither can it be described as one-dimensional, uncomplicated resistance. This is because women writers not only needed to appropriate male-dominated radical discourses in order to gain entry into the project of Chinese modernization, but also had to confront the traditional norms of female conduct that had been first instilled in them through a classical curriculum in their childhood, and which were later replicated to some extent in a modern school system dominated by male modern intellectuals.

This link between the "traditional" and "modern" curricula for women's education can be particularly seen in the similarity between their discourses on female emotions. Although the tendency to reprimand women writers for feminine emotionalism became more prominent in the 1920s and 30s, excessive emotions had been traditionally associated with the female gender in premodern Chinese society. Confucian aesthetics and poetics promoted moderation. Although ideally poetry should express one's intent (*shi yan zhi*), a defining characteristic of high art in the traditional Chinese aesthetic is a constrained and decorous expression of feelings (e.g., Confucius 7, 11). Since women had often been excluded from the production of high art, the aesthetics of moderation had also come to be closely associated with masculinity in the classical tradition. Furthermore, the Confucian idea of "emulation" demands that women curtail their own excessive emotions by imitating their lord and master, the self-controlled man; the Three Cardinal Guides (*sangang*) dictate not only that husband teach and control his wife but also that he do so through his own example (Mencius 11). As a result, numerous traditional handbooks and treatises on women's education from the Han (206 B.C.E.–C.E. 220) dynasty to the Republic period (1912–49), as well as biographical accounts of exemplary women in official historiography, proliferated images of impassive women who modeled on the ideal man to control and moderate their emotions. Naturally, an ideal woman as defined by this group of texts should also adhere to the Confucian gender hierarchy; she not only must obey the kind of social decorum that demands emotional constraint from both men and women but also has to silently submit herself to the man. For instance, the first book for the education of women in China, *Precepts for Women* (*Nüjie*, approx. 100), written by the woman historian Ban Zhao (41–ca. 115) purportedly for the edification of her unmarried daughters and nieces, espoused proper feminine conduct such as living "in purity and quietness (of spirit)" and loving "not gossip and silly laughter" (Swann 83–84). Ban Zhao also admonished her daughters and nieces that a virtuous woman 'should "avoid vulgar language; speak at appropriate times; and not weary others (with too much conversation)" (Swann 86). Subsequent manuals on women's education propagated similar behavioral ideals of emotional constraint and submissive silence for women (see also Martin-Liao 168–89). Although the promotion of these traditional concepts defining women's gender roles was interrupted by the revolution of 1911 and the May Fourth Movement, they had undeniably left an indelible impression on May Fourth women writers from elite families, who had been brought up within this tradition of women's education.

This aspect of women writers' traditional heritage can again be illustrated with the example of Bing Xin. In an essay entitled "Girl Students at a Time of Destruction and Reformation" ("Pohuai yu biange shidai de nü xuesheng," 1919), Bing Xin encouraged girl students to devote themselves to the betterment of society, but asked them to do so only through the fulfillment of their duties within the family. According to her, Chinese society had changed in its reception of girl students: from the "idolization of girl students" to "disgust with girl students." This was because, she further explained, contemporary girl students presented to the pubic "various outrageous and absurd words and deeds," such as vowing to "overthrow Chinese women's old virtues and destroy the fences of Chinese rituals," zealously campaigning for free associations of the sexes, and participating in political activities. To change such an unfavorable public view, Bing Xin issued detailed instructions for the self-improvement of girl students, including telling them how to dress ("Dress in plain and elegant clothes") and behave themselves in public ("Avoid uttering empty words of 'reforming society'"). Moreover, she highlighted the importance of familiarizing themselves with various aspects of family management: "household chores," "children's psychology," and "personal hygiene," though also urging them to pay attention to national and world politics and women's needs in China. Bing Xin's essay forcefully recalls Ban Zhao's *Precepts for Women* not so much because it offers practical suggestions for women's self-cultivation as because such suggestions seem to arise from the same motive to prepare women for their destined domesticate roles.

The return of traditional ideals of female conduct to modern women's writings was by no means limited to Bing Xin's works, though she is generally held to be a woman writer less radical than Feng Yuanjun and Lu Yin. We will see that the more radical women writers had also internalized traditional values to varying degrees. However, women writers can expect little help from their male colleagues in their attempted break from the "tyranny of tradition." As I have mentioned earlier, male criticism of feminine emotionalism surreptitiously reaffirmed the Confucian definition of female decorum and virtue even though male critics ostensibly reprimanded women writers for their "traditionality." As such, women writers had to devise new ways to combat the united forces of traditional and modern discourses on female emotions, both patriarchal in nature though apparently espousing different ideologies. In privileging an emotive first-person narration, their representation of new women reflects their attempts at establishing the female subject through the simultaneous and paradoxical invocation of both "traditional" and "modern" discourses.

Like Bing Xin, Feng Yuanjun and Lu Yin were also new women who were erstwhile disciples of male intellectuals. Both of them graduated from the well-known Beijing Women's Advanced Normal School (later called Beijing Women's Normal College), and had studied with famous male authors such as Lu Xun and Zhou Zuoren at college before becoming writers themselves. But compared to Bing Xin's work, their fiction features more forceful expressions of emotion, and, as a result, was more subjected to the criticism of "emotionalism." In what follows I will study their representations of the new woman by especially examining how they figured "emotions" into their much criticized "sentimental autobiographies." This exercise is useful not only for illustrating how women writers portrayed new women in ways different from male writers through the occupation of a distinctive subject position, but also for investigating to what extent their fiction was shaped by their perception of how their male others saw them.

Feng Yuanjun and her "Autobiography of Emotions"

Feng Yuanjun was not a prolific fiction writer. She wrote only a dozen or so short stories in her entire literary career, and devoted herself almost exclusively to the research of premodern Chinese literature after the late 1920s. Yet her work, although limited in number, illustrates the way women writers of her generation negotiated an independent modern identity for themselves when faced with the marginalization and exclusion of the process of canon formation. This can be particularly seen in the canonization of her short story "Lüxing" ("The Journey," 1923), generally regarded as her representative work and one of the only two stories by her that have been included in the *General Compendium of New Chinese Literature*. Lu Xun praised this story as "a realistic depiction of the young people's psychology at the time of the May Fourth Movement," claiming that it encapsulated that generation's complicated feelings of defiance, uncertainty, and nostalgia even as they rebelled against traditions ("Xuyan" 1481). Furthermore, Lu Xun declared, this story was a significant improvement on Feng Yuanjun's two previous short stories treating the same theme ("Xuyan" 1481): "Gejue" ("Separation," 1923) and its sequel "Gejue zhi hou" ("After Separation," 1923).

In light of Lu Xun's own privileging of an "inner truth" in his fiction and essays (see chapter two), it should come as no surprise that he especially praised Feng's revelation of psychological truth allegedly for the representation of a particular historical period. However, that he favored "The Journey" above the other two stories that were excluded from the *General Compendium* raises an intriguing question. That is, since the three stories collectively narrate the tragic love affair of two college students who are respectively married and engaged to other people, and that all three pieces highlight individual psyche, what exactly made "The Journey" more acceptable to the canon than the other two stories? Sally Lieberman has rightly suggested that "The Journey" was selected because it delineates a heterosexual love affair, and thus exorcises the dominant figure of the mother from the modern woman's life (116–241). I will further illustrate that in addition to this thematic change, it was by managing and modifying the "excessive" emotions prevalent in the other two stories—both of which created a more powerful subversion of the May Fourth discourses of modernity— that Feng Yuanjun succeeded in making "The Journey" into a canonical story through narrative manipulation. Below I will focus on a comparison of "The Journey" and "Separation" while bringing narrative analysis into conjunction with Feng Yuanjun's own justification of her privileging of emotions. I will show that she deployed emotions in her fiction in order to appropriate the dominant May Fourth discourses for the establishment of her own modernity. I have chosen these two stories because they both feature a first-person narrator that is also the female protagonist, while "After Separation" is told from the perspective of the heroine's female cousin who is a witness to her struggle and eventual suicide. Since "The Journey" and "Separation" adopt the same narrative perspective, a comparison of them can not only tease out the nuances of their apparently similar narrative practice but also more effectively reveal the criteria of the canon.

A "typical" May Fourth girl student when she first started writing (Yuan S. 337), Feng Yuanjun's fiction also apparently features the "typical May Fourth love story" by pitting the younger generation's romantic love against the old generation's more conservative attitude (Liu S. 28). However, her unique realization of the theme of romantic love not only enabled her to "legitimately add [her] voice" to the iconoclastic May Fourth discourse of social protest (Lieberman 121), it also distinguished her fiction from the regular fares of the May Fourth fiction that promoted free-choice marriages as a means to women's liberation. Unlike male authors such as Ba Jin and Mao Dun, Feng Yuanjun did not accentuate the revolutionary significance of the Chinese Nora's departure from the patriarchal family. Rather, she made central to the plot the acute agony her heroine experiences at the point of break away from the family. Moreover, it is not the despotic father—a figure that was significantly absent in her work though prevalent in other May Fourth fiction—but the "loving mother" who, far from being "absent" from the life of the new woman as suggested by Lieberman (104), causes the heroine's emotional pain. Feng Yuanjun suggested through her fiction that this is because the heroine insists on the equal sanctity of romantic love and filial love, and cannot make a choice between the lover-lover and the mother-daughter relationships that compete for her commitment. In the extreme case featured in "After Separation," the heroine commits suicide in order to escape the conflict of her love for her mother and her male lover. The centralization of the conflicted loyalties in the new woman's psyche not only challenged the modernization scheme conceived of by radical male intellectuals that often invoked heterosexual love as a weapon to combat patriarchal rule, but also produced a distinctive individual voice and "excessive emotions" that male intellectuals had criticized all along. It is these effects of Feng Yuanjun's stories that they sought to control through both literary criticism and, ultimately, the mechanisms of canon formation.

"The Journey" and "Separation" differ from each other both in plot and in narrative device, though both use an I-narrator to relate the experience of the same heroine. On the plot level, the two stories respectively provide the account of the secret journey made by the heroine and her lover and of its aftermath. The events in "The Journey" take place in some unspecified locale away from the watchful eyes of the lovers' families, but in "Separation," the heroine is grounded at home by her mother because of her rejection of an arranged marriage. In "The Journey" the romance between the two lovers claims center stage, whereas in "Separation" the relationship between mother and daughter plays a more prominent role. But the more important differences of the two stories manifest themselves on the narrative rather than the plot level. "Separation" features an emotive monologue of the heroine, who writes letters to her lover describing her thoughts and emotions while being confined to home. In contrast, "The Journey" more focuses on the *story* of the trip narrated in the first person. As such, the two short pieces adopt different narrative devices that generate distinctive emotional tones.

"The Journey" is more a story *of* the others and *for* the others, whereas "Separation" is a tale that the heroine can claim for herself. A piece of epistolary fiction, the form of "Separation" creates the illusion of a forbidden dialogue, an insular communication only existing between the narrator and the narratee. In other words, since the heroine is writing a secret letter intended only for the eye of her lover, she is apparently pouring out her innermost feelings and thoughts to the only person who is both her fellow sufferer and ally in their fight against the stifling traditional marriage system. But far from merely consolidating the heterosexual relationship, as is more the case with "The Journey," the narrator forcefully claims for herself the position of the subject by establishing herself as the only speaker in "Separation" while designating her lover as a peripheral, albeit sympathetic, audience. Towards the end of her letter, she declares to her lover, "My life has been destroyed in the name of love. Because of my mother's love, I could not simply break off the marriage contract she arranged for me in good conscience. And because of her love, I had to come back to see her. Because of my lover's love, I sacrificed my reputation in society and the joy of being with my family. The author of my tragedy is love. The heroine is myself" ("Separation" 111–12).

As a self-analytical summary of her love affair, the significance of the above statement lies not so much in the fact that the heroine blames her tragedy on love as in the way she positions herself between her mother and her lover by using the concept of love as leverage. It is very telling that she does not address her male lover with either his personal name or the pronoun "you," or even the endearment "my love" (*wo de airen*), as she does elsewhere in the story. Rather, she mentions "my lover" in the third person ("*qingren*") in this passage, thus marking him off as another force external to her, one on par with "my mother" who both nurtures and controls her (112). The heroine thus subtly declares her independence by withdrawing from the intense one-on-one romantic relationship and placing herself at equal distance from the two forces of attraction and restraint in her life. Her weapon is her claim of uttermost commitment to love, which she alleges to have enabled her to act according to her conscience. She tells her lover that she has chosen to come back to her mother out of filial love, just as she has defied social norms to enter into a romantic relationship with him because of her love for him. Therefore, even though she asserts that love is the "author" of her tragedy and herself the "heroine," she actually characterizes herself more as the agent rather than the victim of her tragedy.

The narrator also invokes " humanism" to further elevate the status of filial love and deflect the power of romantic love. It is striking that even where she addresses her lover in a tone more intimate than what is adopted in the self-analysis quoted above, the heroine justifies her voluntary return to home in the name of humanism: "Try putting yourself in the place of a mother already in her sixties who has not seen her child for six or seven year. *Would I still be human* if I did not desire to return home and be close to her while I still can?" (106, my emphasis). By characterizing her action as "humane," the heroine is able to not only make filial love as important as romantic love, but, furthermore, also represent herself as an independent individual possessed of the rational faculty to make critical life decisions. Her demonstration of independence can also be seen in her assertion of her firm belief in the significance of her life and death. She pleads with her lover to "write out the history of our love, from the beginning to the end" and to "organize and publish our six hundred lover letters" in order to "forge a way for other young people and wish them better success [in romance]" (113). Ultimately, it is this call of "destiny" — her self-image as a harbinger of love and freedom — rather than her love for either her mother or her lover that proves to be the anchor of her subjectivity.

In addition to the somewhat detached tone, the narrative modes adopted in "Separation" also accentuate the beauty of the narrator's ideal of love in order to free her from real life entrapments. Feng Yuanjun switched back and forth between the modes of description and summary in this story. As I have mentioned above, the narrator seeks to analyze her dilemma in more philosophical terms in the summary statement towards the end of the letter, but in the first half of her letter she allocates more space to the poetic description of her romance. Gazing at the moon out of her window, she writes a poem reminiscing about her affair, and then provides detailed footnotes to the incidents alluded to in the poem. Interestingly, all the past events are set in scenes of great natural beauty: a park, a garden, a reservoir where "the grandeur and austerity of the autumn landscape seemed to make everything we did beautiful" (109). Natural imagery not only supplies an attractive background for human interactions, but also illustrates the intrinsic bond between the "purity of human souls" (111) and the beauty of nature, the two indispensable and interactive components of her philosophy of love. That is, although the narrator believes that "the purity of our souls is what makes us all human" (111), she regards nature, rather than human behavior, as the more reliable, unsullied mirror and embodiment of "pure soul," free as it is from real life interpersonal entanglements.

In privileging the descriptive mode, Feng Yuanjun decreased narrative speed to accentuate the emotions, rather than the events, in this story. The lyrical prose she thus produced transforms an anxiety-ridden love affair into a series of idyllic vignettes. Moreover, it is the female "I"-narrator's emotions and beliefs that she focused on. Although Feng invoked Western writers such as Ibsen and Tolstoy as well as the names of Werther and Lotte (then one of the most popular and famous pair of fictional lovers ever since Guo Moruo's translation of *The Sorrows of Young Werther* in 1922), she used these examples to enhance the universal appeal of their romance, and thus elevated the narrator's personal experience to a representation of cross-cultural human experiences. Both the description of natural scenery and the use of allusion, as well as the choices of the prevalent narrative tone and mode of "Separation," reveal that the author painstakingly organized the narration in order to create and consolidate the narrator's image as a messenger of ideal love. This is an identity transcendent of the heroine's roles in both her familial and romantic relationships, even though she marshals both to secure her claim to that individualist identity. As such, Feng Yuanjun had rendered this story "unsuitable" for the canon of modern Chinese literature by creating a strong feminine voice in "Separation" through the privileging of individual emotions. This was the case not so much because "Separation" featured a lyrical narrative less consumable for its lack of action. Rather, this story, in centralizing the emotions of the female subject, became more inassimilable to the gender-inflected May Fourth discourses of modernity, which centralized heterosexual love and appropriated female body for the project of nation-building.

In contrast to the self-confident "I"-narrator of "Separation," "The Journey" portrays her as a mixture of courage and trepidation. In a scene describing the lovers' journey on the train, which was later singled out by Lu Xun as an example of Feng Yuanjun's literary achievements, the narrator admits, "I longed to hold his hand but did not dare, except when the train gave an occasional lurch, causing the lights to dim. I was worried that the other passengers would pay undue attention to us" ("The Journey" 169). Because of a similar dread for contemptuous and suspicious looks from other lodgers in the hotel they stay, she and her lover resort to dissimulation, putting up the appearance of renting two separate rooms and claiming to be only classmates to each other. Furthermore, the "I"-narrator betrays her traditional outlook when she expresses jealousy of her lover's wife. She claims to have always been "totally opposed to men who fall in love with other women and abandon their wives without a thought. I had argued that such men are the most inhumane on earth" (172), yet faced with her own dilemma, she changes her tone: "[N]o matter how obvious it is to me that their relationship was established on old ethical codes and practices, I cannot help feeling that the woman, his wife, is my adversary" (172). She secretly hopes that her lover will voluntarily divorce his wife, considering it "the only way to lessen the legal charge against him and the unhealthy criticism society will level against us" (172–73). But she also feels guilty for her wish because the realization of it will lead to the destruction of another, in a sense even more vulnerable, woman's life. Consequently, she deliberately leaves out words such as "marriage," "divorce," or "husband and wife" in her narration, choosing to take refuge in ellipsis marks instead. By omitting these words, the narrator avoids facing not only the negative views of their relationship by society but also her own implicit identification with such views. Her obsession with the legal status of their relationship reveals that she has internalized rather than discarded traditional morality. But more importantly, her animosity towards her lover's wife also questions the kind of romantic love promoted by May Fourth intellectuals that would both cause the conflict between "romantic love" and "universal humanity" and pit a woman against other members of her sex. As such, "The Journey" reveals not only the irreconcilable conflict between the promotions of "individualism" and "humanism" by May Fourth intellectuals, but also brings into sharp relief the male-centered nature of their discourses of Chinese modernity.

Male critics sought to contain the subversive power of "The Journey" by emphasizing its revelation of the heroine's traditionality while eliding its exposure of one source of her "traditional" worldview: the May Fourth version of modernity. They declared Feng Yuanjun's depiction of the narrator's contradictory thoughts and behavior to be a mark of the story's social realism. Lu Xun, for example, praised the heroine in "The Journey" as "realistic" and "completely different" from the protagonists who "boast about their decadent tastes or their literary talents" in works produced by the school of "Art for Art's Sake" ("Xuyan" 1481). Although "The Journey" does provide a picture of a woman wavering between "traditional" and "modern" values, it is also true that male critics emphasized this aspect of the story in order to assimilate it into the male-centered May Fourth discourses of modernity. Ironically, their appropriation of the story was made possible, in no small part, by the narrative features of "The Journey."

As I have mentioned above, "Separation" privileges individual voice to reinforce female subjectivity. In comparison, "The Journey" features an intense dialogue between the narrator and her male lover, while also describing opposite views from their external world in order to accentuate their isolation from and united struggle against a hostile social environment. As a result, in contrast to the self-sufficient "I"-narrator of "Separation," "The Journey" features a female narrator absorbed in a heterosexual relationship in which the woman often has to concede to and depend on her male lover for support. The narrator often invokes and speaks from the location of "we," instead of "I," when seeking to legitimize their love. Yet in her anxiety to demonstrate to her audience the unity in deed and even in thinking of her and her lover, her gaze comes to completely concentrate on her lover to the point of surrendering her own independence. The story exposes the decrease of her agency from the very beginning. Although describing the journey as "a huge wave" and "a resplendent star" in both their lives, she reveals her more passive role by ending the statement with "for him, for both of us" (168). The order of the pronouns, first "him" and then "us," but never "me," indicates that he is the initiator and she the follower. Nevertheless, she emphasizes their connection rather than discreteness, stating that although the journey was first proposed by her lover, it also needs her consent for it to come to fruition. But far from strengthening that claim to (partial) independence in subsequent events, she ironically relives the traditional role of the abandoned wife or lover in the gesture of waiting alone in her hotel room for his return. She complains: "I never liked it when he went out, whether it be to shop or to see friends," and even works herself into a rage when her lover returns to their hotel room after nine o'clock (174).

The narrator's increasing passivity can be best illustrated by comparing the different ways "The Journey" and "Separation" narrate the lovers' first night together in the hotel. The plot remains essentially the same; the reader is told that the narrator's lover starts to undress her, but leaves her side and stands at a distance without taking off her underwear. In "Separation," the narrator cites this incident as one of the many proofs of the "sanctity" of their love and of the purity of humanity: "Is this not rare both in ancient and modern times, within China and abroad? [. . .] It was at that point that I started to believe that the human is fundamentally pure" (111). In contrast to the lyrical, if slightly philosophical, musing tone in "Separation," "The Journey" accentuates the drama of their first night, representing it as a significant and individual "event" and a climax in their relationship. The narrator tells us that the bedding her lover has taken on their trip "amounted to one thin quit and a rug" (171). Well aware of the implication of his apparently innocuous absent-mindedness, she initially resents his presumption and plans to rent more bedding from their hotel once they arrive. But eventually her "calculation was defeated by his" ("Lüxing" 21, not translated in the English version "The Journey"). Somehow they end up in the same hotel room, and a drama of psychological struggles ensues in which she loses more and more grounds.

First, it is striking that in this scene the "I"-narrator surrenders both physical mobility—"sitting on the edge of the bed for well over a quarter of an hour with [her] head bowed" (170)—and emotional independence. She feels so grateful for her lover's self-restraint that she is moved to extol this gesture as "the highest expression of our souls" and as "an expression of purest love" (170). She even elevates this experience to religious heights, for her lover is seen as behaving as if under "sacred solemn supervision, and like a believer praying to God to bless him with good fortune, he reverently left my side and stood at a distance from me" (170). Although Feng Yuanjun also hails love as the expression of purest humanity in "Separation," the ultimate "point" of this account in "The Journey" is not to promote universal love, as is the case with "Separation," but to both emphasize the intimacy of their relationship and to proclaim the moral legitimacy of their affair. Consequently, the narrator emerges more as the apologist for their relationship than as a confident claimer to her own independence.

The "I"-narrator's decreased agency can also be seen in the way she emphasizes the male control of emotions in order to prove the "purity" of their love unsullied by carnal desire. As in "Separation," the narrator also accentuates expression of her emotions, especially anguish, in the scene of their first night together: "I cried, I wept bitterly. But at the same time I felt as though I were alone in a vast network of pitch black caves. With no-one but him to care for me I had no courage to resist his embrace" (171). However, in "The Journey" her male lover alone can purportedly hold off the vast darkness outside of their love nest, not the least because his masculine rationality triumphs over her feminine emotional weakness. Because of his restraint from consummating their sexual relationship, she compares him to Liu Xiahui, a male scholar in Confucius's time who, as legend goes, resisted the temptation of a seductive woman sitting in his lap. It is both ironical and revealing that the "I"-narrator should invoke a canonized Confucian model of self-control and moral rectitude to facilitate their rebellion against Confucian morality, which they have always held responsible for their current dilemma. By crediting her lover alone with the will to refrain from forcing more physical intimacy on her, the narrator not only tacitly yields herself to his power, but also leaves unacknowledged the sexual inhibitions foisted on the individual by social norms, which are actually one original source of her anxiety. In her attempt at proving the "propriety" of their relationship, she in effect becomes a willing helpmate both to her lover and to social conventions.

From the above analysis of the narrative features of "The Journey," it should perhaps come as no surprise that Lu Xun characterized this story as more "conceptual" ("*shuoli*") ("Xuyan" 1481), compared to Feng Yuanjun's other works that have always been considered as "full of powerful subjective feelings and heavy with lyricism [. . .] There is not enough cold, objective description, but much attention to the expression of inner experience" (Luo 73). Indeed, compared to her other works such as "Separation," "The Journey" gestures more towards a rational control of individual emotions.

"The Journey" can be seen as Feng Yuanjun's self-conscious adaptation to male criticism of feminine emotionalism, but her apparent subscription to male definition of good literature arose more from her own sense of mission and identity than from unconditional submission. Like her male comrades, Feng Yuanjun also upheld the mission of literature as one revealing the internal truth. In an essay entitled "Groaning Without Ailment"

("Wubing shenyin"), she contested the derogatory label of "groaning without ailment," or, exaggerating one's misery without legitimate reasons, by questioning the common practice of using an author's biography to judge the authenticity of his or her representation of emotions. Rather than trust biographical accounts that have always been colored by the biographer's own emotions, she argued, critics should instead respect the individual expression of emotions by the author: "The hidden sufferings of one person's life, although seemingly insignificant on the surface, can be severe for the person who experiences them and only he or she can truly understand the impact. The value of art and literature lies in their ability to convey the ineffable pleasures and agonies of life" (163). Feng Yuanjun's defense of what was dismissed as "sentimental" literature utilized the prevalent May Fourth critical discourse that privileged the representation of internal psychological truth. Furthermore, she sought to defend the "emotional" style of her own fiction by claiming for herself the mission of speaking on behalf of the "pitiful people who are filled with sorrow and indignation yet unable to express themselves effectively" ("Wubing sheyin" 163). As such, she represented herself as an author conscientious in fulfilling her social responsibility through the depiction of individual yet representative emotions. As this was also a strategy of self-legitimization utilized by Mao Dun, the criticism of Feng Yuanjun's fiction exposes the double standard employed by male critics. More importantly, it can be seen that both the narrative changes in "The Journey" and her defense of emotional literature in her essay reflect Feng Yuanjun's attempts at carving out a territory for herself through the appropriation of the dominant discursive practices at a time of increasingly rigid control of women's writings.

Lu Yin and Her Self-Corrections

Compared to Feng Yuanjun, Lu Yin not only changed her narrative style more radically but also self-consciously proclaimed those changes in response to the ideological shifts surrounding her. In a chapter entitled "Changes in Thoughts" ("Sixiang de zhuanbian") in her autobiography first published in 1934, Lu Yin divided her writing career into three phases: "Sorrow" ("beiai shiqi"), "Transition" ("zhuanbian shiqi"), and "Innovation" ("kaituo shiqi") (595). She also sought to support this self-proclaimed literary genealogy with concrete examples by slotting her works into these different periods. For instance, Seaside Friends (Haibing guren) was assigned to the first period, The Returning Wild Goose (Guiyan) to the second, and A Woman's Heart (Nüren de xin) to the third. Interestingly, in the same autobiography she characterized her change in style as essentially a change of her "gaze": "Now when I am writing, I hardly ever think of myself. In other words, my gaze has changed directions. I am not just concerned with my own interests, but have also started to pay attention to people around me" ("Sixiang de zhuanbian" 594).

Yet male intellectuals, such as the then much-respected literary critic Mao Dun, remained skeptical of Lu Yin's self-proclaimed transformation. "She has not given us anything new," Mao Dun commented on *The Returning Wild Goose* and *A Woman's Heart*, "They are continuations of her *Seaside Friends*. Although [the heroines in these three works] differ from one another in the degree [of their sentimentality], in essence they are the same. They indulge in fantasies and are very *sentimental* [English in the original]" ("Lu Yin lun"140). Mao Dun especially blamed the production of sentimental characters in Lu Yin's fiction on her auto/biographical tendency: "After reading all of Lu Yin's works, we always feel the limitation of her subject matter. What she shows us is only herself, her lovers, and her friends. Her works are decidedly colored by her autobiography" ("Lu Yin lun" 139). In view of his criticism of other women writers of the time, Mao Dun not only deprecated Lu Yin's literary skills, but also located her lacking within the limits of her gender; apparently, it was her obsession with her limited life — a common failing among women writers according to Mao Dun — that resulted in the flaws of her fiction. Needless to say, the lack of changes in Lu Yin's fiction in the radical 1930s also implied, to her male critics, her adherence to tradition and resistance to the revolutionary discourses of the time. In order to evaluate Lu Yin's modernity or the lack thereof in both her early and late fiction, we need to look at both the contextual and textual evidence.

Lu Yin's proclamation of changes, or, rather, her claim of self-improvement, undoubtedly arose from an anxiety rooted in the sociopolitical environment of the time. Authors in the early 1930s gradually turned from the individual to the collective in their writings, in response to both the national crisis and the pressure from radical intellectuals who promoted "Revolutionary Literature" (geming wenxue) for the sake of national salvation. Lu Yin's autobiography was published in this turbulent historical period, after the bombing of Shanghai by the Japanese Air Force in 1931 and the Battle of Wusong between the Nationalist and the Japanese armies in 1932. In fact, she experienced the political turmoil on a very personal level, as part of her manuscript for the novel *A Woman's Heart* was burned during the Japanese invasion of Shanghai. However, other than the changing fashion of leftist radicalism, Lu Yin's voluntary change of narrative style can also be traced to her continual pursuit for an identity as a creditable writer. From the beginning of her writing career, she had defined "true creativity" as the ability of an author to not only "produce intense associations and passions" but also to "develop [emotions] into some kind of literature able to arouse sympathy and excitement in the reader" ("My Opinions on Creativity" 235). As such, it can be seen that she had always intended the representation of emotions to not only express her individuality but also incite affective responses in her audience. The close association of Self and Other in her conceptualization of literature not only suggests the link between her early fiction and her apparently radically changed late fiction, but also echoes male writers' similar notions about modern literature. As I have mentioned earlier, the conceptualization in modern literature of the essential unity between Self and Other harks back to the premodern definition of individual agency as one and the same with the universal spirit (see chapter one). Therefore, not only was Lu Yin by no means particularly egotistical, despite what some male critics had charged, her "traditionality" also pointed up the similar tendency in radical male intellectuals. In this light, the male criticism of Lu Yin's fiction actually reflects their need to isolate and represent traditionality as a weakness characteristic of their female Other. Furthermore, a close scrutiny of her narrative practice will show that she provoked much male disapproval not exactly because of her use of traditional forms. Rather, she created in her fiction a self-contained, emotion-motivated community of women through such a resurrection of tradition, and thus defied the male-dominated May Fourth discourses of modernity. In what follows I will examine some representative short stories featuring the girl student that were written at different phases of Lu Yin's career in order to further gauge the degree of "modernity" of her narrative style.

What distinguishes Lu Yin's early fiction about the new woman from that of either Bing Xin or Feng Yuanjun is her apparent indifference to the new woman's family background. While Feng Yuanjun dramatized the clash between the new woman's love for her mother and for a male lover, Lu Yin focused more on the woman's troubles in romantic love and her disillusionment with marriage, both of which only have a tenuous connection to the woman's own upbringing. In many of her stories, the heroine's mother is only mentioned in passing, while her emotional as well as physical life away from home is highlighted. Whether this implies Lu Yin's fictional repression of her painful childhood memories of her own mother's neglect and cruelty, as in contrast to her cathartic narrative of childhood trauma in her autobiography (J. Wang 120–56), is open to discussion, but her fiction does appear to do a more thorough job of accentuating women's liberation from the family. Furthermore, of all the May Fourth writers, Lu Yin probably privileged the modern form of first-person narration most in her fiction. She wrote at least four short stories—"The Diary of Lishi" (1923), "Father" ("Fuqin," 1925), "Manli" ("Manli," 1927), and "The Diary of a Mistress" ("Yige qingfu de riji," 1933)—and one novel, *The Returning Wild Goose* (1931), fully or partially in diary fiction form, as well as numerous short stories fully or partially in epistolary fiction form, including "A Letter" ("Yi feng xin," 1921), " "Somebody's Sorrow" ("Huoren de bei'ai," 1922), "After Victory" ("Shengli yihou," 1925), and "A Victim of the Times" ("Shidai de xisheng zhe," 1928). Despite these modern characteristics of her fiction, her works incurred severe male criticism. What male critics really resented, one suspects, was Lu Yin's centralization of female subjectivity through the accentuation of affective identifications among women in her fiction. To that end, Lu Yin not only boldly introduced the topic of romantic love between women (e.g., "Lishi's Diary"), but also utilized both first-person narration and "traditional" lyricism to establish a metanarrative link between the female writer and her targeted female audience, and thus constructed a close-knit and self-sufficient community of women.

On the thematic level, Lu Yin's early fictional works collectively feature a "biography" of the girl student; her stories represent the different stages of the new woman's life. Furthermore, these stories establish an emotional cohesiveness through shared narrative gestures, tropes, and tempo. Above all, her early pieces all emphasize the empathy between the narrator and narratee through innovative uses of first-person narration. Diaries are presumably private writings, intended only for the eye of the diarist. Yet "Lishi's Diary" encloses both a prologue and a postscript by a fictional editor, indicating an afterlife of the diary that survives the death of its own author. Similarly, both "Somebody's Sorrow" and "After Victory" are equally "extroverted," though both simulate the form of private letters. "Somebody's Sorrow" ends with a note written by the cousin of the original letter writer Ya Xia, who, after Ya Xia's suicide, collects her letters and diary and sends them to Ya Xia's friend KY, the intended recipient of her letters. "After Victory" also has a frame for the featured long letter, connecting the life of the recipient with its sender. Furthermore, Lu Yin's fictional diaries or private letters extend the communication beyond the two people directly engaged in correspondence. She typically wove many women's names and lives into her diary or epistolary fiction. Not only do her works highlight women's group activities, but they also develop multiple story lines following each of these women's lives. Moreover, since the epistler frequently cites the love affairs and worldviews of mutual acquaintances to her addressee, other women's lives and opinions are also incorporated into the letter. As such, the letter in Lu Yin's stories invariably breaks the insularity of private correspondence between two parties, conjuring up instead an intricate web of empathy and sympathy among women.

In addition to interweaving multiple paralleled story lines, Lu Yin's early fictional works also employ similar tropes in order to facilitate the exchange and sharing of emotions among women. A perfect case in point is her deployment of the trope of love. To be sure, for Lu Yin as well as for her fictional characters, "to love is an act of supreme honesty and sincerity: stripping oneself of civilized hypocrisy in order to reveal one's true self to the beloved. To love is also a heroic act of defiance, renouncing all the external restraints of artificial society and merging ecstatically with nature" (Lee, *The Romantic Generation* 77). However, even as she celebrated romantic love as a gesture of supreme individualism, she repeatedly represented women's shared experience of suffering psychological ordeals caused by love in their search for both their own identity and the meaning of their life. For instance, in "Somebody's Sorrow," the heroine Ya Xia not only describes in her letters to her friend KY a series of her own unlucky romantic encounters with men, but also frequently refers to similar misfortune of her other female friends involved in heterosexual relationships. She eventually commits suicide because her philosophy of *Carpe Diem* is no match for the powerful social conventions that expect a woman to committee herself to a heterosexual relationship. As the indefinite pronoun "somebody" in the title implies, Lu Yin considered the complication of romantic love a common denominator of women's identity crisis. Her female characters test their philosophy of life by applying it to their romantic relationships, only to see it collapse in the face of reality. Therefore, their subsequent embracing of death, whether by suicide or by illness, is not just a testimony to their failure in love affairs, but more importantly, also a sign of the irresolvable conflicts between their ideal and reality. In this light, Lu Yin represented romantic love in her fiction not so much to privilege love as the commanding force of life as to delve into the dilemma central to the shared life experiences of new women.

Although Lu Yin's alteration of the conventions of diary and epistolary fiction already reveals her divergence from the standard "individualist" fiction, it is the temporal arrangement of her fiction that more explicitly reveals her daring practice of integrating tradition into modern narrative forms. Most of her fiction depends on what Seymour Chatman calls "contingency" rather than "causality" in order to accommodate the representation and signification of female emotions (47). In other words, in her fiction different letters or different entries of the diary in a story usually follow an emotional rather than a causal logic, as they are linked with one another through what Robbe-Grillet calls "accumulative descriptive repetition" (qtd. in Chatman 47). Rather than developing through a series of fast-paced dramatic events, Lu Yin's early stories more often gradually build up a certain mood or atmosphere through the reiteration of similar scenes. As such, her temporal arrangement proves intrinsically circular rather than linear.

Lu Yin usually recorded distinct dates, as required by the conventions of epistolary or diary fiction, to mark a formal division between different parts of the same story. However, the inner sense of the progress of time is often more determined by descriptions of seasonal changes in her works. Since seasonal changes often inspire the letter or diary writer to describe and contemplate the mystery of nature and the meaning of life, this gesture of philosophical meditation virtually transforms the linear story time, namely, the time when events take place one after another, into a synchronic poetic-descriptive time. Furthermore, the writer of the letter or diary frequently cites examples of her friends for the generation of her own philosophical discourse, and also asks for confirmation of this discourse from her addressees. As such, Lu Yin's fiction often establishes an emotional and philosophical community of women by privileging a unique kind of internal time over external time.

To Lu Yin's radical male colleagues, the resurgence of a circular temporal structure in her fiction was undoubtedly a sign of her "traditionality," for they conceived of a modern literature as embodying a new historical consciousness, and only authorized in this literature a "unilinear time" that would confirm the newness and progress of their times according to an overarching evolutionary logic (Lee, "Modernity and Its Discontents" 159). Therefore, Lu Yin challenged the male definitions of both modern literature and modern consciousness as well as established female subjectivity through the paradoxical generation of such a "traditional" lyrical sense of time. The effects of Lu Yin's unique temporal arrangement can be seen most clearly in her short story "After Victory." As it consists of only one long letter that also incorporates other letters, this story best illustrates the way Lu Yin established a circular discourse time to highlight the stagnation of the women characters' lives after their apparent triumph over tradition. As such, it also questions the May Fourth definition of modernity as progress as well as reinforces female subjectivity through the establishment of a community of women with common emotional experiences.

The letter in "After Victory" brings together a group of women by quoting their life stories and comments. The specifics of their life experiences might differ from one other, as one becomes a bored housewife, another a harassed spinster absorbed by her work, and yet another a second wife struggling within an "unnatural" marital configuration. But related by the same letter writer, their lives become testimonials to the same pattern of deterioration; their present invariably compares unfavorably to their past. Not surprisingly, they all express identical negative emotions: "nostalgic about the past, troubled by the present, and fearful of the future" ("After Victory" 147). In addition to the circular structure of the story, Lu Yin also slowed down the narrative speed in "After Victory" by adopting the descriptive mode to produce narrative pauses. Specifically, she transformed the linear narration of events into a series of mutually resonating representations of places. The letter ostensibly begins with its writer Qingzhi's wistful remark about the fleeting of time. However, her letter in fact eliminates the progress of time, since the past and the present congeal into symbolic locations in it. For instance, Qingzhi describes the site of her honeymoon as bountiful in natural beauty, free from the intrusion of society, and comforting for troubled human spirits. By capturing such picture-perfect moments of the past, Lu Yin froze the passage of time into a series of descriptive vignettes.

In contrast to the static representation of time, the story is suffused with volatile human emotions, which constitute the main driving force of the narrative and belie the "traditional" temporal arrangement of the story. Qingzhi's memory of an idealized past is shaped by the emotions she harbors for the present. Precisely because she feels keenly the disappointment of unrealized aspirations, she yearns for the golden past, a lost Utopia that represents all her lost youthful ideals. As such, "After Victory" proves to be a story of two parts; its theme of stagnation and its static narrative tempo contrast sharply with the "modern" discontent it conveys, making it more a protest in despair rather than a sigh of resignation. Furthermore, the unique modernity of "After Victory" consists in its establishment of a communal rather than individual modern identity, for the story again establishes a community of women through the accentuation of their emotions. First of all, it emphasizes the communication between the correspondents by featuring a frame for its centerpiece—the long letter from Qingzhi. Just as "Lishi's Diary" begins and ends with editorial notes and "Somebody's Sorrow" ends with Ya Xia's cousin's short letter to the intended recipient of Ya Xia's letters, "After Victory" also depicts the way Qingzhi's friend Qiongfang receives, reads, and responds to the letter. "After Victory" also accentuates sympathetic reception of the letter by its reader. Just as both Ya Xia's cousin and the editor of Lishi's diary burst into tears after their perusal of the texts, Qiongfang, the recipient of Qingzhi's letter, feels "as if something were lodged in her chest" after reading the letter (147). Lu Yin even had Qiongfang's husband, who has not even read the letter, agree to her expression of disillusionment, thus implying a rapport between the reader and writer of the letter based on a shared emotional *reality* that transcends even the text.

From the above analysis, we can see that Lu Yin's early stories represent women's quest for independent modern identities in ways different from the discourses of Chinese modernity promoted by radical male intellectuals. Particularly, her stories illustrate the affective effects of both modern (e.g., first-person narration) and traditional (e.g., lyrical temporal arrangement) narrative forms, thus not only placing "unsuitable" emphasis on female subjectivity but also demonstrating a new way of integrating tradition into the definition of modernity. In light of Lu Yin's revelation of the link between tradition and modernity in modern literature, male criticism of "feminine emotionalism" and "autobiographical colors" of her fiction can be interpreted as an attempt at containing the subversive power of her stories. Perhaps more importantly, her unique way of configuring time and space for the representation of new women also established a new model of representing basic human experiences in the modern era, thus further revealing the cultural-political ramifications of her conceptualization of female subjectivity.

Compared to the narrative innovation of Lu Yin's early fiction that enabled her to deploy emotions for the negotiation of an independent female identity, her later efforts of self-correction often produced only mediocre specimens. Starting in the early 1930s, Lu Yin self-consciously changed the subject matter of her works in order to shed the title of "autobiographical" writer. Her works of her self-styled transitional period, the novels *Ivory Rings* (*Xiangya jiezhi*, 1934) and *Flames* (*Huoyan*, 1935), apparently more focus on the others than herself. Lu Yin claimed that *Ivory Rings* was "a faithful description" of her friend Shi Pingmei's tragic life and death. *Flames* veers even further from her usual subject matter, offering a report of the Chinese army from the battlefield of the anti-Japanese war. Not coincidentally, she also considerably decreased the use of subjective mode of narration in her later works. However, an examination of the thematic and narrative aspects of her "Diary of A Mistress," a short story that she wrote in the form of diary fiction in the late 1930s, will more clearly demonstrate the impact on her narrative practice caused by her deliberate ideological changes.

The fictional diary in this piece runs from September 3 to November 5 of the same year, covering the sixty days that lead to a turning point in the female diarist's life. She is a clerk by the name Meijuan who works in a government office and harbors a secret love for her married boss, "a leader of the party." Defying the contempt and condemnation of her colleagues, she initiates a romantic relationship with him, only to see him leave her shortly after under the pretext of his mother's illness. His subsequent letters in his absence make her realize that he does not want to risk his own reputation by continuing their affair. In the last two entries of the entire diary the diarist suddenly wakes up from her infatuation. On November 5, after a former colleague tells her about the Japanese atrocity in Manchuria, Meijuan declares: "I want to fulfill the supreme love. I will not only love Zhongqian [her married lover], I ought to love my motherland more" ("Qingfu de riji" 424). The diary ends with her farewell letter to her lover written in her own blood before she leaves to join in the anti-Japanese war.

Lu Yin made self-conscious efforts to create a new, more revolutionary, and more male-oriented narrative in "Diary of a Mistress," to the point that its plot at times strains the reader's credulity. The rationale behind the diarist Meijuan's life-changing decision is inadequately explained in the narrative. Furthermore, as Lu Yin sought to anchor the narrative on a (male) Other, the heroine also appears to lose her agency. In a clear departure from her other diary and epistolary fiction written up to that point, "Diary of a Mistress" includes no editorial notes, preface, or postscript to convey the impression of self-sufficient textual and emotional exchange between its female writer and (female) reader. Rather, the diarist appears to be a woman who desperately wants to be included in the world of men. The title alone indicates the unusual self-image of the diarist; she takes pride in her role as a mistress and defines herself only through her relationship with a married man. Moreover, rather than citing other women's similar opinions to reinforce her own point of view, Meijuan's diary integrates multiple male perspectives and depicts how they dictate her thought and behavior.

Revealingly, the heroine's emotions appear to be debilitating or even diminishing for the female subject. Not only is Meijuan's self-confidence seriously eroded by the condemnation of the public, her sense of self-worth also completely relies on the love of a man. One brief look from her lover Zhongqian overwhelms her: "I was completely dazzled. Some hot, repressed emotions rose in me. I almost fainted and had to lean on the back of a chair to support myself" (407). Her lover's acceptance of her love lifts her out of "the maelstrom of sufferings," prompting her excited announcement: "I am ecstatic, I am smug, I have possessed the most valuable thing in the whole universe: Zhongqian" (415). In establishing her male lover as the center of her universe, Meijuan surrenders her own rights to seek out the meaning of her life. Although Lu Yin apparently granted the heroine certain agency in her gesture of abandoning an old life at the end of the story, she also had Meijuan join in the army because of the rejection by her male lover. Tellingly, Meijuan is initiated into her new life by yet another man, who brings into her isolated world the news of other people's suffering. Ultimately, Meijuan appears to be a woman forever seeking, whether through love or valor, to belong in a men's world, apparently unaware of any kind of female identity other than what is granted and defined by men.

As a story belonging to Lu Yin's third period of "Innovation," "The Diary of a Mistress" conveys an apologetic gesture from the author but nevertheless falls short of her previous literary achievements. Lu Yin had criticized herself in her autobiography in 1934 for works from her first period that were submerged in sorrow: "I was selfish. I decided the world was so [full of sadness] and wanted to drag other people along the same path. I did not think of ways to solve the problem and did not point out a new path for other people" ("Sixiang de zhuanbian" 591–92). Yet in her haste to negate individual emotions for the betterment of the collective, Lu Yin created not only an implausible plot but also a less distinct and independent female protagonist in "Diary of a Mistress." By voluntarily shifting the female subject's emotional experience from the center to the periphery, she actually caused the subjugation of female agency to first a male-centered heterosexual relationship and then an equally male-centered nationalist discourse. But Lu Yin's continual interest in female emotions demonstrated in this story, just as her subpar artistic achievements, also shows the tenacity of her previous view on the nature and effects of literature, which privileges the representation of emotions and creation of affective identifications among the audience. In this light, Lu Yin's later fiction demonstrates not only the limited power of ideology to produce creditable literature but also the enduring link between the old and the new, between tradition and modernity in any individual author's literary endeavors.

As was the case with Bing Xin and Feng Yuanjun, not only Lu Yin's fiction but also her life provided ammunition for gender-inflected literary criticism. Faced with charges of "feminine emotionalism," Bing Xin retreated into the genre of children's literature while Feng Yuanjun dedicated her life to the study of classical Chinese poetry. Lu Yin's life ended in childbirth. Some of her male contemporaries argued that the author's passionate nature made her remarriage, and, by implication, her childbirth and death, unavoidable. It seems that the accusation of "emotionalism" not only haunted Lu Yin's life but also dictated the definition of her death. The experiences of the first generation of May Fourth women writers foretold the inevitability and difficulty of their successors' struggle against both traditional and modern forces of objectification in their own endeavors to establish their independent modern identity. This will been testified by Ding Ling's example in the next two chapters.

SEVEN

The "Bold Modern Girl": Ding Ling's Early Fiction

In an apparent case of life imitating art, Ding Ling (1904–86) followed the path that the new woman had traced in fiction, progressing from girl student to woman revolutionary, and eventually joining in the Communist regime in Yan'an in 1936. Furthermore, she seemed to have thrived on that path, for she emerged as the most consistently prolific and highly regarded woman writer of the May Fourth group. In the 1930s she was unanimously praised as the woman writer who "demonstrated the highest literary skills of all women writers in the representation of the quintessential modern girl" (Qian Q. 226), and since the 1970s she has been elevated to the status of a "feminist" writer of the May Fourth period (e.g., Barlow, "Feminism and Literary technique"). Moreover, the longevity of her writing career presented a sharp contrast to the cases of the other women writers within the May Fourth group, who either gave up fiction writing after only a few productive years (e.g., Feng Yuanjun) or were forced to switch to marginalized genres such as children's literature (e.g., Bing Xin). Not only did Ding Ling's productive years extend into the 1980s—though with an interruption of almost twenty years from the mid-1950s to the mid-1970s when she was persecuted for her alleged "antirevolutionary" political stance—but her fiction has also won much acclaim from male radical intellectuals over the years. In view of Ding Ling's apparent camaraderie with rather than antagonism toward male intellectuals, how are we to assess her relationship to dominant male discourses of Chinese modernity?

Ding Ling's life already presents much mystery, and her writings to some extent compound the difficulty of our inquiry, for she strove to make room for a voice of female experience that was comprehensible and significant within the canon of May Fourth literature as defined by male writers. In particular, she seemed to contribute to the male-centered discourse of "feminine emotionalism" through her own fiction and essays when faced with the barrage of male intellectuals' disparagement of the supposedly "sentimental" and "autobiographical" qualities of female fiction. However, a close scrutiny of the representation of new women in her fiction also reveals that rather than unquestioningly identifying with the male objectification and marginalization of women writers, she appropriated the masculine position for purposes of female empowerment through her own representation and deployment of emotions. As such, Ding Ling's life and fiction encapsulate the unique ambiguity of a woman writer at once enfranchised by and straining to break free of dominant patriarchal discourses.

In this chapter and the next, I will examine the areas of continuity and the significant changes in Ding Ling's fictional representation of the new woman before the turning point of 1936. These two chapters mark a climax in my inquiry in two ways. By delving into Ding Ling's narrative construction of the new woman, I can compare her literary endeavors with those of the male authors mentioned in previous chapters and thus offering a different, if not contrastive, glimpse into the relationship of May Fourth intellectuals to Chinese modernity. More importantly, these two chapters will allow me to take stock of the gender dynamics within the May Fourth literary canon through the study of what is arguably its most complex case. I will concentrate on Ding Ling's early works in this chapter, whereas I devote the next chapter to her later works (c. 1930-36) with deliberate changes in narrative style.

Ding Ling and the New Woman

As mentioned in the previous chapter, many influential women writers of the May Fourth era had been girl students in colleges studying under the tutelage of modern male intellectuals when the May Fourth Movement erupted. In addition to receiving classroom instruction, these women were also exposed to new literary models provided by contemporary male writers, all of which influenced them as they were preparing to venture into the new literary arena. Compared to the more explicit propaganda of critical essays, the narrative representation of the modern Chinese woman that came from the pens of male writers had a more subtle, yet profound impact on female writers' fiction. This was because male authors not only outlined the acceptable themes and subject matter in the portrayal of Chinese women, but also established widely applied narrative forms through their fiction. Therefore, women writers had to confront not only the obvious deprecation of their literary works in male literary criticism but also the more implicit molding of their styles and perspectives by modern male intellectuals when striving for their own identity and literary recognition. A relatively late comer to the literary scene, Ding Ling was exposed to an even larger and more established collection of literary products by radical male intellectuals than the first generation of May Fourth women writers. As such, her quest for an independent, individual modern identity met with even greater difficulty. Emerging from the shadow of male intellectuals and equipped with and confined to using the literary apparatus handed down by them, was she able to use the master's tool to dismantle the master's house?

Ding Ling's appropriation of the male discourse of "feminine emotionalism" in particular demonstrates the triumphs and setbacks she experienced in her attempts at creating an independent modern identity for herself. First appearing on the literary scene in the late 1920s, she stepped right into the center of a maelstrom of political realignments and literary transmutations. As a woman writer, she not only needed to adapt to the turbulent ideological transition from individualism to collectivism, but also had to deal with the increasingly obvious gender prescriptions that limited women's literary endeavors. Ding Ling's strategy, for the most part, was to prove that she was "different" from other women writers by trying to avert charges of "emotionalism." Although the pessimistic tone and first-person narration in her depiction of new women made it possible for male critics to associate her fiction with similar literary efforts by Feng Yuanjun and Lu Yin, Ding Ling herself resisted such a grouping. On the one hand, she voiced her disapproval of female sentimentality in her essays, identifying it as women's unique and self-defeating weakness. On the other, she also changed the narrative form of her fiction in order to promote women's mastery of their emotions. Through an examination of Ding Ling's self-conscious and gradual disassociation from "feminine" emotional writing, we will see that her change of narrative style epitomizes not only the ideological vicissitudes of the time but also the gender politics in the May Fourth representation of the new woman. Before in-depth narrative analysis of her individual works, a brief sketch of Ding Ling's fiction written before 1936 is in order.

Ding Ling's fiction underwent significant changes in both content and style in the course of her career. Her fiction dealing with new women before her Yan'an period (1936–49) can be roughly divided into three types according to both themes and chronology. The first type is represented by "Shafei nüshi de riji" ("Miss Sophia's Diary," 1928) and "Yecao" ("Yecao," 1929), both of them discussed in this chapter, but this type also includes her first story "Mengke" ("Mengke,"1927), "Zisha riji" ("Suicide Diary," 1928), and "Ri" ("Day," 1929). Stories of this type often depict the frustrations and dilemmas faced by young women living alone in the city without, however, offering any obvious resolutions to their questions or their misery. Unlike the girl students create by the first generation of May Fourth writers such as Feng Yuanjun and Lu Yin, the modern women by Ding Ling's pen are usually female writers, teachers, revolutionaries, or urbanites with no apparent educational or occupational affiliations. Furthermore, because of their increased exposure to more complex and challenging social relationships beyond school life, Ding Ling's new women more frankly and fervently express their discontents and desires than those depicted by Feng Yuanjun and Lu Yin. Chapter eight will examine the other two types of her fiction featuring new women. The second of these types generally delineates heroines who leave behind their bourgeois lifestyle, especially romantic love, to embrace Marxist ideology and devote themselves to revolutionary causes, such as "Shafei riji di'er bu" (Sophia's Diary, Part II, 1931), and the novellas "1930 nian chun Shanghai zhiyi, zhi'er" ("Shanghai, Spring 1930, Part I and II," 1930) and "Wei Hu" ("Wei Hu," 1930). The third type provides a rather idealized picture of the new woman's life after she joins the revolution. The representative work of this type, "Tianjia Village," portrays a revolutionary woman who, after breaking away from her gentry family, mobilizes peasants in the countryside, and is eventually executed by the Nationalist government. Although less typical of Ding Ling's pre-Yan'an fiction in terms of both setting and narrative style, "Tianjia Village" not only attracted a great deal of attention at the time of its publication, but also foreshadowed the more radical thematic and stylistic changes in Ding Ling's works written in Yan'an, which I will discuss in the Epilogue. Through this chapter and the next chapter, I will show that rather than following the apparently linear and teleological progression of her life that some critics and biographers suggest it to be, the fiction that Ding Ling composed at different periods of her career reveals a multifaceted and sometimes even conflicted interaction of gender politics and party politics, Self and Other, and convention and innovation.

Diary of a Lonely City Dweller: "Miss Sophia's Diary"

Although Ding Ling started her writing career in 1927 with the publication of her first short story "Mengke" in *Short Story Monthly*, she made her name as the woman writer who most successfully depicted "modern girls" only with the appearance of "Miss Sophia's Diary." An integrated textual and contextual analysis of this story will provide us with not only a useful vehicle to explore the complex gender negotiations in Ding Ling's early fiction but also invaluable insights into her later narrative innovations under changed sociopolitical circumstances.

Described as "a bomb thrown into the silent literary arena" for its bold description of female sexual desires (Yi, "Ding Ling nüshi" 223), "Miss Sophia's Diary" predictably stirred up male efforts at appropriation and containment. Mao Dun, for instance, categorized Sophia, the heroine of this story, as merely a type reflective of a specific set of sociopolitical conditions, identifying her as "a young woman bearing the scars of her times and crying out in rebellion, a representative of the young women emancipated by the May Fourth Movement and yet still harboring contradictory sexual desires" ("Nü zuojia Ding Ling" 253). Qian Qianwu also declared Sophia to be a typical "bourgeois woman intellectual" suffering from a kind of *fin-de-siècle* malaise (*shiji mo bing*) (227). A different, albeit no less reductive, interpretative approach adopted by male critics was to praise the portrayal of Sophia as a sign of Ding Ling's exceptional literary skills as a woman writer, for she allegedly "went beyond the gentleness of women's literature, and instead boldly delineated sexual psychology with depth and in detail" (Hu

Yunyi, qtd. in Yuan L., "Xin shiqi Ding Ling xiaoshuo" 27). Although apparently praising her artistic talent, Ding Ling's contemporary male critics all attempted to elide the issue of female subjectivity raised by this story through the neutralization of Ding Ling's descriptions of female sexuality. They either emphasized the social realism of such descriptions, or, praised the work as an exceptional literary achievement, thus in effect using her gender as a tool to trivialize women's literature as a whole as merely the expression of "soft" feminine emotions instead of the "hard" representation of violent psychological conflicts that Ding Ling allegedly accomplished.

In view of the gender-inflected interpretation of "Miss Sophia's Diary" at the time of its publication, it is all the more important for us to adopt a productive approach in our investigation of the role sexuality plays in the process of female subject formation in this story. We cannot simply regard this story as a kind of "metanarrative diary fiction" (Hyun 105) that exposes the mechanisms and failings of this genre while dismissing the cultural and political forces that shaped its narrative forms. Although this story features, as Yi-tsi Feuerwerker points out, a unique self-deconstruction by revealing that the act of writing defeats rather than supports the diarist's attempt at forming a coherent narrative about the self ("The Changing Relationship" 49-52), to claim that "Miss Sophia's Diary" is *only* an intriguing generic specimen could easily result in abstracting this story from its sociopolitical context, and risks the elision of the gender politics underlying the text. But nor can we adequately examine Sophia's subjectivity by simply claiming her as the first "autonomous female subject of observation, thinking, and speech in the text" of modern Chinese literature (Liu S.141) without paying attention to the deep ambiguity embodied in the narrator's expression of her own desire; for her diary mobilizes different, and even contradictory, value systems and gender roles, as well as shifting temporal and speech locations.

In contrast to the various kinds of reductive interpretations of the story mentioned above, the category of gender has consistently proven to be richly useful in the reading and rereading of this complex text that it enables. Many recent scholars have combined the insights of gender studies with psychoanalytic, historic, or linguistic approaches in their discussions of this story. Particularly significant and fruitful among those inquiries are the works by Tani E. Barlow, Rey Chow, and Lydia Liu, who have tackled the question of female sexuality in "Miss Sophia's Diary" from different perspectives. Barlow's foundational work alerts readers to the role of Western influence in the production of gender discourses in modern Chinese literature. She remarks on "the pollution of their [women characters'] consciousness" that has led the "merely female women [...] to the womanish preference for dreams over reality" in Ding Ling's early fiction ("Feminism and Literary Technique" 92), but later argues that Ding Ling appropriated this type of disenchanted and sexualized female character from Western bourgeois culture for the construction of a narrative of Westernized and eroticized Chinese womanhood (Introduction 27). However, in Ding Ling's later works such as her unfinished novel *Muqin* (Mother), Barlow states, Ding Ling "restored the question of female identity to a concretely Chinese framework" ("Gender and Identity" 15) by revealing the notion of "Chinese woman" before the May Fourth period to be a product of "a system of social relationships (the *guiju* and *lishu*) without reference to a female physiology or psychology" ("Gender and Identity" 12). Although reprimanded by Rey Chow for "prescribing [for] the West's 'other women' their own national and ethnic identity" and thus causing the non-Western women's "exclusion from having a claim to the reality of their own existence" (*Woman and Chinese Modernity* 163), Barlow has rightly brought to our attention the role of what she calls "Western sexual universalism" (Introduction 15) — which promotes a deep (hetero)sexuality as a mandatory element of the modern person — in the formulation of the female modern Chinese subject. For Chow, the contradictions in Sophia's sexual desire are not unintended side effects of the author's appropriation of Western discourses but rather revealing illustrations of the problematic inherent in the representation of female subjectivity in the process of Chinese modernization, for, she argues, in this story "the psychic, ideological contradictions [...] are embedded in a Westernized Chinese woman writer's attempt at self-representation" (*Woman and Chinese Modernity* 163). Turning the Freudian model of divided male libidinal investment of sensuality and affection (see chapter five) on its head, Chow lists yet another redeeming feature of this story, stating that Sophia's desire for women, based not on degradation but identification, suggests the possibility of women's "conjunction in femininity" and signals an "alternative aesthetic that is based on a sympathetic feminine interlocutor/spectator/reader" (169). Although concurring with Chow's observation of the "feminine talk" promoted in "Miss Sophia's Diary," Lydia Liu points out that this is ironically a utopian desire that fails to be realized in the narrative because of the death of Yun, the intended female reader of Sophia's Diary, in a loveless conventional marriage (*Translingual Practice* 179).

Insightful and copious as the existing discussions of Sophia's sexuality and subjectivity have been, I argue that we must also take into account the narrative progression in the representation of Sophia's desire, embodied in Ding Ling's construction and deployment of two interactive triangles of desire: the first one linking Sophia, her female friend Yun, and Sophia's rarely mentioned family, and the second involving Sophia and her two male suitors, a Chinese man by the name of Weidi and Ling Jishi, a Singaporean Chinese. In describing and arranging these two triangles in her diary, Sophia attempts at replicating a (fantasized) prior model of self-validation in a heterosexual sexual economy. However, Sophia eventually fails to create a coherent subjectivity through the writing of her diary, for she is entrapped in the Western narrative of modern, heterosexual love in which the underlying native/traditional model of female subject formation is denied its efficacy and relevance. Ultimately, by representing Sophia's self-conscious use of diary writing for the realization of a (Western-style) subjectivity, as well as by showing the strengths and weaknesses of such an undertaking, Ding Ling not only endorsed the female subject's pursuit for autonomy and power, but also exposed the limitations of the Western model of subject formation as expressed in the form of diary fiction, thus preparing herself for the further exploration of new paths for Chinese women to follow in their quest for independence. Therefore, my semi-structuralist scrutiny of the constitution of Sophia's subjectivity in this story will not only excavate the different layers of "traditional," "modern," "masculine," and "feminine," prototypal narrative forms that both informed and were modified in this story, but also reflect on the historical and literary parameters of Ding Ling's narrative efforts that shaped her representation of the female Chinese subject.

In Ding Ling's two triangular arrangements, the heterosexual triangle between Sophia and her two male suitors is foregrounded through the synchronic narration of a psychological drama in her diary-writing, while the triangle between Sophia, Yun, and Sophia's family is placed in the past, is intriguingly "bodiless," and maintained through a practice of *letter*-writing frequently invoked in the present time of Sophia's diary composition. These two triangles play crucial roles in Sophia's articulation and enforcement of her subject position because their interaction figures *the process* of her search for self-knowledge, one of the most prevalent themes produced by the May Fourth discourses of individualism. We will see that by describing Sophia's attempts at integrating the two triangles in order to better understand herself, Ding Ling in effect brought the Western imagining of the individualist self into conjunction with the image of the more "traditional" Chinese female, and thus bringing a more native model of female self-validation to bear on the new woman's grappling with the exigencies of the modern heterosexual model.

Ding Ling has often been praised for depicting in Sophia a liberated modern Chinese woman who "is capable of desiring women as well as men, and speaks of her body and sexuality with an openness new to the works of Chinese women writers" (L. Liu, *Translingual Practice* 172). However, Sophia's diary also presents a revealing genealogy of her desire by placing her love for a woman in a golden nostalgia-filled past, antedating her tumultuous heterosexual affair of the present. Moreover, just as her desire for Ling Jishi is physical, combative, and corrosive to her own sense of self-worth, her love of Yun is emotional, reciprocal, and conducive to self-validation. As such, although the temporal progression of the two triangle apparently enables a Freudian heterosexual narrative of female "maturation": love for one's family, love for same-sex friend, and heterosexual love, Sophia's struggle and eventual failure to replicate the first triangle in the second, heterosexual triangle actually destabilize this conventional narrative.

The dynamic interactions both within and between the two triangles signify the complex relationships between Sophia's past and present, between her desire for women and for men. In the first triangle comprised of

Sophia, Yun, and Sophia's family, Yun is described not only as a "very emotional and passionate person" (62) but also someone who "understands" and nurtures Sophia's emotional self. Sophia recalls that in the past she often "lost [herself] in unrestrained sobs" in front of Yun (72) and Yun, faced with Sophia's emotional distress, would "hold [her] in her arms. 'Oh, Sophia, my Sophia,' she'd cry. 'Why can't my valor rescue Sophia from so much suffering?'" (74). Yun's role carries evident maternal overtones and Sophia admits to having often exaggerated her own "most trivial dissatisfactions to work on [Yun's] tearful anxiety and get [Yun] to fondle [sic] [her]" (73). Yet Sophia emphasizes that Yun is not so much a doting surrogate mother who caters to her every whim as a source of understanding and validation of her subjectivity. For Yun not only provides unconditional love but also responds to and even celebrates Sophia's psychological uniqueness without passing on any moral judgment. Within their shared emotional life, Yun also unreservedly accepts Sophia's constant summons and her intrusion upon her own subject position. For Sophia, it is Yun's affirmation of her emotional and psychological reality alone that makes it possible for Yun to not only substitute for but also surpass the apparitional, third vertex of the triangle: her family.

Compared to the relatively full image of Yun, Sophia's family exists in a hazy past from which it is even harder to retrieve them. Sophia rarely mentions her family members in her diary except to complain of their blind devotion to her without any understanding of her character, but she enjoys imagining her family's grief for her impending death: "I spend days and nights dreaming up ways I could die without regret. I imagine myself resting on a bed in a gorgeous bedroom, my sisters nearby on a bearskin rug praying for me, and my father sighing as he gazes quietly out the window" (56). In this light, Yun is a superior replacement for Sophia's family not just because Yun alone can both sympathize with *and* understand her unique emotional interior, but also because Yun provides a stabilizing continuity in Sophia's life away from her native family without destroying her fond memories of them. That is to say, Yun simultaneously re-enacts and improves on the role of nurturer in Sophia's experience, enabling the coexistence of Sophia's emotional ties to her family and to her same-sex friend, and thus facilitating Sophia's own efforts of coming to terms with her rootless existence outside of home. Furthermore, the triangle of Sophia, Yun, and Sophia's family authorizes Sophia as its agent and guiding force: she leaves her loving yet inadequate family behind to seek self-knowledge, and pursues and possesses a superior object of love in Yun, who not only re-enacts the (imagined) nurturing role of the family but also affirms Sophia's subjectivity by accepting and reciprocating her desire.

In Sophia's diary-writing, the second, heterosexual triangle figures more prominently. This triangle represents her attempt to recreate the prior model of reciprocal love and identification between herself and the Other, though the grounds for the existence of the previous triangle have already shifted. Sophia claims to have started the diary because Yun insisted that she share her life with her in this way. Writing for this female object of love, Sophia records her efforts to establish more socially acceptable but equally satisfying relationships after a series of psychological ordeals that have happened before the start of the diary: Yun was "tricked by God" into marrying an indifferent husband (who happens to be the elder brother of Sophia's male suitor Weidi), and she herself has also experienced several painful "previous liaisons" (66) at school that subjected her to cruel rejection by a female schoolmate she had admired (52–53). Therefore, she claims in her diary, she is at the time seeking someone "who'll hold [her] and let [her] sob, someone who'll listen to [her] cry" (67–68), namely, a duplicate of Yun who understands and embraces her emotional turmoil as an essential part of herself. However, the heterosexual triangle she chronicles in her diary defeats her efforts at transferring her affections. This is not just because her two male suitors are incapable of the same emotional sensitivity and responsiveness as Yun; authorized by different discourses, this heterosexual triangle also functions with a very different dynamic: it features bitter competition between two *desiring* male suitors rather than the (imagined) symbiotic existence of Sophia's two *desired* objects, as is the case with the first triangle.

Sophia initially aims to establish in this triangle the same dynamics that sustained the previous triangle in order to achieve a similar sense of autonomy. She wishes to reject Weidi, a faithful but obtuse suitor, who, like her family, supplies a sense of security with his blind devotion but also limits her development in his equally steadfast refusal to see the real her. On the other hand, she wishes to pursue and possess Ling Jishi, whose air of a "medieval knight" at first implies a correspondingly "noble soul"—the kind of spiritual superiority possessed by Yun—and hence the capability of confirming her subjectivity. But not only do the inadequacies of the two male suitors upset her typecasting, but even when she apparently acquires a certain degree of power over them, she finds herself reaffirming rather than overcoming the restrictions placed on her gender. In her diary writing, we can see that she has internalized a male-centered consciousness even as she struggles to confront both the traditional Chinese gender codes and the conventions of modern heterosexual love, both of which are organized around male-centered consciousness.

To be sure, Sophia manages to gain some informal, provisional power through the manipulation of the traditional construct of femininity. Although she is presented as a "Westernized" woman from the very beginning, both in her exotic name Sophia and in her occupation of a space outside of the traditional Chinese family structure, she is fully aware of the burden placed on her by the traditional social norms governing her gender. She acknowledges that she has to yield to public views and behave with the "propriety" required of a "respectable" woman. Therefore, when she first meets Ling Jishi, her instant attraction is checked by this knowledge: "[In] this society I'm forbidden to take what I need to gratify my desires and frustrations, even when it clearly wouldn't hurt anybody" (55). She also often reins in her uninhibited words and behavior in front of Ling, considering them unsuitable for a decent woman and worried that they would cost her his respect. Moreover, she deliberately plays the weak female to capture Ling Jishi's interest when she discovers that Ling is "only able to respond to [her] helplessness, [her] vulnerabilities" (71). The diary also shows that Sophia often plays on other people's misplaced gender expectations of her to secure their attention and affection. For example, when pursued by Weidi, she encourages him to linger in order to alleviate her boredom even while internally mocking his obtuseness. Sophia is equally disingenuous in her dealings with her friends Yufang and Yunlin. In order to get closer to Ling Jishi, she pretends that she hopes to live near her female friend Yufang, whose boyfriend Yunlin is a neighbor of Ling Jishi. Later, during a sudden relapse of her tuberculosis, she deliberately asks her friends to fetch her the box where she keeps all their letters, and declares her wish to take them with her to the hospital, thus earning their gratified tears.

However, the male gaze, once internalized by Sophia, exerts insidious influence on her conception and performance of gender. This can be seen in her different requirements of her relationships with women and with men. While Sophia savors the emotional exchange between women, sometimes even displaying a masochistic delectation of the cold snubs given her by other women (52–53), she is even more in favor of physical expressions of desire between the sexes. Not only does she wish to "mark every part of his [Ling Jishi's] body with [her] lips" (147), but she is also willing to submit to male domination solely on the strength of Ling's "male beauty" despite the lack of an emotional tie between them: "If he wanted nothing more than sexual satisfaction, he might conceivably have seduced me with his sensuous beauty" (79). Furthermore, Sophia does not consider it necessary to withhold her emotions in her relationships with Yun, while with her male suitors, she claims that her "self-respect [...] surfaces and controls [her] emotions, allowing [her] to choke back the words ['My lord and master! Grant me one kiss']" (75). The withholding of her emotions in heterosexual relationships not only constitutes part of her strategy of self-empowerment but also reveals the deep ambiguity that underlies her conceptualization of masculinity and femininity.

Of course, Sophia's division of emotional and physical satisfaction as mutually exclusive experiences in her relationships reflects her recognition of the objectification of women as sexual objects by men within the heterosexual couple in a male-dominated society. For when Sophia tries to break down the psychological and emotional barrier between her and her male suitors and replicate the transparent and free exchange between herself and Yun, she always meets with bitter disappointment. Weidi misreads her diary merely as a refusal of his love and a declaration of her love for another man, a conventional interpretation according to the rules of the heterosexual triangle. Ling Jishi, on the other hand, proves to possess a "cheap, ordinary soul" (68), and is only passionate about "the Debate Club, playing tennis matches, studying at Harvard, joining the foreign service, becoming an important statesman, or inheriting his father's business and becoming a rubber merchant. He wants to be a capitalist [. . .] that is the extent of his ambition!" (68). In other words, neither of them is capable of the deep emotional and psychological engagement with which Yun had previously provided her. As a result, Sophia feels her subjectivity compromised and debased by their desire for her.

However, Sophia also subconsciously insists on the control of emotions as an essential component of masculinity and, furthermore, as the only path to power. As I have mentioned earlier, Sophia enthuses over a shared emotional bond between herself and Yun as the definitive factor of their relationship. Curiously, she finds Weidi's tears and misery merely nuisances and frequently taunts him to his face for "acting like a child" (67). Although she often relents and comforts him "in a sisterly way" later (54), she nevertheless considers his crying jags futile efforts to appeal to her "feminine and weak" side (54). In contrast, she initially becomes infatuated with Ling Jishi not only because of his physical beauty but also because he can apparently absent himself and control his own desires and emotions, and thus making him a more attractive and masculine "European medieval knight." What is most striking in her relationships with Weidi and Ling Jishi is not the contrast between familial and sexual dynamics that she plays out through them, nor is it just a matter of her fantasy of "a Chinese man with a Caucasian man's sex appeal" (L. Liu, *Translingual Practice* 174), but rather her internalized self-image as a "feminine" woman whose sexuality can only be defined by the pursuit of a masculine man. Weidi annoys her not only because he is emotional, but also because by acting emotional and therefore "effeminate," he undermines her position as the sexually desirable female and forces her into the role of a (desexualized) mother.

Not only does control of emotions signify masculinity, for Sophia the masculine separation of affection and sexual desire also generates (masculine) power. Sophia withholds her emotions not just because of her fear of the disciplinary force of gender stereotypes but also because the control of her emotions facilitates her quest for power. As I have mentioned above, Sophia often masks her emotions not only in deference to social conventions but also for the acquisition of informal power. Furthermore, her textual possession of Ling Jishi also repeats the masculine practice, suggested by Freud (see chapter five), of excluding respect and affection from erotic fantasy. Her description of Ling Jishi is curiously both emasculating and objectifying. Not only does Sophia describe his general appearance as "pale, delicate, fine," but she also forms a fixation on his "soft, red, moist" lips. Throughout the diary Sophia transports the masculine language of desire into her daydreams of Ling Jishi, turning him into a sexual object. Revealingly, she finds herself attracted to Ling's "tall lean body, his delicate flower-soft skin, his soft lips and provocative eyes" (68) even as she discerns and despises his lack of sincere feelings and understanding of love. Revealingly, Sophia's account of her pursuit of Ling Jishi by disguising herself as a demure female is paradoxically heavily invested in the masculine metaphors of battle and conquest:

> It's like planning a battle. Now I'm concentrating all my energy on strategy. I want something, but I'm not willing to go and take it. I must find a tactic that gets it offered to me voluntarily. I understand myself completely. I am a thoroughly female woman, and women concentrate everything on the man they've got in their sights. I want to possess him. I want unconditional surrender of his heart. I want him kneeling down in front of me, begging me to kiss him. I'm delirious. I go over and over the steps I must take to implement my scheme. (58–59)

Sophia meanders through different gender positions in this paragraph; although presenting a façade of helpless femininity to the external world, she describes this as a strategic move that promises masculine power. As such, she holds, both in life and in writing, the power to release or withhold her emotions as a weapon to gain and defend a powerful and independent subject position.

Yet, even as Sophia's appropriation of the masculine model of emotional regulation demonstrates her resourcefulness in manipulating male-centered gender codes for self-empowerment, the freedom supposedly provided by such self-determination is simultaneously curtailed. For her self-restraint can also be seen as a result of her negation of spontaneous emotions, which have been defined as the core of her individuality in her relationship with Yun. In this light, her eventual disenchantment with Ling Jishi confirms the failure of her efforts to re-enact, through the medium of this heterosexual relationship, the dynamic of mutual response and validation shared by her and Yun. Not only this, it also renders problematic her previous advocacy of free emotional expression as the ultimate barometer of individuality and subjectivity.

Therefore, the narrative progression enacted by the two triangles, especially Sophia's failure to successfully replicate the dynamic interaction of the earlier triangle in the later, exposes the constraint of a woman's independence in a male-dominated society by showing the unlikelihood of her ever completely realizing her individuality within a conventional heterosexual relationship. Moreover, Ding Ling's unique triangular arrangement also shows the contradictions and impossibilities of the Freudian model of feminine "adjustment" of progressing from homosexual to heterosexual love. But more importantly, the interaction between the two triangles reveal the risk a Chinese woman runs in seeking independence through writing in an appropriated Western form. As I will show below, Sophia's failure to formulate a coherent subjectivity can also be attributed to her failed attempt at grafting a more native model of female interaction and mutual validation onto the Western form of diary fiction. Prototypes for Ding Ling's depiction of the relationship between Sophia and Yun can be found in a relatively less stern native literary tradition. Although we do not have to follow Barlow's interpretation of Yun's name as the "homophonic reference" (*Woman* 49) to the wife who dies of love for a courtesan in *Six Chapters of the Floating Life* (*Fusheng liuji*), a late-eighteenth-century Chinese memoir, it is obvious, as Matthew Sommer argues, that female homosexuality enjoyed more latitude than male homosexuality in imperial China. Premodern Chinese narratives, both in the classical and vernacular language, also describe love between different wives of the same man without causing any major moralistic or institutional censorship. Moreover, the privileged emotional bond between Sophia and Yun also draws inspiration from the Ming drama *Peony Pavilion* (71–72), even as Sophia consciously rejects the classical scholar-beauty romance it portrays (L. Liu, *Translingual Practice* 179). As such, Ding Ling's depiction of heterosexual triangle that supersedes and in effect destroys the first triangle also enacts, in Sophia's failed quest for a coherent and viable subjective position, the expulsion and replacement of a native form of female emotional intimacy by the Western discourse of romantic modern love. The impediment that the form of diary fiction presents to the achievement of female autonomy becomes even more distinctive if we more closely examine the effects of Ding Ling's deployment of the conventions of diary fiction—a genre that represents what Sidonie Smith calls the "androcentric enterprise" (15) of the Western autobiographical writings—for the constitution of a female subject.

Significantly, Ding Ling had Sophia reject the native form and adopt the Western form of diary fiction in the representation of her emotions. Sophia scoffs at the "talented women" who can write insipid and artificial poems about "'how depressed I am,' 'Oh, the tragic sufferings of my heart'" (73), and insists on searching out a more powerful vehicle for her untrammeled passions. But, of course, the representation of her emotions through diary writing does not lack artifice, either. From the beginning, the reader feels overwhelmed by Sophia's obsession with the small details in her daily life as a new woman trapped alone in a Beijing hostel:

> Nothing to do after the paper except sit alone by the stove and work myself into a rage. What infuriates me is the daily routine. I get a nervous headache every day as I sit listening to the other inmates yell at the attendants. Such loud, braying, coarse, monotonous voices, "Attendant, bring hot water!" or "Wash basin, attendant!" You can imagine how ugly it sounds. And there is always somebody downstairs shouting into the telephone. Yet when the noise does let up, the silence scares me to death. Particularly inside the four whitewashed walls that stare blankly back at me no matter where I sit. If I try to escape by lying on the bed, I'm crushed by the ceiling, just as oppressively white. I can't really find a single thing

here that doesn't disgust me: the pockmarked attendant, for example, the food that always tastes like a filthy rag, the impossibly grimy window frame, and that mirror over the washbasin. Balancing from one side you've got a face a foot long; tilt your head slightly to the side and suddenly it gets so flat you startle yourself.... (51)

As the opening of the first entry, this passage sets the tone for Sophia's entire diary. The extremely subjective quality of Sophia's narrative is illustrated in her subjective and emotional interpretation of the outer world: Her external world only exists in terms of its role in causing her misery. Her sight, hearing, taste, and thought are all mobilized to collaborate in an immense discontent. For her, other than the tedious ritual of warming up milk five or six times a day in order to kill time, the only distraction is to find new sources of complaint. She admits to longing for new misery to break the tiresome uneventful run of her life: "Still I'd really like a few fresh complaints and dissatisfactions. Novelty, for better or worse, always seems just out of reach" (51). The power of "Miss Sophia's Diary" lies precisely in such vivid representation of Sophia's subjective emotions. As a piece of diary fiction, "Miss Sophia's Diary" simulates emotional spontaneity by masking the separateness of the protagonist and the narrator: an *acting* Sophia laughs and cries, while a *writing* Sophia recalls and improvises. Ding Ling especially capitalized on another generic requirement of diary fiction, the privileging of internal reflection, to elaborate upon the emotive effects of the story. Sophia's emotions are allowed to play out, to rationalize, and even to anticipate her later wayward behavior.

As with the distinction between the experiencing and narrating Sophia, Ding Ling also glossed over the difference between story time (i.e., the time when events happen in the story) and discourse time (i.e., the time when the story is told) in order to reinforce Sophia's subjectivity. A diarist always presents facts after the fact. The gap between story time and discourse time means that the presentation of past events is always informed by hindsight and determined by the situation in which the discourse is made. The diarist's storytelling, then, is by necessity motivated by the here and now, instead of being a "factual" representation of her past. For the reader, this also suggests the possibility of the narrator's conscious or subconscious resignification of past events, for what the reader sees is the already mediated and re-ordered life that the diarist chooses to put forth. In "Miss Sophia's Diary," Sophia also tells her story from the vantage point of the present, producing interpretations of past events to meet the present demands of reinforcing her own subject position. But rather than revealing the discrepancy between the discourse time and the story time in Sophia's narration, Ding Ling again utilized the genre conventions of diary fiction by making the diarist's psychological time into the only dominant discourse time of her impassioned narrative. In this way, she not only averted the possibility of the same incident being told from different points of view, and therefore possibly subverting Sophia's version, but also made it possible for

Sophia to create an alternative image of herself within an alternative reality based on the imagined uniqueness and strength of her emotions. Indeed, the privileging of the diarist's psychological time afforded Ding Ling the kind of insulation needed to optimize the affect of the story for the purpose of female subject formation.

Ding Ling thus created in Sophia a heroine adroit at manipulating both the Western discourse of individualism and the form of diary fiction to accentuate her remarkable inner strength and to avoid showing any external signs of weakness. However, the limitation of this useful function of diary fiction is clearly illustrated in the last entry of the diary. In her final encounter with Ling Jishi, Sophia admits: "The lust in his eyes scared me" (79). The story as related in the last entry shows that her purported emotional strength fails to grant her any power of action, as she discovers to her shame and horror that her body betrays her, and she lets Ling kiss her and stands "poised to toss away all [her] self-esteem and pride" (80). After the encounter, however, she uses a series of "I should have said" declarations to express regret for her temporary lapse of control. Moreover, she again marshals different narrative devices to transform her (lack of) action into meaningful emotional experience.

Sophia meticulously inventories the range of emotions she has experienced in order to construct a coherent or even masculinized self *after the fact*. First of all, she expresses, instead of gratification, intense loathing for both Ling Jishi and herself. Ling Jishi's mouth, once the object of intense longing for Sophia, loses its attraction after the kiss, when Sophia ridicules Ling Jishi's vanity about "the warmth and tenderness of his lips, their smooth delicacy" (80). Sophia thus takes up a traditionally masculine role in her appropriation of the objectifying undertone and fetishistic, fragmentary body imagery for her description of Ling Jishi. Moreover, she also highlights her will to dominate. According to her account of the event, not only did she open her eyes wide and silently chant "I've won" during the kiss, but she also believes that her behavior under the circumstances proves her difference from "some women" who would swoon in their lovers' arms (80).

More importantly, this kind of reflection on her emotions enables her to evaluate not only her diary but also her life:

> Rather than calling this diary a record of my life, it's more accurate to regard it as the sum of all my tears. At least that's the way it feels. But now it's time to end the diary because Sophia doesn't need it as a vent or consolation, since now she understands that nothing has any meaning whatever and that tears are only the most elegant proof of that lack. Yet on this last page of diary, I ought fervently to toast the fact that suddenly from the depth of disappointment I did achieve the satisfaction that should rightly have killed me with ecstasy. I . . . I . . . all I felt out of that satisfaction was victory. From victory came a terrible sense of sorrow and an even profounder understanding of how pathetic and ludicrous I am. And so the "beauty"

that has been the focus of my tangled dreams for months was dissolved away, revealed as nothing more than the image of a tall man's exquisite bearing. (78–79)

This passage is a postscript to real life events even though it occupies the position of prologue in the entry itself. In other words, it chronologically comes after Sophia's encounter with Ling Jishi, though placed at the beginning of the entry and before the description of that fateful night. That the narrator should conspicuously reverse the order of external events and internal contemplation already indicates a conscious effort of re-ordering life through writing. Furthermore, she reconstructs herself by paradoxically and deliberately dispersing herself among different speech locations. At one point the diarist refers to herself by the personal name "Sophia," which may suggest to some the possibility that this gesture signals a schizophrenic breakdown. However, since the whole passage is set apart from the remainder of the final entry as a kind of retrospective preface, we can deduce that here she is consciously stepping back from her old self to assess what has happened before. Specifically, a contrast is deliberately set up between two consecutive sentences. In the first sentence, the diarist bitterly mocks Sophia, the infatuated woman finally kissed by the man of her fantasies, jeeringly saying, "[She] ought fervently to toast the fact that suddenly from the depth of disappointment [she] did achieve the satisfaction that should rightly have killed [her] with ecstasy" ("Shafei nüshi de riji" 61, "Miss Sophia's Diary" 78; the English translation of the pronouns here changes the original Chinese version). In the next sentence, however, she reverts to the pronoun "I" and almost clinically records her cooling down from the fervent emotions of infatuation: "[All] I felt out of that satisfaction was victory. From victory came a terrible sense of sorrow and an even profounder understanding of how pathetic and ludicrous I am" ("Miss Sophia's Diary" 79). The change of pronouns from third-person to first-person reveals the process of analysis and re-integration of the self. Finally, the diarist claims that she has woken up from her past "dream" and now realizes her own absurdity. By switching abruptly from internal, psychic time to external, historical time at this point of her narrative, the diarist transforms the moment of deep disillusionment into that of profound self-enlightenment.

In the end Sophia defines her diary as a folly of the past—"the most elegant expression of [. . .] meaninglessness" (78) that she has outgrown. She apparently decides to transcend even writing itself by letting her actions speak for themselves: "I've decided to take a train south, somewhere where no one knows me, where I can squander the remaining days of my life" (81). However, the birth of the new self still very much depends on the validation of true emotions. Revealingly, her last words are: "I feel so sorry for myself. How pathetic you are, Sophia!" (81). Furthermore, Sophia's search for a new beginning is already doomed since, as I have mentioned before, the emotionally motivated triangle comprised of Sophia, Yun, and Sophia's family had already broken down even before she started the diary in an effort to recapture the experience of women's mutual validation. Moreover, since Sophia previously intended to use her diary "to mourn Yun" and to provide a "testimonial to all the things she told me while she was alive" (73), the voluntary termination of diary writing, more than Yun's death, forcefully confirms the destruction of the earlier model. In the end, Sophia rejects her diary, "the sum of all [her] tears" (78), just like Lin Daiyu, the heroine from the vernacular novel Dream of the Red Chamber, who on her deathbed burns all her poems written on her handkerchiefs that are said to bear her bitter tears. This final gesture of renunciation not only reaffirms the irrevocable loss of the emotional support for her subjectivity from her female Other, but also questions the efficacy of Western discourses and narrative forms in Chinese women's quest for autonomy and liberation.

Ding Ling's representation and deployment of emotions in "Miss Sophia's Diary" ultimately subvert rather than support the Western discourse of individualism. This is not merely because Ding Ling's depiction of Sophia's complete isolation from other people and her impotent rage, though presumably providing fertile ground for the generation of her diary, demonstrates the new woman's entrapment in the "modern" genre. More importantly, "Miss Sophia's Diary" reveals, through the portrayal of the destruction of a more native model of female emotional bond by modern heterosexual economy, that the Western discourse of individualism privileges only one form of subjectivity: a kind of bourgeois masculine subjectivity that presents the self as "under siege from hostile Others, threatened and in danger of abjection" (Gagnier 221), a subjectivity that is affirmed, among other things, by a feminized Other positioned antagonistic to the Self. In this respect, "Miss Sophia's Diary" also reveals the dangers of appropriation, for women writers could too easily allow the male-centric basis of the genre to impede women's struggle for a more appropriate and enduring model of female subjectivity. Ding Ling seemed to realize the potential weakness in Sophia's subjectivity constructed through writing. But instead of attributing Sophia's failings to the gendered nature of the discourses that organized literary genres, she blamed it on female emotionalism. Influenced by public discourse, particularly contemporary male literary criticism of women's emotions, Ding Ling earnestly set out to correct the lapses of her heroine.

The Woman Writer in "Yecao"

Ding Ling gradually moved away from the extremely subjective narrative style of "Miss Sophia's Diary," and juxtaposed an internal and an external vision in "Suicide Diary" (1928), "Day" (1929), and "Yecao" (1929). "Suicide Diary" adopts an external perspective that provides a frame of reference and contrasts with the diarist's internal monologue, though the two perspectives carry equal weight in the narrative. "Day" features an omniscient narrator that depicts the heroine's psychological development in a series of vignettes. "Yecao" proves by far the most complex story of the three. Through the centralization of a woman writer's act of writing, it illustrates the way she strives to preserve her autonomy through the control of her emotions, thus foreshadowing Ding Ling's production of works of Revolutionary Literature and her further radicalization in the 1930s.

To be sure, "Yecao" suggests writing, rather than radical politics, as a way for the urban, female intellectual to establish an independent identity for herself. Yet, at the same time, it also implies the similarity between the functions of writing and revolution in regulating individual emotions for the empowerment of women. This can be seen in the way Ding Ling employed the trope of writing in her exploration of female subject formation. "Yecao" is Ding Ling's earliest story in which the new heroine's occupation is described in detail and made central to the plot. As the story begins, the title character Yecao, a twenty-four-year-old woman writer living alone in Shanghai, is having some trouble with her writing. Apparently, the heroine in her novel behaves in an inconsistent manner, and Yecao blames this lapse of good writing on the intrusion of her own memories of the past. While fretting over her lack of self-control and weakness of character, she receives a letter from a male admirer by the name of Nan Xia, in which he asks her to rendezvous with him at a park. Yecao goes to the appointed site and strikes up a stilted conversation with him, during which her thoughts constantly drift back to her writing. In spite of her preoccupation, he insists on expressing his passionate love for her, a performance that she finds pitiful and unmoving. They then go for a walk, during which Yecao briefly recalls her love affair with another man three years early, the drama of which had partly unfolded at the same park. She falters in her decision to remain aloof, momentarily wishing that Nan Xia would be physically more demonstrative. But as they emerge from the dark trail into bright lamplight, Yecao collects herself and looks at Nan Xia with cold distaste. In the end, she refuses another date, and goes home with the happy thought that she has worked out some phrases for her novel during the meeting with Nan Xia.

The most striking change in the characterization of this heroine, another new woman like Sophia, is the emphasis she places on her work, rather than on romantic or sexual relationships, in her self-definition. Yecao is no literary dilettante or amateurish "talented woman." She takes her work seriously—so much so that she feels more passion for her novel than for her amorous admirer. Equipped with a sense of purpose and mission, Yecao chooses when and where to go, and whom to meet, and she rarely allows her social life to interfere with her work. However, even as her career provides her with increased autonomy, she finds her emotions an obstacle to her work and a threat to her sense of independence:

> Today she was terribly upset because she had endowed an extremely level-headed and rational woman in her novel with unduly passionate emotions. Also, she had let a slight touch of melancholy [for

the past] slip in. This definitely was not the character she had intended to create, but it was the flaw in women that she was able to understand best. She didn't know what would be better, to tear up the manuscript and start over, or to go on writing, but not sympathize with the woman. She couldn't stop thinking about this perplexing problem, but gradually, she turned her thoughts to the social environment that caused women to overemphasize emotions, then to how pitiable women are. In a moment of self-examination, she began to detest herself. Could she stifle her own emotions? Even though it seemed that she needed nothing other than her writing, still there were times when, freed from external aggravation and lost in prior joys and happiness, she would think of the past—this was something so painful and so tinged with remorse that she could never bring herself to speak or think of it. She thought of the past with resentment and longing, and then, finally, with indifference. (106)

This passage epitomizes the complex relationship of the woman writer to the act of writing because it not only describes Yecao's inability to separate her life from her literary production but also demonstrates how she overcomes the challenges in her life through writing. Ding Ling adopted an omniscient narrator stance to relate the self-reflection of the professional writer in the story, simultaneously exposing her inadequacy and establishing the narrator/author's superiority with the deft maneuvering between the heroine's internal and external worlds. Yecao feels that she fails to create a credible character because she loses control of her own emotions. However, the narrator adds, her emotions are not entirely self-centered; they also arise from her understanding of women's plight in real life: "This definitely was not the character she had intended to create, but it was the flaw in women that she was able to understand best" (106). Ding Ling thus not only used the narrator to corroborate Yecao's observation of social problems, but also implicitly designated Yecao as representative of all women, whose emotionalism, like theirs, is conditioned by "the social environment that caused women to overemphasize emotions" (106). In so doing, Ding Ling not only re-introduced and privileged the theme of women's shared life situations and emotional experiences, as embodied by the relationship between Sophia and Yun, but also situated her representation of such experiences in a larger social context. This was to become a common practice in Ding Ling's later fiction written in Yan'an. Nevertheless, even with the knowledge of the sociopolitical forces shaping women's lives, at this point Ding Ling still accentuated the protagonist's self-signification through writing rather than through any service to the Party and the people. As we can see from the above passage, although initially upset with the intrusion of personal emotions upon her creation of a character, Yecao soon finds writing a useful exercise to divert and to wash away her fixation on the past. She turns "her thoughts to the social environment," and, finally, is able to think of the past "with indifference" (106).

Ding Ling delineated the process of Yecao's exorcism of her troublesome and enervating emotions through an ingenious use of the omniscient narrator. Presenting a character's psychological development from an external perspective was not a new feature in Ding Ling's fiction at this point in her writing career. However, it was the first time Ding Ling employed an omniscient narrator to represent the interior reflections of a woman writer on herself. While "Miss Sophia's Diary" lingers on each minute psychological change the character underwent, it is told from an internal perspective in an apparently random manner. By contrast, Yecao's internal world is not only meticulously described from an external point of view, but also supplied with temporality and causality; her past is contrasted with her present, and the past is used as the reason to explain her present mental and emotional state. The description of the heroine's psyche is thus transformed into the recounting of a psycho-narrative. Furthermore, this psycho-narrative in "Yecao" at the same time reveals the writing process of the heroine in order to examine the benefits and limits of writing for the purpose of self-creation and self-definition. Yecao proves to be stronger than Sophia, for she possesses not only self-respect but also the faculty of rationality: She is said to be "blessed with the ability to analyze herself" (106). And analyze herself she does, not only to improve her writing, as demonstrated in her self-criticism for allowing her melancholy to spill into her work, but also to organize her life. It is writing that enables her to detach herself from the past, to overcome uncertain emotions, and to view the past "with indifference" (106). As such, Yecao's practice of rational self-reflection as well as her profession as a writer puts her in the unique position of proxy narrator in this story. That is, by reflecting on her own thoughts and emotions, she not only demonstrates the process of writing but also partly performs the function of the omniscient narrator.

However, even as Yecao's rational temperament and profession of writing grant her some power over life, the story also reveals the uncertainty of such power through the description of her vulnerability when separated from her writing. As is shown in this story, she in fact substitutes writing for many other life experiences. The reader is led to wonder whether such tenuous control of emotions achieved by avoiding human company offers the most effective means of self-empowerment. "Yecao" does not give a clear answer to this question. The beginning of the story sets up a significant contrast between the small, confining room Yecao stays in and the sight of the open ground right in front of her window. While outside spring unfolds in its irrepressible glory, Yecao has "shut herself up in a small room alone, worrying over the characters in her novel. She had forgotten spring" (105). Instead, she conjures up what she cannot have in life through writing her novel, where "there was a spring day, filled with ecstatic and impassioned love, raging like fire" (105). The image of Yecao shut in her room and absorbed in her writing may invoke the figure of the male romantic genius who shuns society in order to preserve the purity of his spirit. Yet, unlike the idealized romantic genius, Yecao cannot trust her spontaneous emotions alone but has to summon up rational self-discipline in order to produce works of art that ironically describe passionate love and uncontrolled emotions. Her name, meaning "wild grass" in Chinese, implies that she controls the wild exuberance of herself by focusing on the safer blank page under her pen, distancing herself from the joyful spring outside of her window.

Although inside her study Yecao manages to control her unruly feelings through writing, her encounter with Nan Xia at the park reveals the precariousness of her self-mastery. At first, she keeps control of the situation, as if to both avenge her humiliation in her disastrous love affair in the past and to demonstrate that writing has instilled in her masculine resolution. When Nan Xia bursts into an impassioned declaration of his hopeless love for her, also confusedly accusing her "you love only yourself and your work" (109), Yecao remains coolly detached. She pities Nan Xia, but she still finds him not a little ridiculous. She believes that he should take charge of his own emotions and not allow them to show in front of others. In a scene that uncannily recalls Sophia's scorn of a weeping Weidi, she silently scolds him: "Ai, you are no child!" (109). But in this story, the female protagonist does not turn to an image of masculinity, such as Ling Jishi, for self-definition, but rather depends on writing as a source of power. During their meeting she also experiences moments of emotional weakness. When they walk onto a faintly lit trail, for one moment she "wished he would let himself go so that she would once again experience that intoxicating feeling [of love]" (110). She even feels regret when Nan Xia does not act in the bold way her former lover did. Interestingly, such a lapse is to be countered first by her intense emotions of loathing and hostility towards Nan Xia, and then by thoughts of her writing: "she was preoccupied with various ways of describing a night scene" (110).

It can be seen that Yecao's writing indeed provides a means to suppress emotional upheavals and to grant her a certain freedom to establish her career. But in her case, writing is both pivoted on and results in the repression of a part of her even as it creates a sense of control and power. The ending of the story is revealing in its ambiguity. The omniscient narrator withdraws from the territory of Yecao's psychology, content with a cryptic external description: "On the way home she sang, apparently very happily, her newly composed, well-turned phrases" (111). The word "apparently" calls into question Yecao's actual emotional state. She is returning to her cheerless and stuffy small room, and will conceivably meet with another emotional assault from Nan Xia in the future. She might have found an ideal resolution for the heroine in her work, but will she always be able to sublimate and rechannel her own emotions? If emotional writings of the kind done by Sophia only create confusion and despair, does a more controlled way of writing provide resolution to women's unique predicament of "emotionalism"? If Sophia can be dismissed as "merely a woman" (Barlow, "Feminism and Literary Technique" 99), does Yecao sufficiently prove herself "more than a woman" through her writing? Literary explorations and life circumstances prompted Ding Ling to answer the question of women's identities in new ways yet, which I will examine in the next chapter.

EIGHT

The Revolutionary Age: Ding Ling's Fiction of the Early 1930s

Ding Ling's unwavering commitment to the pursuit of Chinese women's self-empowerment, as well as her own quest for identity, came to concentrate even more sharply on the issue of women's emotions in the early 1930s. In prose essays she repeatedly expressed concern over what she considered to be women's unique weakness: self-defeating emotionalism. Distinctly echoing her fictional writer Yecao, Ding Ling claimed that she wrote about women's emotions only because "as a woman, I understand their weakness better" ("Wo de chuangzuo jingyan" 106). Furthermore, she characterized her own description of women's emotions as objective: "Actually I strongly dislike these weak points in women [...] I may not feel sympathetic towards the women in my writings, but I am unable to write in accordance with my opinion" ("Wo de chuangzuo jingyan" 106). The more significant and complex changes in her deployment of emotions took place in her fiction. Ding Ling's different portrayal of new women in the 1930s signals an important transitional point in her literary career.

Although previously known for her portrayal of neurotic female city dwellers in diary fiction and other forms of first-person narratives, starting in the early 1930s Ding Ling turned to the representation of the intellectual-turned-revolutionary and used more objective narrative modes. Yi-tsi Feuerwerker points out that in Ding Ling's fiction "After 1930 love is rejected not in favor of literature [as in "Yecao"] but of political action" ("The Changing Relationship" 298). Her novellas "Wei Hu" and "Shanghai, Spring 1930" indeed propose a different path to achieving individual empowerment for women: the simultaneous practice of control of emotions and participation in the revolution. However, Ding Ling's apparent rejection of her own past fiction as well as the works of an earlier generation of women writers must be construed in the light of her goal of establishing her credibility as a woman writer. In the 1930s, she needed to adjust to her new life situation, which included the secret arrest and execution of her husband Hu Yepin (1903–31) for his Communist association and her new affiliation as a member of the Chinese Communist Party. Due to the increasing influence of

Marxist ideology on the political consciousness of China's intellectuals, she was also surrounded by radical male critics who, although her colleagues in revolution, voiced their disapproval of excessive female emotions in literature with the more powerful political weapon of promoting Marxism for national prosperity. Ding Ling's fiction at that time demonstrates not only her accommodation of her new political identity but also the deliberate changes she made in order to speak for women as a legitimate interest group participating in this new phase of Chinese modernization.

Revealingly, Ding Ling's works from this period that represent urban revolutionary intellectuals were not her personal favorites. In a public speech delivered at Guanghua College in Shanghai in May 1931, she deprecated "Wei Hu" as "unsuitable": "[It is] a story of 'Revolution Plus Love' (*geming yu lian'ai jiaocuo de gushi*)" ("Wo de zibai" 98). The "unsuitability" of this novella, which she did not elaborate on during the public speech but explained later, lies in the fact that it turned out to be an unintended "vulgar" (*yongsu*) imitation, its formula courtesy of Jiang Guangci, the then-popular writer of "Love Plus Revolution Literature" ("Wo de chuangzuo shenghuo" 110). The source of Ding Ling's chagrin was more than a mere concern for originality. In 1932, as a new Communist Party member, she had to struggle to achieve two somewhat contradictory ends. On the one hand, she considered it her mission to free her heroines and herself from what she perceived as the tyranny of bourgeois love and to seek out a new path to women's liberation. On the other, she also resisted the categorization of her works as examples of Revolutionary Literature, a fashionable school of writing she viewed as having little literary merit. In other words, she had to strike a fine balance between "revolution" and "love," so as to both steer clear of the banal propaganda of Revolutionary Literature and to provide deliverance for women through her writings. Ding Ling apparently found a point of leverage in dealing with this problem: She claimed that her works were truthful biographies of her friends—a claim also made by Ba Jin about his fiction.

This strategy reflected Ding Ling's need to change her image as a woman writer who focused only on her own emotions. By her own account, she first started writing to air her grievances against society after many setbacks in her quest for a worthy cause in life ("Wo de chuangzuo shenghuo" 110). Influenced by Marxist ideology in the 1930s, however, she began to transform the personal into the collective; she sought to utilize her intimate knowledge of Chinese women's plight, gained by her as an experiencing subject, in order to find a solution for them. Yet Ding Ling faced a unique dilemma in the 1930s. Even as she distanced herself from her early works in her essays by echoing the male opinion that excessive emotion was disadvantageous to women, in fiction writing she was unwilling or unable to subscribe to the genre requirements of Revolutionary Literature dictated by the Communist Party. This was not only because of some vestige of her past belief in "individualism," as radical male critics charged, but also because the successful representation and privileging of women's unique emotions in her early fiction had instilled in her a set of narrative habits quite distinct from the standard fares of Revolutionary Literature. Revolutionary Literature, widely popular among radical intellectuals at the time, was envisioned as writing about the proletariat and the peasantry to endorse the Marxist vision of the oppressed masses as the motivating forces of history. However, an author's choice of proletarian characters or the subject matter of revolutionary activities was not in itself sufficient to guarantee favorable reception by radical critics. As mentioned before, both Yu Dafu's depiction of a tobacco factory worker and Mao Dun's portrayal of intellectuals' participation in revolutionary causes were criticized as not sufficiently revolutionary. Revolutionary Literature further required writers to erase their authorial ego, particularly the writers' bourgeois beliefs, and to voice optimism about the ultimate victory of the proletariat and the realization of a socialist society. As yet to fully invest herself in this Marxist Utopian vision, Ding Ling took refuge in the claim of psychological realism, characterizing her fiction as the emotional "biography" of her radical intellectual friends in order to prove her fiction to be both truthful and revolutionary.

In a move that should remind us of Ba Jin, Ding Ling declared that all her works had real life models, though they were not at all autobiographical: "People always think that myself is transformed into my writings. This is not correct" ("Wo de chuangzuo shenghuo" 110). The claim to writing "biographical" fiction enabled her not only to depart from the emotional "autobiography" of an earlier period, which she had by then deemed weak and feminine, but also to stand apart from the propagandistic Revolutionary Literature about the proletarian Other that she found uninspired. On the one hand, being biographical had the advantage of appearing "realistic" without submitting her psychology to the surveillance of male critics. She could thus assume detachment from her characters' emotions and strengthen her claim to a critical view of feminine emotionalism. On the other, Ding Ling's proclamation that she had written "biographies" of friends enabled her to claim a "truth" that she considered missing from Revolutionary Literature. She declared that she had nothing against "selfless" (*wuwo*) literature, but "in principle I am opposed to writing from pure fantasy [without any personal experience]" ("Wo de zibai" 99). Speaking from the authoritative position of the experiencing subject, she challenged the truthfulness of the then fashionable fiction on the proletariat: "What is the point of writing about a peasant or a factory worker, if we know nothing about their lives?" ("Wo de zibai" 99).

The same desire to produce truthful literature also prompted Ding Ling to remonstrate with some critics who considered her "Wei Hu" a piece of "Proletarian Literature." She asserted that her motive for writing this novella did not differ significantly from that behind "Miss Sophia's Diary," stating: "I did not intend to create a hero in [the character] Wei Hu, nor to write about revolution. I only wanted to write about some people [I knew] before the May Thirtieth Movement [May 30, 1925]" ("Wo de zibai" 99). She emphasized in the lecture given at Guanghua College that the main incidents in "Wei Hu" had happened to one of her "dearest fellow writers," making an oblique reference to Hu Yepin, her common law husband who was executed by the Nationalist government ("Wo de zibai" 99). She later explained that the story in "Wei Hu" was also based on the affair between her school friend Wang Jianhong and the well-known Communist literary theorist Qu Qiubai, again accentuating the novella's biographical nature and hence truthfulness ("Wo suo renshi de Qiubai tongzhi" 149–51). In using the claim to psychological realism to counter male criticism of her lack of revolutionary spirit, Ding Ling created her own definition of Revolutionary Literature. As such, she in fact established her own modern identity not on a complete self-effacement demanded by radical intellectuals but on an authorial agency that she claimed to enable her unique contribution to revolutionary causes.

Like the change in her notion of fiction, the alteration of Ding Ling's narrative style illustrates not only her resourcefulness in adapting to political pressure but also her continual commitment to women's self-strengthening through the exploration of new strategies. In other words, Ding Ling's promotion of women's independence in general and her attempt at self-determination in particular had been the crucial motive behind both her disapproval of emotionalism as a form of feminine weakness in her essays and her adoption of a more objective narrative style in her fiction. Even before 1932, Ding Ling's fictional exploration of the woman writer's relationship to the literature she produced (e.g., "Yecao") already implied her preference for a more self-sufficient female subject. Furthermore, in "Miss Sophia's Diary," she established a model of narrative ventriloquism in representing Sophia as a woman who appropriates a masculine position for the sake of subject formation and self-empowerment. Applying Sophia's strategy to her own narrative practice, Ding Ling appropriated narrative conventions established by male writers in order to both construct a powerful woman in fiction and to establish herself as a worthy woman writer at the same time.

"Wei Hu" and "Shanghai, Spring 1930" are two examples that demonstrate both the gains and drawbacks of Ding Ling's creative appropriation of narrative modes established by radical male writers. These two novellas marked a transition from her individualist diary fiction to the literature of her Yan'an period. In both novellas, not only did Ding Ling portray urban intellectuals who embrace Marxist ideologies and seek solidarity with the oppressed masses, she also distanced herself from the subjective narrative mode by adopting an omniscient narrator. In "Wei Hu" she portrays a dedicated male revolutionary, Wei Hu, who leaves his girl friend Li Jia to join in the revolution in Guangdong, so that he can devote himself completely to the revolutionary cause without romantic distractions. Inspired by his example, Li Jia also vows to mend her old ways as a self-absorbed girl student and "do something good with [her] career" (121). Although Ding Ling already proposed radical ideological changes in "Wei Hu," such as promoting the sacrifice of romantic love for the revolutionary cause while validating a male-centered consciousness, in her "Shanghai, Spring 1930" she presented ideology through more compelling stylistic changes. This novella consists of two parts, which are in fact two short stories connected apparently only by the shared location (Shanghai) and time frame (Spring 1930) of their occurrence. Both stories introduce the elements of love and revolution, but each configures them differently.

In the first story Zibin and Ruoquan, both young male writers and former good friends to each other, begin to drift apart because of their different conceptions of the function and nature of literature. Whereas Zibin believes in "Art for Art's Sake" and lives comfortably with his lover Meilin on his income from writing, Ruoquan plunges into the mobilization of factory workers and organization of political rallies to the point of neglecting his literary career. During the course of their debate and conflict, Meilin gravitates towards Ruoquan's viewpoint until, in the end, she leaves home and joins in the political demonstrations on the street. The second story in the novella depicts the conflict between love and revolution experienced by the hero Wang Wei. Mary (transliterated into Chinese as "Mali"), his sometime lover, is portrayed as a defector who deserts him because of his dedication to revolutionary causes. Like Wei Hu, Wang Wei is deeply infatuated with his lover. Also like Wei Hu, he spends so much time with her that he even neglects his work. Unlike Wei Hu, however, he does not take the initiative to break up with Mary. Rather, Wang Wei gradually and subtly withdraws from Mary and returns to his work. Mary leaves him when she can no longer bear the loneliness and boredom when Wang Wei is off doing his revolutionary work. The story ends with Wang Wei being arrested in a political rally and dragged away by the police. Suddenly, he catches sight of a woman coming out of a department store on the other side of the street, wearing extravagant clothes and carrying with her all kinds of parcels. Recognizing Mary, Wang Wei says to himself, "Good, she's happy again. That's the kind of person she is, and I don't have to worry about her anymore. Goodbye, Mary!" ("Shanghai, Spring 1930" 171).

From these plot summaries, we can see that in both stories in "Shanghai, Spring 1930," Ding Ling deployed the figure of the female city dweller to accentuate the rising importance of revolutionary causes in the lives of modern intellectuals. Ironically, the two stories also expose a connection between radical discourse and a male-centered consciousness, for women lose their central position in her narratives the same time the thematic importance of revolution increases. "Shanghai, Spring 1930" accentuates group activities and group identities. Ding Ling veered from the concentrated depiction of women's psychology to focus on the men in their lives and, finally, on the looming presence of ideology.

Very tellingly, condescending or even misogynistic attitudes towards women become increasingly visible within this purportedly revolutionary work. Whereas the unrevolutionary Zibin predictably "treat[s] [his lover Meilin] like a child" ("Shanghai, Spring 1930" 126), self-proclaimed male revolutionaries also matter-of-factly deprecate women. Ruoquan regards himself as the guide and protector of Meilin. Having previously thought of her as "naïve, pampered, and definitely not bad looking" (134), he is quite surprised at her initiative in requesting a meeting with him. As an interesting footnote to Ruoquan's enthusiasm about the revolutionary cause and his encouragement of Meilin to end her stifling relationship with Zibin, the narrator describes that, at their meeting, "Ruoquan watched her high-heeled, brown leather shoes as she minced along. She had on flesh-toned stockings. Were her feet really that tiny, or did the elegantly crafted shoes make them look so pathetic and feminine, he mused" (134–35). Like Ruoquan, who displays more interest in the bourgeois woman's sexual appeal than her "awakened" class-consciousness, the male revolutionary in the second part of the novella, Wang Wei, also fails to take his lover Mary seriously as an intelligent human being. Just like the unrevolutionary Zibin in the first story, he frequently uses sweet talks to cajole Mary, rationalizing that "women were always like this; it was better to move them by love than to convince them by reason. This phenomenon was the opposite of what he'd hoped to find in women. However, since Mary was like this, he was glad to handle it this way, and to prove as well that he really loved her" (164). Therefore, the reader may question the amount of sacrifice Wang Wei has actually made when giving up Mary for revolution, since his "love" for Mary does not seem to involve either a respect for her powers of reasoning or any deep emotional commitment on his part. In this light, Wang Wei proves to be an uncanny double of Zibin in terms of their attitude towards the women they allegedly love.

Ding Ling's description of the cavalier treatment of women by male revolutionaries and the chauvinistic attitude shared by both revolutionary and unrevolutionary males can be interpreted as a criticism of the patriarchal nature of the revolutionary group. However, she also partly identified with that male gaze and contributed to the decentralization of women in her fiction, particularly by replacing bourgeois women with proletarian women as role models. A significant departure from her previous stories is that in these two stories it is mostly male characters that are portrayed as the center of consciousness. Although Meilin and Mary do reflect on the events in their lives, ultimately it is the men who form the commanding forces in their lives, forces by which they are either motivated or rejected. By privileging male psychology, Ding Ling gravitated towards a more masculine perspective in the representation of women. Ding Ling's change of perspective can be seen most clearly in the new way she depicted male-female relationships, especially triangular relationships in her fiction.

In "Miss Sophia's Diary," Ding Ling had reversed the gender roles featured in the more traditional version of heterosexual triangles that had been the standard fare of male authors' works. She established Sophia, a woman, as the center of consciousness that commented on and compared the two men in her life: the timid Weidi and the dashing Ling Jishi. In the first story in "Shanghai, Spring 1930," although Ding Ling used the same reversed triangular structure, she made two men into representatives of conflicting ideologies rather than rivals for the woman's love. As a result, the woman character Meilin is not the reason for the men's competition; nor is she an active pursuer of the men. In sharp contrast both to Mao Dun's fiction and to her own "Miss Sophia's Diary," the woman in this story is neither a desirable object nor a self-determining subject. Ding Ling revised the triangle arrangement mostly to strip it of romantic and emotional undertone and thus to convey revolutionary messages more effectively. However, the effect is that Meilin becomes a signifier of the correctness of one man's ideology as compared to the other's. She is mostly represented as a faithful worshipper of first Zibin and then Ruoquan. Her approving gaze not only establishes the legitimacy of both male characters at different periods, but also sanctifies the radical ideology that Ruoquan represents. Consequently, Meilin does not appear as a convincingly strong woman even in her most independent moments. Ding Ling also contrived to have Meilin's erstwhile lover Zibin stubbornly opposed to revolutionary ideas. His belligerence is necessary both to establish the opposing ideological orientations in the story (a distinct echo of Mao Dun's positioning of two women as symbols of traditional and modern values), and to praise Meilin's revolutionary consciousness. Yet such an eager reception of revolutionary discourses on Meilin's part lacks substance, since little narrative space, if any, is given to Meilin's psychological development, especially to the possible conflict between her affection for Zibin and her determination to find her own place out of her home. She has never voiced any serious complaint about Zibin as a good provider, who has lived with her for several years and has, by all accounts, been a loving and caring mate. If he manifests a male chauvinist attitude towards her from time to time, he is certainly no worse than the more revolution-inclined Ruoquan and much more forthright about it. Meilin's devotion to the revolutionary cause seems to be based on either a naïve trust in the superior morality of male revolutionaries or a blithe disregard for personal autonomy, or both. Her conversion to the revolutionary cause thus appears to be the product of her romantic vision of revolution, neither entailing any intelligent digestion of new ideas nor offering any reinforcement for her subject position. The final effect is that Ding Ling has created a much weaker woman character by focusing the narrative attention more on ideological strife than on the woman's psychological struggle. Therefore, even though Ding Ling did not make the woman character into an explicit sexual object for male consumption, as did Mao Dun, she still elided Meilin's subjectivity, rendering her along a preformed ideological contour rather than as a rounded person.

The second story in "Shanghai, Spring 1930" illustrates the banishment of urban women intellectuals who behave differently towards revolution than Meilin. In it, the main female character, Mary, an educated woman, proves to be the impetus for a rite of passage for the male revolutionary Wang Wei; his resistance to her charms serves to illustrate his growth both as a political worker and as a man. The positioning of the woman in this story not only closely resembles the male authorial scheme of othering women for the illustration of the maturation of the revolutionary man, especially exemplified in fiction by Ba Jin, but also shows that ideology dictates romantic love. The representation of women in this story undermines the May Fourth promulgation of Nora as women's role model. Mary is portrayed as vain, impetuous, and inconstant, whereas in previous decades she could have been portrayed as another Nora deciding to leave a confining relationship in order to seek her independent identity. The authorial denunciation of the bourgeois Mary, like the approval of Meilin, who leaves her bourgeois lover, demonstrates that the dominance of Marxist ideology resulted in a discourse on women's liberation rather distinct from the version that had been popular before. Whereas previously a woman's modernity could be vouched for by her actions of seeking modern education, defying arranged marriages, or seeking a career to support herself, now she had to join in revolution to prove herself a "new" woman.

Parallel to the fall in stature of the bourgeois woman in the novella, the rise of the proletarian woman provides yet more evidence of the triumph of Marxist ideology over the earlier May Fourth discourse of individualism. In the first story, Meilin encounters at a meeting of the Communist study group a female textile worker who wants to study literature with her. Although Meilin is "quite comfortable [chatting with her casually,] because they were all 'comrades,'" she also feels "inexpressible shame. Everyone there, she felt, had a better grasp of politics than she did and was more capable than she" (136–37). At the meeting Meilin cannot speak up when asked to contribute her opinions on a current situation. Yet she immediately takes heart: "But she was quite sure that before too long she could be retooled and her ignorance remedied" (137). In contrast to the conventional May Fourth depiction of the oppressed woman, including Yu Dafu's more "revolutionary" work such as "Intoxicating Spring Nights," the woman intellectual here is speechless *vis-à-vis* her Other, the proletarian woman. Moreover, she feels inadequate not because she feels too helpless to change the Other's miserable life, but because the Other presents such an awesome role model for her to emulate. Meilin is willing to be "retooled" (137), a mindset that once again confirms women's status as "girl students," albeit students of the proletariat. In this light, Meilin leaves a domineering lover only to be made into a copy of her female proletarian Other, for she is asked to submit herself unquestioningly to the revolutionary cause. Not only is the bourgeois woman depicted as inadequate in revolution, she is also to lose grounds in romance. Apparently, male revolutionaries prefer proletarian women as lifelong partners. In the second story, one of Wang Wei's comrades courts a female ticket-seller, who to Wang Wei's admiring eyes seems "a true revolutionary" (169). Holding Mary's image at bay, he thinks enviously of his comrade, the lover of the ticket-seller, "Ah, his former dream [for a companion in revolution] had now been realized by Feng Fei!" (169).

The emergence of proletarian women as positive role models indicates changes in Ding Ling's conceptualization of the relationship between the intellectual and the masses, but it also brings into focus another thorny question: the role of radical politics in new women's quest for an independent identity for themselves. While the oust of the bourgeois Mary at both the plot and the narrative levels suggests Ding Ling's increased identification with Marxism, the experience of Meilin also reveals that within revolutionary groups women are subjected to other forms of patriarchal dominance by their male colleagues. Can women establish themselves as independent subjects by joining forces with radical male intellectuals? Or should they give up any thought to their individuality but devote themselves completely to the collective project of revolution? Although Ding Ling did not revisit the issue of the new woman's identity within revolutionary communities such as the Communist Party until her relocation to Yan'an in 1936, her more autobiographical short stories written at the same period as "Shanghai, Spring 1930" shows that she continued to devise new strategies for her heroines to gain power. She proposed, through her fiction, that they control their emotions at all times, including in their writings, desist from manipulating the men in their lives, and mold themselves into stronger revolutionaries ready for any challenge in life.

Ding Ling's short stories that are more autobiographical either in content or in narrative form contrast revealingly with her earlier works in the diary form, especially with regard to the configuration of women's emotions. These later stories include "From Night to Dawn" ("Cong yewan dao tianliang," 1931) and "Sophia's Diary (II, Unfinished)" ("Shafei riji di erbu [weiwan gao]," 1931). Her depiction of the woman revolutionary in "Tianjia Village" ("Tianjia chong," 1931) will also be examined below, since it foreshadows the more definitive changes in narrative style in the fiction of her Yan'an period. Both "Sophia's Diary (II)" and "From Night to Dawn" feature as the center of consciousness a woman writer who has recently lost her husband and sent their infant child to stay with her mother. The reader who knows about Ding Ling's own life can all too easily read autobiographical references into them. More importantly, the two stories reveal how Ding Ling negotiated the conflicting demands of literature, personal life, and politics in a more successful manner through a revamping, rather than complete changeover (as in "Shanghai, Spring 1930"), of her previous narrative deployment of emotions.

"Sophia's Diary (II)"

"Sophia's Diary (II)" provides us with a perfect opportunity to explore the transformation in Ding Ling's narrative style. As an unfinished piece published posthumously, it presents a less adorned version of Ding Ling's experimentation with new narrative methods in order to steer her life in a new direction. The trauma of her first husband's execution had aroused in her intense grief and anger against the Nationalist government. Restless for action and change, Ding Ling became concerned over the perceived gap between her "old style" and the "new (revolutionary) content" of her fiction. In 1932, she wrote, "I felt agonized last year [1931]. I couldn't write for several months at a time. I was extremely annoyed with my old literary style. I felt it inappropriate to convey new content with old devices. Although I did write a bit [in the old style] later, I felt the writing was forced [*mianqiang*]" ("Wo de chuangzuo jingyan" 106). Written in 1931, "Sophia's Diary (II)" was the joint product of Ding Ling's need for change and the influence of radical revolutionary discourses, particularly contemporary male literary criticism of feminine emotionalism. In this story, Ding Ling earnestly set out to correct the lapse of the same heroine that she had constructed through the centralization of emotions in the earlier "Miss Sophia's Diary." In an apparently complete reversal of her earlier "Miss Sophia's Diary," in "Sophia's Diary (II)" Ding Ling emphasized Sophia's action of denouncing and exorcising the emotional old self in her new diary in order to represent her growth.

Sophia adopts a far more detached tone in "Sophia's Diary (II)" than in "Miss Sophia's Diary." Whereas in "Miss Sophia's Diary" the diarist records her emotions meticulously to both console and reinvent herself, here she is not only remarkably reticent about her feelings but also openly discredits the more "embellished" representation of emotions in the old diary. As if to bear out Ding Ling's own struggle with the newly emerged conflict between her narrative form and content, the diarist in "Sophia's Diary (II)" claims, "No, no, I really can't write this way. This does not read like a diary at all. My writings have changed completely because of my changed mood [*xinjing*]" (310). Yet, even as she admits that she can no longer produce a diary in compliance with the proper generic conventions as featured in "Miss Sophia's Diary," she criticizes "Miss Sophia's Diary," dismissing it as "embellished, far more exaggerated and profound than what happened in real life" (311).

More significantly, in the later work Ding Ling self-consciously cast off the simulation of private writing and emotional spontaneity, both important parts of the generic formula of diary fiction, in order to better illustrate the diarist's performance of the narrative control of emotions. "Sophia's Diary (II)" consists of only two entries respectively dated May Fourth and Fifth, describing the diarist Sophia's life after a four-year's lapse between her first and second diary. Eschewing diary fiction's conventional avowal of soul-searching and self-evaluation, the diarist in "Sophia's Diary (II)" claims to write this diary as a way of self-rehabilitation: "I am just using some leisure time to write casually as a way of relaxation" (309). Corresponding to her utilitarian view of diary writing, Sophia also shows consideration for her audience. She alleges that she writes the second diary in order to inform her readers that "Sophia had not escaped to some place where nobody knew her and wasted the remaining of her life, as she claimed in the first diary" (309). She even self-consciously attaches a preface to the narration of her new life proper: "I feel it a good idea to enclose a little personal history here, in case somebody will read this some day" (309). She then incorporates a number of "realistic" details from the author Ding Ling's own life up to that point. She mentions her earlier cohabitation with a nineteen-year-old poet (Hu Yepin), their baby son, her common-law husband's execution, and her sending their baby to her mother in Hunan after his death. She even brings up the actual title of Hu Yepin's work, *The Light Is in Front of Us* (*Guagnming zai women mianqian*) in the story. By supplying such details of her life, the diarist is apparently targeting the less informed audience—those who know nothing about her life beyond her first diary—but she is also demonstrating the control of her emotions by transferring the narrative attention from the self to others. Further debunking the claim to emotional spontaneity of diary fiction, she exposes and parodies the conventionality of the diary form. "It is a rule to talk about weather in a diary first," she remarks. "So I will talk about the weather now" (311). The perfunctory and uninspired sentences about the sky and the clouds that follow this statement provide a perfect buffer of banality against the rawness of emotions. As such, in contrast to the insularity of the narrative perspective in "Miss Sophia's Diary," in "Sophia's Diary II" Ding Ling violated the diary fiction's convention of simulating private writing, and turned the diary into a piece of reportage on the more mundane aspects of the diarist's life.

The abandonment of all pretence of spontaneity leads to a different temporal consciousness in the second diary fiction, which also contributes to the detached tone of the story. While the narrator in "Miss Sophia's Diary" more often makes the gesture of directly confronting her emotions here and now, the new Sophia regards herself as the product of her past experiences and consequently strives to free herself from the fetters of old emotions. Not the immediacy of life events but the awareness of life as a continuous and sustained process makes up the internal temporal logic of "Sophia's Diary (II)."

The story begins with the May Fourth entry, in which the diarist resumes diary writing after a lapse of several years. Gazing at her old diary—presumably "Miss Sophia's Diary"—she remarks: "my shadow left on these yellowed pieces of paper [of my old diary] seems a completely different person from what I am now" (308). The difference, as she perceives it, should result in her liberation from her past: "What has passed is not only the time; all my dreams, passions, sentiments, and enjoyment of love are gone. They have flown by so naturally that the process has not caused me any shock or nostalgia. With what exhilaration and nimbleness have I jumped to my current state of life!" (308). Yet she follows with a humble concession, "Of course I am still not perfect. There is probably still too much of the past left in me, unbeknownst to me yet sometimes unconsciously manifested in my behavior" (308). She then vows to keep a vigilant watch over her present emotional state while invoking the rhetoric of crisis: "The present is key; it is a dangerous time," because, she claims, she could all too easily "be more decadent [*duoluo*] than in the past" (309).

At first glance, the diarist seems to be stressing the importance of the present, the presumed starting point for the writing of any diary. However, she is even more invested in facilitating a break of the present from the past in order to march towards the future. With this move the present *per se* is actually disregarded. In other words, instead of presenting life as something one encounters and ponders in daily segments, as is the convention of diary fiction, the diarist in "Sophia's Diary (II)" tends to take a comprehensive view of life as a continuous whole, and hopes to transcend the present by this exercise. She wants to prove herself not a diarist inundated by the emotional currents of the present but a rational observer who writes the diary for the purpose of self-mastery. This new Sophia alleges that she is aiming for a self-interrogative confession, "I am willing to spare a small amount of time every day to record what happens to me, what I think and how I feel. I am writing a faithful confession, as frank as my confessions in the past. But I also have to interrogate myself, overcome myself, improve myself, for I am no longer a young girl who knows only about feeling upset and worried" (309). The diarist actually adopts an "evolutionary" view of time, emphasizing her present difference from, or, more precisely, her improvement on her past.

In keeping with her accentuation of time as a continuous process, the diarist privileges the mode of summary, and is thus able to condense certain periods of her life in order to prove her personal growth after the trauma of her husband's death. For instance, the entry on May Fourth compresses the diarist's life of the last four years into one paragraph, sketching her past romance, her husband's death, her grief, and her gradual recovery. This kind of configuration of the past, besides providing a background for the present, helps to demonstrate her status as a victorious survivor—instead of a victim of circumstances—who relates the past with control, another sharp contrast with the helpless rage manifested in "Miss Sophia's Diary."

Ding Ling's deliberate violation of the generic conventions of diary fiction is significant in that it results in a different positioning of the diarist with regard to both her life and her writing. As I have mentioned before, the new Sophia does not consider writing this diary different in nature from any of the other forms of self-rehabilitation she suggests for herself, such as taking cold showers. Dismissing the "embellished" tale narrated in "Miss Sophia's Diary," she claims self-interrogation to be her sole motive for writing this diary (309). Moreover, self-interrogation in her eyes will enhance self-discipline, especially in moments of emotional disturbances. She specifically names writing her diary as the best thing to do when she is feeling too emotional. According to her, reading is too taxing and writing serious fiction is also tiring, but "to restrain myself from running all over the city, writing a diary is the best way" (311). Writing a diary not only enables her to practice self-discipline, it also paves the way for her to actively make positive changes in her life. She claims a change in her lifestyle concurrent with the writing of the diary, manifested in her behavior such as taking cold showers and not lingering in bed in the morning. She explains, "I often ruined my own health in the past. Now I take care of myself, because I feel I have a lot to do" (312). As Sophia regards her diary as a tool to tame strong feelings and take control of her life, she has also come to see her production of nonautobiographical literary works as both a responsibility towards others that she must fulfill and a yardstick of her progress on the path to becoming a less egocentric author. "I wrote five pages yesterday and three today," she happily records in the entry of May Fifth (312).

Ding Ling deviated from the generic conventions of diary fiction not only in replacing the psychological drama highlighted in "Miss Sophia's Diary" with rational contemplation and organization of a continuous life, but also in effecting a subtle self-effacement through that shift of narrative focus. She apparently included particular autobiographical details and the diarist's daily routines—and thus applying the principle of "Realism"— only in order to portray a stronger female "I"-narrator: "My heart calms down day by day. I'm becoming more rational. I don't want myself to waste all my time mourning for the deceased, as others have predicted [I would]. It is high time that I started reading, working, and being a person again. I want things of the past to pass without a trace. I am going to only march towards the future, never looking back" (310). But in so doing, the author has "othered" not only the old self of the diarist but also her own old style of subjective writing in her bid to both demonstrate the birth of a new type of heroine in life as well as in fiction and to construct a conversion narrative for both her character and herself.

Ding Ling's own explanations of her writings imply that her departure from subjective style in "Sophia's Diary (II)" was a deliberate move to disassociate herself from the "autobiographical" and "emotional" female fiction. A revealing piece of information regarding Ding Ling's attitude towards the earlier "Miss Sophia's Diary" since its publication in 1928 is her denial of having ever made any autobiographical identification with the character Sophia. In a letter to her friend Xu Xiacun, she claimed that the character Sophia was based on one of her old classmates from high school in Hunan (Ding Y. 29-30). Moreover, in the public lecture given at Guanghua College in 1931 already mentioned, she claimed to have never put herself in her works, while emphatically denying rumors of her "washing her face with her tears all day" (zhongri yilei ximian) after Hu Yepin's death ("Wo de zibai" 97). Around the same time in an essay discussing her literary experiences she also expressed her "detestation" (*zengwu*) of feminine hysterics ("Wo de chuangzuo jingyan" 105-7). In this light, "Sophia's Diary (II)" demonstrates Ding Ling's experimentation with a new form of diary fiction: a combination of both an "objective" tone and the inclusion of a considerable amount of personal information to replace vivid description of individual emotions. But this experiment obviously proved unsatisfactory to her. For she not only did not finish and publish "Sophia's Diary (II)," but also, with the exception of "Yang Ma de riji" (The Diary of Yang Ma, 1931), virtually gave up the form of diary fiction after 1931, as she moved irrevocably towards leftist radicalism. Ding Ling refrained from using first-person narration for the depiction of female emotions until her Yan'an period, when she eventually created an I-narrator that sustains her analytical faculty through an empathetic relationship with another woman. But meanwhile, she also experimented with third-person narration for the representation and regulation of women's emotions.

"From Night to Dawn"

Narrated in the third person, "From Night To Dawn" also draws on Ding Ling's own life. It relates the emotional turmoil of a woman writer who has recently lost her husband to government persecution, again believed by readers and tacitly acknowledged by the author as the representation of Ding Ling's own trauma ("Cong yewan dao tianliang" 318, note 1). In terms of narrative practice, it differs from "Sophia's Diary (II)" in that it enacts "a process of life as it becomes literature, a process of making moral and artistic sense out of seemingly random experience" (Feuerwerker, "The Changing Relationship" 287). In so doing, it heightens the "spontaneous" and "authentic" presentation of the narration, in contrast to the self-conscious, controlled narrative of "Sophia's Diary (II)." Interestingly, these narrative effects are accomplished without the use of an I-narrator or any autobiographical form such as diary fiction. "From Night to Dawn" employs a limited third person point of view that is voiced by an omniscient narrator, or a covert narrator (i.e., a narrator that is not specified with a name but remains closely identified with the center of consciousness). The contrast between the narrators in this story and in "Sophia's Diary (II)" demonstrates the way Ding Ling performed the control of emotions through yet another venue.

Of course, the "I"-narrator in "Sophia's Diary (II)" also illustrates the woman's mastery of her emotions by accentuating the ideological and emotional distance between the diarist and the central character of the same name. Not only does that narrator assess the character's thought and behavior, she also evaluates the character's past life and foretells her future, a practice that further differentiates a transcendent narrator from a presently situated character. In other words, the "I"-narrator in "Sophia's Diary (II)" assumes a conceptualizing voice of reason that leaves the realm of story time and functions in her own discourse time, summarizing, interpreting, and judging. In contrast, "From Night to Dawn" concentrates on the turbulent psyche of one character in the story but adopts a covert/omniscient narrator. Therefore, even as Ding Ling apparently resurrected the practice of representing spontaneous emotions, she not only delegated apparently disarrayed and effusive emotions to a third-person character, but also placed these unruly emotions into the custody of the narrator.

The covert narrator in "From Night to Dawn" performs many tasks in the objectification of individual emotions. This narrator not only emphasizes the heroine's reflections on her own behavior, but also marks the various levels of her consciousness through distinctive modes of representation. The narrator differentiates between the heroine's self-reflection and instinctive reaction. It uses the mode of internal monologue, namely, thoughts directly presented in quotation marks, to represent the conscious self-interrogation of the heroine. By contrast, her more impulsive reactions to past memories and her sensory impressions of the external environment appear more in the form of a "stream of consciousness"; accompanying the character's physical action, they are randomly ordered, appearing with no quotations marks and giving the impression of free association induced by internal and external stimuli. Not only does the narrator alternate between these two means of relating the character's thoughts, it also makes sparing use of static description. The story includes descriptions of the heroine's gestures and movements, but no static portraiture. The narrator avoids summary and commentary completely. Although all these narrative devices produce the effect of direct and spontaneous presentation of emotions, such an artistic achievement per se reveals the author's painstaking strategizing.

The heroine has apparently mastered her psychological agony eventually, as the ending of "From Night to Dawn" turns out to be a celebration of the triumph of the heroine's will over the emotional chaos caused by the events in her life. In this highly symbolic scene, the woman writer finally seats herself in front of her writing desk as the dawn is breaking, after a whole night's restless wandering and thinking. She takes a last look at the baby clothes she has bought impulsively, prompted by the memory of her faraway child, and resolutely turns back to her manuscript on the desk. "Hypocritical reason! You only want to eliminate humanity," she laments. But she immediately plunges into writing anyway, "Good, let it be so!" "From Night to Dawn" ends with a description: "The story [she was writing] is now already at page fifteen" (318). The torment of emotions is thus transformed into the motivating force for her writing.

Ding Ling herself often used the same strategy of gaining self-control by re-ordering her life on paper. This is demonstrated not only by the fact that she wrote such stories as "Sophia's Diary (II)" and "From Night to Dawn" apparently as attempts at catharsis, but also by the high frequency with which the image of writing and the writer occur in her fiction in general. As Feuerwerker remarks, "It is striking to note how many of Ding Ling's stories conclude with the main character physically picking up a pen or composing sentences. He or she has overcome despair, has resolved a conflict, is making a fresh start, or has reached a state of acceptance or awareness" ("The Changing Relationship" 287). What is even more unusual about "From Night to Dawn" is that Ding Ling included one of her own works, a short story later published under the title "Tianjia Village" (Tianjia chong) as the story that the character is writing. In this respect, it echoes "Sophia's Diary (II)," where autobiographical detail is also utilized. But "From Night to Dawn" is prophetic as well as autobiographical. Through the inclusion of "Tianjia Village," it foretells the direction of Ding Ling's life as well as of her writing; like the heroine in this story, Ding Ling would move away from the city to the countryside, both in her fiction and in her life.

"Tianjia Village"

One of the last stories written before Ding Ling's Yan'an period, "Tianjia Village" suggests a few new developments in her fiction that were to become fully fledged in her later fiction written in Yan'an. First of all, the setting of this story is in the countryside. As the story begins, a peasant family is eagerly awaiting the arrival of the daughter of their landlord. This young woman from the city, called "Third Young Mistress" (San Xiaojie) by her father's tenants, has been banished to the country by her family because she has been taking part in radical political activities. After arriving in the countryside, Third Young Mistress continues her work underground, attending secret meetings and mobilizing peasants, until she is eventually arrested and secretly executed.

The figure of Third Young Mistress suggests the emergence of a new type of female character in Ding Ling's fiction: the intellectual woman revolutionary who has not only firmly rejected her family and class background but also moved to rural locale for revolutionary work. In "Shanghai, Spring 1930" she had already portrayed urban intellectuals who turn towards revolutionary activities. However, the setting of her stories thus far had often been the city, and the female intellectual had not finished their "retooling" yet. Third Young Mistress is the first full-fledged woman revolutionary in Ding Ling's fiction whose action takes place in a country setting. She is also a political organizer, neither a writer nor an urban drifter, another new feature in Ding Ling's representation of the new woman. In the portrayal of Third Young Mistress, Ding Ling distinguishes her from other, more sexually attractive female characters conversant in the arts of cosmetics and couture, such as Meilin and Mary. To be sure, Third Young Mistress is reminiscent of Ding Ling's earlier representation of the untraditional, untrammeled woman who does not care for feminine vanities. Sophia, after all, was said to be "a strange girl" who "wear[s] tattered gloves, [does] not perfume [her] dresser drawers, [and] at times for no reason [she's] been known to tear up [her] new cotton-padded jacket" ("Miss Sophia's Diary" 75). However, here, for the first time Ding Ling delineated a woman who sought to disguise her femininity for the sake of work, rather than as a gesture in defiance of social norms; as we are told, Third Young Mistress stops wearing embroidered shoes and begins to dress in men's clothes in order to move more freely around the countryside ("Tianjia chong" 326, 330).

The more significant changes in this piece take place in the area of narrative devices. In a move very unusual for Ding Ling's works up to that point, a fourteen-year old peasant girl by the name Yao Mei forms the center of consciousness in the story. Moreover, this girl provides, for the most part, a biased perspective due to her young age. In her eyes, the countryside appears to be an idyllic place that boasts beautiful scenery, happy families, and enjoyable housework. Her worship of the beautiful "Miss" from the city and her naiveté also prevent her from understanding the risky undercurrents that run beneath Third Young Mistress's secretive exterior. Consequently, not only do Third Young Mistress's political activities remain in the background, but the representation of her death is also both truncated and likened to the passing away of any other human life rather than being signified as an atrocious political persecution like that represented in Ding Ling's "A Certain Night" ("Mouye").

The temporal arrangement of this story, as well as its perspective, also seems to facilitate the reduction of emotional anguish. Ding Ling primarily employed the mode of description in this story, a practice that produces frequent narrative pauses. The story begins with Yao Mei's excitement as she awaits the arrival of Third Young Mistress, and this phase is depicted as a long and anticipatory period with little action. Third Young Mistress's stay with the family is also related at a leisurely pace. Third Young Mistress becomes Yao Mei's adored companion and helps her with daily tasks such as feeding the chickens and ducks, while Yao Mei fails to realize the significance of her friend's frequent mysterious disappearances. However, the narrator abruptly changes tempo when narrating Third Young Mistress' death, a traumatic event reminiscent of Hu Yepin's execution. The narrator uses only one sentence, "She did not come back that night" ("Tianjia chong" 356), to indicate the event, and immediately moves on to relate the changes in the peasant family several months later. The reader is then told that the peasants gradually shake themselves free of their grief, and start to take charge of their own lives by organizing meetings among themselves to air their grievances against the unjust system. As such, here the mode of summary replaces the descriptive mode prevalent in previous scenes. This sudden shift of modes calls attention to the presence of an external narrator/author, for, whereas descriptive passages are generally construed as necessary background for the core events, summary alerts the reader to narrative manipulation. Seen in this light, both the deliberate omission of the woman revolutionary's death and the sudden conversion of the conservative and timid peasant family to radicalism at the end of story reveal imposed authorial intention. We can see that Ding Ling displayed revolutionary optimism through "Tianjia Village," as mandated by the doctrines of Revolutionary Literature; in this story she not only downplayed "negative" emotions of pessimism, suffering, and melancholy through various narrative devices, but also pointed out that the martyrdom of the woman revolutionary has resulted in the rise of the peasants' consciousness.

"Tianjia Village" met with a mixed success. He Danren, for example, applauded Ding Ling's effort at depicting the process of "progressive intellectuals moving from individualistic nihilism to proletarian revolution" (250). However, he expressed dissatisfaction with her literary techniques, claiming that an "old realism" has caused the story to be full of "pre-conceived and abstract observations and romantic distortions" (250). Ding Ling defended herself by citing the "realistic" source material of the story and even making use of personal narrative to relate her own life in the country ("Wo de chuangzuo shenghuo" 110). However, she in fact spent her formative years traveling through and residing in big cities, and her childhood, spent within a gentry family in the country, was obviously different from the life of the common peasantry depicted in "Tianjia Village." Critics such as He Danren would have to wait for a "new realism" to emerge in Ding Ling's fiction. Not until the 1940s, when Ding Ling had settled down in Yan'an, did she make another major stylistic change in her representation of both intellectual and peasant revolutionaries in order to explore women's liberation.

To summarize, even as Ding Ling moved towards leftist ideology and adopted a more male-centered, objective narrative style in her fiction starting in the 1930s, her quest for female autonomy persisted. This sense of mission, central to the self-perception of her identity as a woman writer, would continue to sustain her literary and political endeavors in Yan'an, enabling her to declare herself both an authority on the plight of the Chinese woman and an unbiased advocate of women's rights in the patriarchal Yan'an context.

EPILOGUE

Ding Ling in Yan'an: A New Woman within the Party Structure?

Of all the radical male and female writers within the May Fourth group who represented new women in fiction, Ding Ling's life and work present by far the most complex case of negotiations of gender position, radical politics, and narrative style. The demands of such negotiations are registered in the changes we have seen in the theme and style of her fiction before 1936, particularly the shifts in her narrative deployment of emotions, as she adjusted to literary and political restrictions while continuing her pursuit of Chinese women's liberation as well as the establishment of her status as a serious writer. In this chapter I will examine the new development in Ding Ling's representation of new women after her induction into the Communist community of Yan'an in order to explore not only the relationship between her literary endeavors and political allegiance but also some general issues central to the May Fourth construction of the figure of the new woman.

Before Ding Ling joined in the Communist government in Yan'an, her fiction had already exposed the problematic of the male-centered May Fourth discourses of Chinese modernity and the male formula of othering the Other for self-representation. After her initiation into the Communist Party system, she continued to produce controversial works, even as she attempted to comply with Party policies. In the 1940s she was criticized in Yan'an for her story "When I Was In Xia Village" ("Wo zai xiacun de shihou," 1940) and "In the Hospital" (Zai yiyuan zhong," 1940). These two stories reveal the backwardness of the masses at Communist-controlled Yan'an instead of presenting a positive picture of the peasant Other, and thus violated the edict issued by the Party to form a united front with the peasants. Ironically, in these two stories Ding Ling also made greater efforts to adopt the objective narrative style required by the Party. Ding Ling's political mishap at Yan'an raises the question of how, if at all, a woman writer could maintain an independent identity when faced with increasingly totalitarian control of literature. To answer this question, we need to examine some of the narrative aspects of these two stories that demonstrate Ding Ling's attempts at accommodation. But first, a general survey of the sociopolitical and personal circumstances that prompted Ding Ling's relocation to Yan'an and, as a result, brought the new changes in Ding Ling's fiction will provide a necessary and illuminating background.

In 1948, Ding Ling's long-time friend and Communist literary critic Feng Xuefeng attempted to explain Ding Ling's conversion to Communism. He claimed to have detected a "crisis" in the author's career at the precise point when she made a success with "Miss Sophia's Diary" (295). This was because, he explained, compared to Lu Xun's "Regret for the Past," which "uncovers the deep sociopolitical origin of the characters' tragedy" (295), Ding Ling's story only portrayed a worshipper of romantic love in Sophia. Sophia "is separated from the revolutionary social forces. Sophia's emptiness and despair prove exactly that she does not have the strength to grow with the times, though her ideals of love are also the product of the times" (294). Feng Xuefeng further pointed out three ways for Ding Ling to cope with this crisis. One was to remain isolated from the revolutionary cause and society and continue to write "playful works full of sentimentality, nihilism, and despair" (295), works that would only be weaker and inferior simulacrums of "Miss Sophia's Diary." Another way was to stop writing altogether. And the third way for Ding Ling, which Feng Xuefeng advocated as "the true path," was to move from love to revolution: "Passionate pursuit of romantic love has fulfilled the need of young people liberated by the May Fourth Movement. It has inherent revolutionary significance in that it answered to the call of the time. Therefore, it is very natural, very proper [for a writer] to move [from the pursuit of love] to revolution" (295). Feng declared, "This should be a turning point for Ding Ling" (295).

Feng Xuefeng's mapping of the three routes proved accurate for radical writers, especially women writers, of the May Fourth group. For those who had once promoted doctrines of individualism and romantic love, the option at the time was to convert to leftist radicalism, or suffer negative reception or even exclusion from the canon of modern literature, a fate well demonstrated in the cases of Feng Yuanjun and Lu Yin. Of course, the disciplinary force of revolutionary discourses was by no means limited to women writers. For instance, Lu Xun, called by some the founding father of modern Chinese literature, was attacked violently for his "pessimistic" depiction of the spiritual ailment among the Chinese masses. But compared to women writers, male writers were better equipped to defend their own "unrevolutionary" writing styles in the name of revolution because of their august position as the chief creator of modern knowledge. Furthermore, they had also constructed for themselves a positive public image against the figure of the unenlightened Chinese woman and through the invocation of an enlightenment project. Mao Dun, for example, invoked the concept of "Realism" to justify his eroticization of the female body under the rubric of raising revolutionary consciousness, claiming, "this kind of women will join revolution if their circumstances change" ("Cong Guling dao Dongjing" 13).

As a woman writer who overcame large odds against her gender, Ding Ling's life and fiction presented a far more complex case than the straightforward teleology outlined by Feng Xuefeng. Like her fellow women writers, Ding Ling demonstrated her individual agency by appropriating discursive patterns established by radical males in order to establish her modern identity. Furthermore, her unwavering pursuit of Chinese women's independence led her to devise new strategies to adapt to the rise of Marxism in the 1930s. In life Ding Ling chose Marxism due to both the national crisis and personal upheavals in the decade between 1930 and 1940. The radical 1930s saw the Japanese bombing of Shanghai (1931), their seizure and occupation of Manchuria (1931), and, consequently, the rise of Chinese nationalism to a new height. For May Fourth intellectuals, the promotion of national salvation had always enabled them to claim the moral superiority and political power otherwise denied them in their turbulent and changing society. The very real threat of a full-scale Sino-Japanese war also substantiated their narrative of national crisis, and thus aggrandized rather than diminished their image as the moral guardian of the nation. This can be seen in the revolutionary rhetoric and "National Defense Literature" (*guofang wenxue*) that they passionately endorsed in order to call on all social strata to join forces to fight against imperialist invasion. A member of the May Fourth group, Ding Ling also designated herself as participant in Chinese modernization as well as advocate of women's rights, but she had more personal stake in leftist radicalism. Not only was her husband Hu Yepin executed by the Nationalist government in 1931, leaving behind her and their infant son, she herself was also put under house arrest by the Nationalists for three years before finally escaping to Yan'an in 1936.

Although the events in Ding Ling's life already suggest the interplay of individual agency and sociopolitical forces, the changes in Ding Ling's fiction reveal more clearly her attempts at self-determination, for they demonstrate her continual quest for female empowerment rather than a simplistic turning "from love to revolution," as described by Feng Xuefeng. Generally speaking, Ding Ling's fiction after 1931 displays increasing narrative self-effacement, as she eschewed subjective modes such as the genre of diary fiction in favor of third-person narration. However, not only did the content of her fiction expose the discriminatory treatment of women within the patriarchal Party structure, but she also sought to speak from the location of an authoritative experiencing female subject. Ding Ling was accused of clinging to bourgeois individualism and forsaking collectivism precisely because her concern for the fate of Chinese women remained the guiding force of her literary endeavors.

Ding Ling's political misfortune at Yan'an was also attributable to her narrative construction of a new voice for the authorial self, one that had evolved from her fiction written in the early 1930s. Before moving to Yan'an, Ding Ling had attempted to solve the dilemma that women faced in works such as "Yecao," where she proposed that women control their emotions through writing in order to gain power. Her increasing indoctrination in Marxist ideology, however, alerted her to the broader social base underlying the individual's fate. Applying the Marxist interpretation of the relationship between the individual and society, Ding Ling declared that women could not overcome emotionalism and obtain liberation on their own. In her "Sanba jie yougan" ("Thoughts on March 8," 1942) written at Yan'an, she stated, "Women are incapable of transcending the age they live in. They are incapable of resisting all the temptations of society or all the silent oppression they suffer here in Yan'an" ("Thoughts on March 8" 319). Rather than issue a call for women's passive submission to the Party as their savior, she encouraged them to proactively strengthen their body and mind while appointing herself spokesperson on behalf of all Chinese women: "I myself am a woman, and I therefore understand the failings of women better than others, but I also have a deeper understanding of what they suffer" (319). Predictably, her separation of women as an independent interest group and, particularly, her self-image as a representative of women fighting against any oppressive force brought her stern criticism from the Party. Always emphasizing the unity of all oppressed people under the banner of socialist revolution, the Party at the time especially aimed at mobilizing all social strata in the Communist controlled region in order to ward off the attacks by both the Japanese and the Nationalist army. Women's interests, they ordered, should not be separated from the goal of the liberation of the Chinese people as a whole. By accentuating women's unique plight and interests and affirming her solidarity with other women, Ding Ling came to be considered a seditious element that instigated one portion of the people to rebel against the collective.

Reflective of the particular milieu at Yan'an, the reception of Ding Ling's two stories "When I Was in Xia Village" and "In the Hospital" epitomizes not only the political tension of her position but also her attempts at accommodation through narrative strategy. These two stories apparently have very little in common, except for the historical background (the Sino-Japanese war) and geographical location (Communist-controlled Northwestern China). Whereas "Xia Village" depicts the ordeal of a peasant girl and the "I"-narrator's friendship with her, "In the Hospital" tells the story of a female intellectual, a trained obstetrician assigned to work in an ill-equipped hospital close to the battlefield. Moreover, while "Xia Village" employs a first-person narrator, "In the Hospital" features a narrative completely in the third-person. However, both stories centralize the theme of the entrapment or liberation of the new woman through particular configurations of women's emotions.

In "Xia Village," the "I"-narrator, a cultural officer of the Communist army, goes to Xia Village to convalesce. Here she meets a village girl by the name of Zhenzhen, with whom she develops a friendship. Raped and abducted by the Japanese army during a raid on the village, Zhenzhen has become a secret agent for the Communist government, collecting Japanese military information and passing it along to the Communists. When she comes home after one year's absence with a sexually transmitted disease, the people in her community greet her with contempt, hostility, and pathological fascination. However, Zhenzhen emerges as a true heroine despite all the obstacles. Not only has she stoically endured the incredible sufferings at the hands of the Japanese, she is also able to overcome the confinement of familial and romantic love through the application of rational reflection. Eventually, she decides to go against her family's wishes for her to marry her former lover, and leaves to seek a full recovery from her illness and an education. Upon hearing of Zhenzhen's decision, the narrator comments, "I was amazed. Something new was coming out of her" ("When I Was in Hsia Village" 315).

In contrast to the forbearing peasant girl Zhenzhen, the heroine in "In the Hospital," Lu Ping, expresses much pessimism and frustration about her thoroughly alienating working environment. In the hospital, she encounters bureaucratic and impersonal leaders, negligent staff, vulgar, conniving, or malicious colleagues, and slow-witted peasant patients. Her brief stay at the hospital would have ended in complete disaster, as she stumbles against and struggles with numerous obstacles at every turn, if not for her fortuitous conversation with a male patient in the hospital. The man, a soldier whose feet had been amputated, advises Lu Ping on strategy: "You're too young! Don't be impatient! Go slowly" ("Zai yiyuan zhong" 291). Miraculously, Lu Ping's complaints reach the ears of her superiors in the Ministry of Health. She is sent away to continue her studies, as she has wished all along. The story ends with a moral, which was said to have encouraged countless young people in Yan'an at the time of the story's publication: "People, like iron, must pass through numerous tempering fires before their real worth can be proven. A person matures amidst hardship" (291).

Both of these two stories highlight the leitmotif of the intellectual learning from the people, advocated by Mao Zedong and later more systematically articulated in his "Talks at the Yan'an Forum on Literature and Art" (1942). In "In the Hospital," Lu Ping's path to a better life is predicted by a male solider, and in "Xia Village" much emphasis is placed on the fact that the intellectual self is inspired by the peasant Other because the Other overcomes seemingly impassable obstacles to build a fulfilling life. The contrast between the emotional yet ineffectual female intellectual in "In the Hospital" and the peasant girl full of heroic forbearance in "Xia Village" also conveys the necessity of intellectuals' re-education by the people. However, the two stories, in expressing Ding Ling's concerns about women's status, still detracted from the Party's policies. Not only did Ding Ling describe women's victimization by the Party in these two stories, as one heroine's sexuality is exploited and the other stifled by the ignorance and indifference of Party bureaucracy, she also continued to explore the role of female emotions in women's self-strengthening. This can be seen not only in the plots but also in the narrative forms of these two stories. Ding Ling emphasized the "I"-narrator's admiration for the peasant heroine's stoic forbearance in "Xia Village." Moreover, in "In the Hospital" she chose the more objective third-person narrative mode to depict a character that was more similar to herself in educational background and life experiences, as if hoping to set up a more clear-cut boundary between the authorial self and the character in order to rein in her own emotions.

Precisely because of her continual advocacy of women's independence, Ding Ling's deliberate change to more objective narrative modes did not prevent her fiction from being classified as subversive by the Communist regime. Partly, this was also because Ding Ling potentially posed more threat to the Communist regime by making an effort to appear more objective. She was apparently abandoning the limited vision of the intellectual elite in order to expose social problems from a more objective perspective. Ding Ling was thus able to launch more powerful attack on the ignorance, prejudice, and cruelty of the peasants as well as the flaws of the Communist regime, having enhanced the credibility of her fiction by apparently answering the Maoist calls for learning from the people and abandoning bourgeois beliefs. At the same time, Ding Ling did not realize that the Communist Party placed more emphasis on the content of fiction than on its form; the Party resurrected and doggedly adhered to the Confucian concept of literature as a tool to convey a version of "Truth" as prescribed by the Party alone. Ding Ling's change of style failed to win approval, for she actually used the objective narrative modes to espouse ideas that clashed with Party ideologies.

The reception of these two stories at Yan'an revealed the perils Ding Ling had to face when voicing different opinions to the Party. The Chinese Communist Party, in presenting itself as the only legitimate representative of the people, did not tolerate any detracting force. Under this regime, literature was expected to serve the stated goals of the main political campaigns. Even though Ding Ling deliberately distanced herself from an "individualist" position in narrative form, she defied the Party control by taking on the task of impeaching the failings of the Party and speaking for the victimized and the oppressed within the revolutionary community. Precisely because Ding Ling designated herself as guardian of women's interests, a topic about which she claimed to have intimate knowledge, she also occupied a particularly vulnerable position. In placing women's interests above those of the Party but particularly by asserting her individual authority over party policies, she was treated as the ringleader of an otherwise relatively silent body of women.

Ding Ling's experience at Yan'an shows that women writers were unable to remain "liberated" within the patriarchal Communist Party structure. Nevertheless, Ding Ling's act of speaking out on behalf of women in literature signals not only her desire for an independent voice in the face of Party strictures but also her persistent strategy of appropriating male formula for female empowerment. Just as she had appropriated narrative conventions established by May Fourth male writers to formulate female subjectivity before her Yan'an period, in Yan'an she adopted objective narrative modes in order to express her concerns for Chinese women. Ding Ling's "feminist" consciousness, albeit perhaps more "collectivist" than "individualist," was always sustained by a versatile narrative ventriloquism.

Ding Ling's Yan'an experience is typical in its illumination of the complex configuration of gender and party politics that shaped her representation of the new woman in fiction. In fact, due to its encapsulation of the unique alchemy of gender and modernity of the May Fourth period, Ding Ling's fiction provides us both a vehicle to examine the problematic inherent in the representation of new women by radical May Fourth intellectuals and a springboard for further inquiries into the self-other relationship both within and outside of the May Fourth canon, and beyond the short period of the1920s–1930s that is the focus of this book.

First of all, the changes in Ding Ling's representation of new women at different phases of her writing career not only demonstrate the creation and consolidation of a modern identity through the invocation of discourses of Chinese modernity but also expose the gender politics at play in such undertakings. As I have mentioned before, male May Fourth intellectuals particularly advocated the liberation of Chinese women from the "Confucian" family and the construction of the fictional counterpart of those new women in order to promote national modernization through the creation of a modern Chinese literature. However, representation of the psychologically more complex new woman, as compared to the more "simple-minded" peasant woman, in Chinese fiction was also paradoxically one of the ways in which male writers of the era explored, negotiated, and laid claim to their own emerging identity as modern intellectuals. By expressing their own "modernist" discontent and lodging political protest against social injustice through the representation of the new woman, male intellectuals sought to demonstrate their own emotional sensitivity and humanistic inclination. Moreover, in representing the new woman they ostensibly appropriated Western narrative forms such as first-person narration in order to demolish the traditional elitist tradition. Yet their self-explanation and legitimization often betray a classical heritage that defines literature as a vessel of the universal Truth. Lu Xun, Yu Dafu, Ba Jin and Mao Dun all cited the morality of their public missions (e.g., to enlighten the masses, to promote nationalist awareness, to indict the old system, or to depict the psychological crisis of revolutionaries) to defend their literary practices. Furthermore, the narrative forms that male intellectuals adopted for the representation of new women often reveal their male-centered consciousness and "traditional" sensibilities. May Fourth male writers not only resurrected the premodern scheme of allegorizing women for both self-representation and political propaganda, but also created synthesized forms through an unself-conscious application of their own premodern cultural heritage as well as a self-conscious adaptation of techniques gained from the study of Western literatures. By turning the male schematization of a female Other on its head for the creation of an independent female subject, Ding Ling's literary endeavors bring into sharp focus the male exploitation of images of women for both political and personal ends, thus exposing a male-centered consciousness deeply rooted in China's history of patriarchal rule.

By constructing new women through the appropriation of dominant discursive patterns, Ding Ling's fiction also illustrates the way women writers within the May Fourth tradition contributed to the definitions and meanings of Chinese modernity. Women writers' literary achievements, ranging from the broaching of previously taboo topics such as women's sexuality to the creation of a female subject in fiction, not only made up an indispensable part of twentieth-century Chinese literature but also established the authors' status as participants in the creation and dissemination of discourses of Chinese modernity. However, women writers had to overcome various constraints imposed by the very modern male intellectuals who had initially promoted Chinese women's break away from tradition. A particularly revealing example was male intellectuals' gender-targeted literary criticism of "feminine emotionalism" that prescribed for women writers the only acceptable form of modernity. Feng Yuanjun and Lu Yin, although having produced only limited amount of fiction, established a model of articulating modern consciousness through the integration of an emotional logic into the Western form of first-person narration. In comparison, Ding Ling illuminated the gendered nature of the modern form of diary fiction and its limitation of women's liberation. Her continual efforts of espousing women's control of emotions, though influenced by the dominant male discourses of female emotionalism, further confirmed her commitment to the pursuit of women's interests and independence.

By displaying the complex interaction of dominant discourses and individual agency, Ding Ling's case also provides a new way to look at the apparent compatibility between the May Fourth legacy and totalitarian politics. On the one hand, Ding Ling's life and fiction reveal the link between cultural radicalism and political radicalism. Her case reveals that May Fourth intellectuals' antitraditionalism not only originated from a Confucian heritage of speaking for the people and exposing the immorality of the existing political regime, but also made them more susceptible to regimes of cultural conservatism and patriarchal dominance such as the Communist Party, precisely because they inherited such a self-image as representative and advocate of the people along with premodern discursive habits. On the other hand, Ding Ling's life and fiction also suggest that rather than follow the simplistic paradigm of resistance versus domination, we must instead assess individual agency, especially female agency, in light of the individual's appropriation and subversion of dominant discourses through narrative maneuvering.

In this light, the study of this particular group of May Fourth fiction will also facilitate further inquiries on modern China. By combining the textual and extratextual, the literary and the political, as well as insights from the different narrative strategies used by male and female writers, this book hopes to shed new light on the crucial significance of both the "modern woman" and "modern fiction" at an important point in Chinese history. But more importantly, it illustrates a way to obtain insights into the ideological and literary orientations of contemporary Chinese society by unraveling the mesh of interests that make up the politics of the narrative form, and thus bringing the personal into conjunction with the political, and tradition with modernity.

Appendix A

Chronological List of Fiction Discussed in Each Chapter

(Dates represent year of completion of the work unless otherwise noted.)

Chapter One

FENG MENGLONG 馮夢龍 (1574–1646)
"Du Shiniang nuchen baibao xiang" 杜十娘怒沉百寶箱 (Du Shiniang sinks her jewel box in anger)
"Maiyou lang duzhan huakui" 賣油郎獨占花魁 ("The Oil Peddler Who Courts the Courtesan")

CAO XUEQIN 曹雪芹 (1715–64)
Honglou meng 紅樓夢 (*Dream of the Red Chamber*) c. 1740–1760

WU WUOYAO 吳沃堯 [WU JIANREN 吳趼人] (1866–1910)
Ershi nian budu zhi guai xianzhuang 二十年目睹之怪現狀 (Strange Phenomena Witnessed during the Past Twenty Years)

ZENG PU 曾樸 (1872–1935)
Nie haihua 孽海花 (Flowers in a Sea of Sins)

Chapter Two

LU XUN 魯迅 (1881–1936)
"Xingfu de jiating" 幸福的家庭 ("A Happy Family") 1924.2.18
"Feizao" 肥皂 ("Soap") 1924.3.22
"Gao Lao Fuzi" 高老夫子 ("Master Gao") 1925.5.1
"Gudu zhe" 孤獨者 ("The Misanthrope") 1925.10.17
"Shangshi" 傷逝 ("Regret for the Past") 1925.10.21
"Dixiong" 弟兄 ("Brothers") 1925.11.3

Chapter Three

YU DAFU 郁達夫 (1896–1945)
"Yinhui se de si" 銀灰色的死 (Silver-Gray Death) 1921.7.7
"Chenlun" 沉淪 ("Sinking") 1921.5.9
"Nanqian" 南遷 (Migration to the South) 1921.10.15
"Mangmang ye" 茫茫夜 (Endless Night) 1922.2
"Chunfeng chenzui de wanshang" 春風沉醉的晚上 ("Intoxicating Spring Nights") 1923.7.15
"Xueye: Riben guoqing de jishu zizhuan zhi yizhang"

雪夜：日本國情的記述，自傳之一章 (Snowy Night: One Chapter in My Autobiographical Records of the Milieu in Japan) 1936

Chapter Four

BA JIN 巴金 (1904–)
  Jia 家 (*Family*) 1931.4–12
  "Wu" 霧 ("Fog") 1931
  "Yu" 雨 ("Rain") 1932.8
  "Dian" 電 ("Lightning") 1933.12
  Chun 春 (*Spring*) 1938.2
  Qiu 秋 (*Autumn*)

Chapter Five

MAO DUN 茅盾 (1896–1981)
  "Huanmie" 幻滅 ("Disillusionment") 1927.9
  "Dongyao" 動搖 ("Vacillation") 1928.1
  "Chuangzao" 創造 ("Creation") 1928.2.23
  "Zhuiqiu" 追求 ("Pursuit") 1929.6
  Hong 虹 (*Rainbow*) 1929.3.10

Chapter Six

FENG YUANJUN 馮沅君 (1900–1974)
  "Gejue" 隔絕 (Separation) 1923
  "Gejue zhi hou" 隔絕之後 (After Separation) 1923
  "Lüxing" 旅行 (Journey) 1923

LU YIN 盧隱 (1898–1934)
  "Huoren de beiai" 或人的悲哀 (Somebody's Sorrow) 1922
  "Lishi de riji" 麗石的日記 (Lishi's Diary) 1924
  "Shengli yihou" 勝利以後 (After Victory) 1925
  "Yege qingfu de riji" 一個情婦的日記 (Diary of a Mistress) 1933

Chapter Seven

DING LING 丁玲 (1904–86)
  "Shafei nüshi de riji" 莎菲女士的日記 ("Miss Sophia's Diary") 1928
  "Yecao" 野草 ("Yecao") 1929.5

Chapter Eight

DING LING 丁玲
  "Wei Hu" 韋護 ("Wei Hu") 1930
  "1930 nian chun Shanghai (zhiyi, zhier)" 一九三零年春上海 ("Shanghai, Spring 1930, Part I and II") 1930.6, 10
  "Shafei riji dier bu" 莎菲日記第二部 ("Sophia's Diary (part II)") 1931

"Cong yewan dao tianliang" 從夜晚到天亮 ("From Night to Dawn") 1931.4.23

"Tianjia chong" 田家沖 ("Tianjia Village") 1931

Epilogue

DING LING 丁玲

"Wo zai Xiacun de shihou" 我在霞村的時候 ("When I Was in Xia Village") 1940

"Zai yiyuan zhong" 在醫院中 ("In the Hospital") 1940

Appendix B
Glossary

Aiqing sanbuqu 愛情三部曲
Aiya 哎呀
Aiyou 哎呦

Ba Jin 巴金
Bai Juyi 白居易
baihua 白話
Ban Zhao 班昭
Bao Tianxiao 包天笑
Baosu 抱素
beiai shiqi 悲哀時期
Bing Xin 冰心

cainu 才女
Caiyun 彩雲
Cai Yuanpei 蔡元培
Chen Duxiu 陳獨秀
Chen Ermei 陳二妹
Chen Pingyuan 陳平原
Chen Zhen 陳真
Cheng Fangwu 成仿吾
Chenlun 沉淪
"Chenlun" 沉淪
Chengdu 成都
"Chuangzao" 創造
chuangzao lian 創造臉
Chuangzao she 創造社
Chuangzao zhoubao 創造週報
"Chuguan" 出關
Chun 春
"Chunfeng chenzui de wanshang" 春風沉醉的晚上
congliang 從良
"Cong yewan dao tianliang" 從夜晚到天亮
Daguan yuan 大觀園
Den'en no yuutsu 田園 憂鬱
"Dian" 電
Ding Ling 丁玲

"Dixiong" 弟兄
Dongfang wenku 東方文庫
"Dongyao" 動搖
Du Shiniang 杜十娘
duoluo 墮落

Fang Luolan 方羅蘭
fanxing 反省
"Feizao" 肥皂
Fen 墳
Feng Fei 馮飛
Feng Xuefeng 馮雪峰
Feng Yuanjun 馮沅君
Fu Sinian 傅斯年
Fu Xuewen 傅學文
Funü pinglun 婦女評論
Funü sheng 婦女聲
Funü shibao 婦女時報
funü wenti 婦女問題
Funü zazhi 婦女雜誌
Funü zhoukan 婦女週刊
"Fuqin" 父親
Fusheng liuji 浮生六記

gailiang zhuyi 改良主義
"Gao Lao Fuzi" 高老夫子
Gao Lao Taiye 高老太爺
"Gejue" 隔絕
"Gejue zhi hou" 隔絕之後
geming wenxue 革命文學
geming yu lianai jiaocuo de gushi 革命與戀愛交錯的故事
geren zhuyi 個人主義
Gong Shaoqing 貢少芹
"Gudu zhe" 孤獨者
guanchang 官場
Guanghua daxue 光華大學
Guangming zai women mianqian 光明在我們面前

guiju 規矩
guixiu pai 閨秀派
Guiyan 歸雁
Guo Moruo 郭沫若
guofang wenxue 國防文學
Guomindang 國民黨
guominxing 國民性

Haibin guren 海濱故人
Hong 虹
Honglou meng 紅樓夢
Hu Guoguang 胡國光
Hu Shi 胡適
Hu Yepin 胡也頻
Hu Yunyi 胡雲翼
Hua Mulan 花木蘭
huaben xiaoshuo 話本小說
"Huanmie" 幻滅
Hui 慧
Hui Siling 惠司令
Huoyan 火焰

Jia 家
Jiang Guangci 蔣光慈
jidiao 基調
Jiliu sanbuqu 激流三部曲
Jin Ping Mei 金瓶梅
Jin Wenqing 金雯青
Jing 靜
jiusi yisheng 九死一生
Juansheng   涓生
Juehui 覺慧
Juemin 覺民
juewu 覺悟
Juexin 覺新
Junshi 君實

Kaiming (bookstore) 開明
kaituo shiqi 開拓時期
Kang Youwei 康有為
keguan 客觀
keju zhidu 科舉制度
Kongkong daoshi 空空道士

Li Dingyi 李定夷
Li Jia 麗嘉
Li Peizhu 李佩珠

Li Shizeng 李石曾
Li Wuji 李無極
Liang Gangfu 梁剛夫
liangjia funü 良家婦女
Liang Qichao 梁啓超
"Liangge jiating" 兩個家庭
Liangyou huabao 良友畫報
lianhe zhenxian 聯合陣線
Libai liu 禮拜六
lienü zhuan 列女傳
Ling Jishi 凌吉士
"Lisao" 離騷
Lishi 麗石
"Lishi de riji" 麗石的日記
lishu 禮數
Liu Manqing 劉曼卿
Liu Xiahui 柳下惠
Liu Yuchun 柳遇春
luchen 陸沉
Lu Ping 陸萍
Lu Yin 盧隱
"Lüxing" 旅行

Mali (Mary) 瑪麗
"Manli" 曼麗
"Mangmang ye" 茫茫夜
Mao Dun 茅盾
Mei 梅
Meijuan 美娟
Meili 梅麗
Meilin 美琳
Mei Xingsu 梅行素
"Mengke" 夢珂
min 民
Ming 明
Mingfeng 鳴鳳
"Moluo shi li shuo" 摩羅詩力說
"Mouye" 某夜
Mudan ting 牡丹亭
Muqin 母親

Nahan 吶喊
"Nanqian" 南遷
Nan Xia 南俠
nigu 擬古
Ni Huanzhi 倪煥之

Niehai hua 孽海花
"Nuola zouhou zenmoyang"
　娜拉走後怎麼樣
nü xuesheng 女學生
Nü xuesheng 女學生
Nü xuesheng zhi baimian guan
　女學生之百面觀
Nü xuesheng mimi ji
　女學生秘密記
nuanhuo 暖和
Nübao 女報
Nüjie 女誡
Nüren de xin 女人的心
nüxing de wenzhang 女性的文章
nüxing shuxie 女性書寫
Nüzi shijie 女子世界

pantu 叛徒
Panghuang 彷徨
pingdan 平淡
"Pipa xing" 琵琶行
"Pohuai yu jianshe shiqi de nü xuesheng"
　破壞與建設時期的女學生
Qian Qianwu 錢謙吾
Qian Xingcun 錢杏村
Qiang Weili 強惟力
qianshi 僉事
qianze xiaoshuo 譴責小說
Qin 琴
Qin Yunyu 秦蘊玉
Qin Zhong 秦重
Qing 清
qing jiaotu 清教徒
qingnian zhidaozhe 青年指導者
Qinzhi 沁芝
Qiongfang 瓊芳
qipao 旗袍
Qiu 秋
Qiu Jin 秋瑾
Qu Qiubai 瞿秋白

Refeng 熱風
rensheng pai 人生派
"Ri" 日
rougan 肉感

Ruijue 瑞珏
Ruoquan 若泉

San Xiaojie 三小姐
"Sanba jie you gan" 三八節有感
sangang 三綱
sanwen shi 散文詩
Sato Haruo 佐藤春夫
Shafei 莎菲
"Shafei riji dier bu"
　莎菲日記第二部
"Shafei nüshi de riji"
　莎菲女士的日記
shangchang 商場
Shanghai shibao 上海時報
"Shangshi" 傷逝
Shangwu yingshu guan
　商務印書館
Shao Lizi 邵力子
shi 士
Shi Jun 史俊
Shi Pingmei 石評梅
Shi sanbuqu 蝕三部曲
Shi Taizhao 史太昭
Shi Xun 史循
"Shi yu sanwen" 詩與散文
"Shidai de xisheng zhe"
　時代的犧牲者
shidai xing 時代性
shijimo ming 世紀末病
Shimonoseki 馬關
Shuihu zhuang 水滸傳
shuoli 說理
shuqing wen 抒情文
Shuying 淑英
"Sichou shi" 四愁詩
Sili taosheng 死裡逃生
"Sixiang de zhuanbian"
　思想的轉變
Song 宋
Sun Fuyuan 孫伏園
Sun Wuyang 孫舞陽
suowei de 所謂的

"Tan" 曇
"Tianjia chong" 田家沖

Tianren heyi 天人合一
tongzhi 同志

"wan e zhiyuan" 萬惡之原
Wang Canzhi 王燦芝
Wang Dungen 王鈍根
Wang Jianhong 王劍虹
Wang Meiniang 王美娘
Wang Shitao 王詩陶
Wang Wei 望薇
Wang Yunwu 王雲五
Wang Zhongzhao 王仲昭
Wanyou wenku 萬友文庫
watakushi shosetsu 私小說
"Wei Hu" 韋護
Wei Hu 韋護
wei rensheng de yishu
　爲人生的藝術
Weidi 葦弟
Wei Yu 韋玉
wenku 文庫
wenrou 溫柔
Wenxue yanjiu hui 文學研究會
wenyan 文言
"Wo zai Xiacun de shihou"
　我在霞村的時候
woxing wosu 我行我素
"Wu" 霧
Wuhan 武漢
Wu Renmin 吳仁民
Wu Zhihui 吳稚暉
"Wubing shenyin" 無病呻吟
wuwo 無我

xiahui fenjie 下回分解
xianbi 閑筆
Xiangya jiezhi 象牙戒指
Xianxian 嫻嫻
Xiaoshuo yuebao 小說月報
xiezi 楔子
Xinchao 新潮
Xin funü 新婦女
xin guixiu pai 新閨秀派
Xin Meiniang 莘美娘
Xin nüxing 新女性
xin nüxing 新女性

xin nüxing pai 新女性派
Xin qingnian 新青年
xin wenyuan 新文苑
"Xingfu de jiating" 幸福的家庭
xini 細膩
xinjing 心境
Xinsheng 新生
Xiong Zhijun 熊智君
Xu Guangping 許廣平
Xu Xiacun 徐霞村
Xu Zhenya 徐枕亞
Xue Sao 薛嫂
Xuesheng zazhi 學生雜誌

Ya Xia 亞俠
Yan'an 延安
Yan Fu 嚴復
Yan Jiayan 嚴家炎
"Yang Ma de riji" 楊媽的日記
Yang Xingfo 楊杏佛
Yang Yinyu 楊蔭宇
yanqing 言情
Yao Mei 幺妹
Ye qiangwei 野薔薇
"Yecao" 野草
Yecao 野草
"1930 nian chun Shanghai"
　一九三零年春上海
"Yinhui se de si" 銀灰色的死
"Ying de gaobie" 影的告別
yongsu 庸俗
Yosano Akiko 与謝野晶子
"Yu" 雨
Yu Dafu 郁達夫
Yu Zhifu 于質夫
yuanyang hudie pai 鴛鴦蝴蝶派
Yufang 毓芳
Yuli hun 玉梨魂
Yun(jie) 蘊（姊）
Yunlin 雲霖

"Zai shujia zhong" 在暑假中
"Zai yiyuan zhong" 在醫院中
Zeng Pu 曾樸
zengwu 憎惡
Zhang Heng 張衡

Zhang Manqing 張曼青
Zhang Qiuliu 章秋柳
Zhang Taiyan 章太炎
Zhaohua xishi 朝花夕拾
Zheng Boqi 鄭伯奇
zhengshi rensheng 正視人生
Zhejiang 浙江
zhenshi 真實
zhenshi xing 真實性
Zhenzhen 貞貞
zheyang 這樣
Zhina ren 支那人
zhishi fenzi 知識分子
zhiyin 知音
Zhongguo funü wenti taolun ji 中國婦女問題討論集
Zhongguo jindai wenxue daxi 中國近代文學大係
Zhongguo xin wenxue daxi 中國新文學大係
Zhongguo zuoyi zuojia lianmeng 中國左翼作家聯盟
zhongjian wu 中間物
Zhongqian 仲謙
zhongri yi lei ximian 終日以淚洗面
Zhou Ruolan 周若蘭
Zhou Rushui 周如水
Zhou Zuoren 周作人
Zhu Yingtai 祝英臺
zhuanbian shiqi 轉變時期
zhuangyuan 狀元
zhuguan 主觀
"Zhuiqiu" 追求
zhurengong 主人公
Zijun 子君
"Zisha riji" 自殺日記
Ziye 子夜
Ziyou du 自由毒
zuoren 做人

Works Cited

Anderson, Benedict. *Imagined Communities: Reflections on the Origin and Spread of Nationalism.* London: Verso, 1983.

Anderson, Marston. *The Limits of Realism: Chinese Fiction in the Revolutionary Period.* Berkeley: U of California P, 1990.

Anderson, Marston. "The Specular Self: Subjective and Mimetic Moments in the Fiction of Ye Shaojun." *Modern China* 15.1 (1989): 72-101.

Apter, David, and Tony Saich. *Revolutionary Discourse in Mao's Republic.* Cambridge: Harvard UP, 1994.

Armstrong, Nancy. *Desire and Domestic Fiction: A Political History of the Novel.* New York: Oxford UP, 1987.

Ba Jin. *Family.* Trans. Olga Lang. 1972. Prospect Hill: Waveland, 1989.

Ba Jin. 巴金 "*Aiqing de sanbu qu* zongxu." 愛情的三部曲總序 (General Preface to *Love Trilogy*, 1935). *Ba Jin yanjiu ziliao.* Ed. Li Cunguang. Fuzhou: Haixia wenyi, 1985. Vol. 1, 305-48.

Ba Jin. "Da Faguo *Shijie bao* jizhe wen." 答法國世界報記者問 (Answers to the French Journalist from *Le Monde*, 1979). *Ba Jin zixu.* Ed. Chen Qiongzhi. Beijing: Tuanjie, 1996. 321-31.

Ba Jin. "Guanyu *Jiliu*." 關於激流 (On *Torrent*, 1980). *Ba Jin yanjiu ziliao.* Ed. Li Cunguang. Fuzhou: Haixia wenyi, 1985. Vol. 1, 435-48.

Ba Jin. "He duzhe tantan Jia." 和讀者談談家 (Talking about *Family* with My Readers, 1957). *Ba Jin yanjiu ziliao.* Ed. Li Cunguang. Fuzhou: Haixia wenyi, 1985. Vol. 1, 387-93.

Ba Jin. *Jia*. 家 Beijing: Renmin wenxue, 1982.

Ba Jin. "*Jia*" 家 (On *Family*, 1937). *Ba Jin yanjiu ziliao.* Ed. Li Cunguang. Fuzhou: Haixia wenyi, 1985. Vol. 1, 371-84.

Ba Jin. *Wu, yu, dian.* 霧，雨，電 (Fog, Rain, and Lightning). Shanghai: Xin wenyi, 1956.

Ba Jin yanjiu lunji. 巴金研究論集 (Collected Papers on Ba Jin). Chongqing: Chongqing, 1988.

Bakhtin, Mikhail M. *The Dialogic Imagination: Four Essays.* Ed. and trans. Michael Holquist. Austin: U of Texas P, 1981.

Bao Tianxiao. 包天笑 *Nü xuesheng* 女學生 (Girl Student) 1 (1931): 1.

Barlow, Tani E., and Angelo Zito, eds. *Body, Subject, and Power.* Chicago: U of Chicago P, 1994.

Barlow, Tani E. "Feminism and Literary Technique in Ting Ling's Early Short Stories." *Women Writers of 20th-Century China.* Ed. Angela Jung Palandri. Eugene: Asian Studies P, U of Oregon, 1982. 63-110.

Barlow, Tani E. "Gender and Identity in Ding Ling's Mother." *Modern Chinese Women Writers: Critical Appraisals.* Ed. Michael Duke. Armonk: M.E. Sharpe, 1989. 1-24.

Barlow, Tani E., ed. *Gender Politics in Modern China: Writing and Feminism*. Durham: Duke UP, 1993.

Barlow, Tani E., ed. *I Myself Am a Woman: Selected Writings of Ding Ling*. Boston: Beacon, 1989.

Barlow, Tani E. Introduction. *I Myself Am a Woman: Selected Writings of Ding Ling*. Ed. Tani E. Barlow. Boston: Beacon, 1989. 1–45.

Barthes, Roland. "L'effet de réel." *Communications* 11 (1968): 84–89.

Beahan, Charlotte L. *The Women's Movement and Nationalism in Late Ch'ing China*. Ph.D. dissertation, Columbia U, 1976.

Bing Xin. 冰心 "Liangge jiating" 兩個家庭 (Two Families). *Beijing chenbao* 北京晨報 (Beijing Morning) 18–22 September 1919.

Bing Xin. "Pohuai yu biange shidai de nü xuesheng" 破壞與變革時代的女學生 (Girl Students at a Time of Destruction and Reformation). *Beijing chenbao* 北京晨報 (Beijing Morning) 4 September 1919.

Boscaro, Adriana, Franco Gatti, and Massimo Raveri, eds. *Literature, Visual Arts, and Linguistics*. Volume 1 of *Rethinking Japan*. Sandgate, Folkestone, Kent: Japan Library Limited, 1991.

Brown, Carolyn T. "Women as Trope: Gender and Power in Lu Xun's 'Soap.'" *Modern Chinese Literature* 4 (Spring/Fall 1988): 55–70.

Cao Xueqin. 曹雪芹 *Honglou meng*. 紅樓夢 (*Dream of the Red Chamber*). Beijing: Renmin wenxue, 1985.

Chambers, Ross. *Story and Situation: Narrative Seduction and the Power of Fiction*. Minneapolis: U of Minnesota P, 1984.

Chan, Stephen Ching-kiu. "The Language of Despair: Ideological Representation of the 'New Woman' by May Fourth Writers." *Gender Politics in Modern China: Writing and Feminism*. Ed. Tani E. Barlow. Durham: Duke UP, 1993. 13–32.

Chan, Wing-ming. "The Self-Mocking of a Chinese Intellectual: A Study of Yu Dafu's 'An Intoxicating Spring Night.'" *Interliterary and Intraliterary Aspects of the May Fourth Movement 1919 in China*. Ed. Marián Gálik. Bratislava: Veda Publishing House of the Slovak Academy of Sciences, 1990. 111–17.

Chang, Kang-I Sun. "Ming-Qing Women Poets and Notions of 'Talent' and 'Morality." *Culture and State in Chinese History: Conventions, Accommodations, and Critiques*. Ed. Theodore Huters, R. Bin Wang, and Pauline Yu. Stanford: Stanford UP, 1997. 236–58.

Chatman, Seymour. *Story and Discourse: Narrative Structure in Fiction and Film*. Ithaca: Cornell UP, 1978.

Chen Duxiu. 陳獨秀 "Dong Xi minzu genben sixiang zhi chayi." 東西民族根本思想之差異 (The Fundamental Differences in Thought between the East and the West). *Qingnian zazhi*. 青年雜誌 (The Journal of Youth) 1 (1916): 4.

Chen Pingyuan. 陳平原 "Xiaoshuo de shumianhua qingxiang yu xushi moshi de zhuanbian." 小說的書面化傾向和敘事模式的轉變 (The Literarization of Fiction and the Changes in Narrative Patterns). *Ershi shiji* zhongguo wenxue shilun. Ed. Wang Xiaoming. Shanghai: Dongfang chuban zhongxin, 1997. Vol. 1, 220–49.

Chen Pingyuan. Zhongguo xiaoshuo xushi moshi de zhuanbian. 中國小說敘事模式的轉變 (The Change of Narrative Modes in Chinese Fiction). Shanghai: Shanghai renmin, 1988.

Chen, Pingyuan. "Literature High and Low: 'Popular Fiction' in Twentieth-Century China." *The Literary Field of Twentieth-Century China*. Ed. Michel Hockx. Honolulu: U of Hawaii P, 1999. 113–33.

Chen Qiongzhi, 陳瓊芝ed. *Ba Jin zixu*. 巴金自敘 (Ba Jin Talking about Himself). Beijing: Tuanjie, 1996.

Chen Xianghe. 陳翔鶴 "Yu Dafu huiyi suoji." 郁達夫回憶瑣記 (Miscellaneous Records on the Memory of Yu Dafu, 1947). *Yu Dafu yanjiu ziliao*. Ed. Wang Zili and Chen Zishan. Tianjin: Tianjin renmin, 1981. Vol. 1, 101–17.

Chien, Ying-ying. "Revisioning 'New Women': Feminist Readings of Representative Modern Chinese Fiction." *Women's Studies International Forum* 17.1 (1994): 33–45.

Chow, Rey. "Against the Lures of Diaspora: Minority Discourse, Chinese Women, and Intellectual Hegemony." *Gender and Sexuality in Twentieth-Century Chinese Literature and Society*. Ed. Tonglin Lu. Albany: State U of New York P, 1993. 23–45.

Chow, Rey. "Introduction." *Modern Chinese Literary and Cultural Studies in the Age of Theory: Reimagining a Field*. Ed. Rey Chow. Durham: Duke UP, 2000. 1–25.

Chow, Rey, ed. *Modern Chinese Literary and Cultural Studies in the Age of Theory: Reimagining a Field*. Durham: Duke UP, 2000.

Chow, Rey. *Woman and Chinese Modernity: The Politics of Reading Between West and East*. Minneapolis: U of Minnesota P, 1991.

Confucius. *The Analects*. Trans. Raymond Dawson. Oxford: Oxford UP, 1993.

Denton, Kirk. "The Distant Shore: the Nationalist Theme in Yu Dafu's 'Sinking.'" *Chinese Literature, Essays, Articles, Reviews* 14 (1992): 107–23.

Denton, Kirk. General Introduction. *Modern Chinese Literary Thought: Writings on Literature, 1895–1945*. Ed. Kirk Denton. Stanford: Stanford UP, 1996. 1–68.

Denton, Kirk. Glossary. *Modern Chinese Literary Thought: Writings on Literature, 1895–1945*. Ed. Kirk Denton. Stanford: Stanford UP, 1996. 493–500.

Denton, Kirk. Introduction. *Modern Chinese Literary Thought: Writings on Literature, 1895–1945*, Part III, *Revolutionary Literature 1923–1930*. Ed. Kirk Denton. Stanford: Stanford UP, 1996. 257–62.

Denton, Kirk, ed. *Modern Chinese Literary Thought: Writings on Literature, 1895–1945*. Stanford: Stanford UP, 1996.

Denton, Kirk. *The Problematic of Self in Modern Chinese Literature: Hu Feng and Lu Ling*. Stanford: Stanford UP, 1998.

Ding Ling. 丁玲 "Cong yewan dao tianliang" 從夜晚到天亮 (From Night to Dawn). *Ding Ling wenji*. Changsha: Hunan renmin, 1983. Vol. 2, 310–18.

Ding Ling. *Ding Ling wenji*. 丁玲文集 (Anthology of Ding Ling's Writings). 5 volumes. Changsha: Hunan renmin, 1983.

Ding Ling. "In the Hospital." Trans. Gary J. Bjorge. *Modern Chinese Stories and Novellas, 1919–1949*. Ed. S. M. Joseph Lau, C. T. Hsia, and Leo Ou-fan Lee. New York: Columbia UP. 279–91.

Ding Ling. "Miss Sophia's Diary." Trans. Tani E. Barlow. *I Myself Am a Woman: Selected Writings of Ding Ling*. Ed. Tani E. Barlow. Boston: Beacon, 1989. 49–81.

Ding Ling. "Shafei nüshi de riji" 莎菲女士的日記 (Miss Sophia's Diary). *Ding Ling wenji*. Changsha: Hunan renmin, 1983. Vol. 2, 45–86.

Ding Ling. "Shafei riji dier bu (weiwan gao)" 莎菲日記第二部（未完稿）(Sophia's Diary II [Unfinished]). *Ding Ling wenji*. Changsha: Hunan renmin, 1983. Vol. 3, 308–12.

Ding Ling. "Shanghai, Spring 1930." Trans. Shu-ying Tsao and Donald Holoch. *I Myself Am a Woman: Selected Writings of Ding Ling*. Ed. Tani E. Barlow. Boston: Beacon, 1989. 112–71.

Ding Ling. "Tianjia chong" 田家沖 (Tianjia Village). *Ding Ling wenji*. Changsha: Hunan renmin, 1983. Vol. 2, 319–57.

Ding Ling. "Wei Hu" 韋護 (Wei Hu). *Ding Ling wenji*. Changsha: Hunan renmin, 1983. Vol. 1, 1–122.

Ding Ling. "When I Was in Hsia Village." Trans. Gary J. Bjorge. *Modern Chinese Stories and Novellas, 1919–1949*. Ed. S. M. Joseph Lau, C. T. Hsia, and Leo Ou-fan Lee. New York: Columbia UP. 265–75.

Ding Ling. "Wo de chuangzuo jingyan." 我的創作經驗 (My Experience in Writing, 1932). *Ding Ling yanjiu ziliao*. Ed. Yuan Liangjun. Tianjin: Tianjin renmin, 1982. 105–07.

Ding Ling. "Wo de chuangzuo shenghuo." 我的創作生活 (My Life of Writing, 1933). *Ding Ling yanjiu ziliao*. Ed. Yuan Liangjun. Tianjin: Tianjin renmin, 1982. 108–11.

Ding Ling. "Wo de zibai." 我的自白 (My Confession, 1931). *Ding Ling yanjiu ziliao*. Ed. Yuan Liangjun. Tianjin: Tianjin renmin, 1982. 97–102.

Ding Ling. "Wo suo renshi de Qiubai tongzhi." 我所認識的秋白同志 (The Comrade Qiubai That I Knew, 1980). *Ding Ling xiezuo shengya*. Ed. Huang Yixin. Tianjin: Baihua wenyi, 1984. 131–54.

Ding Ling. "Wo zai xiacu de shihou" 我在霞村的時候 (When I Was in Xia Village). *Ding Ling wenji*. Changsha: Hunan renmin, 1983. Vol. 3, 221–42.

Ding Ling. "Yecao." Trans. Charlotte Calhoun. *I Myself Am a Woman: Selected Writings of Ding Ling*. Ed. Tani E. Barlow. Boston: Beacon, 1989. 104–11.

Ding Ling. "1930 nian chun shanghai (zhiyi)" 一九三零年春上海（之一）(Shanghai, Spring 1930 [Part One]). *Ding Ling wenji*. Changsha: Hunan renmin, 1983. Vol. 2, 230-64.

Ding Ling. "1930 nian chun shanghai (zhier)" 一九三零年春上海（之二）(Shanghai, Spring 1930 [Part Two]). *Ding Ling wenji*. Changsha: Hunan renmin, 1983. Vol. 2, 265-309.

Ding Ling. "Zai yiyuan zhong" 在醫院中 (In the Hospital). *Ding Ling wenji*. Changsha: Hunan renmin, 1983. Vol. 3, 243-65.

Ding Yanzhao. 丁言昭 *Zai nanren de shijie li: Ding Ling zhuan*. 在男人的世界裡：丁玲傳 (In the World of Men: Biography of Ding Ling). Shanghai: Shanghai wenyi, 1998.

Doleželová-Velingerová, Milena, ed. *The Chinese Novel at the Turn of the Century*. Toronto: U of Toronto P, 1980.

Doleželová-Velingerová, Milena. "Narrative Modes in Late Qing Novels." *The Chinese Novel at the Turn of the Century*. Ed. Milena Doleželová-Velingerová. Toronto: U of Toronto P. 57-75.

Dooling, Amy, and Kristina Togeson, eds. and trans. *Writing Women in Modern China: An Anthology of Women's Literature from the Early Twentieth Century*. New York: Columbia UP, 1998.

Duke, Michael, ed. *Modern Chinese Women Writers: Critical Appraisals*. Armonk: M.E. Sharpe, 1989.

Duke, Michael. "Past, Present, and Future in Mo Yan's Fiction of the 1980s." *From May Fourth to June Fourth: Fiction and Film in Twentieth-Century China*. Ed. Ellen Widmer and David Der-wei Wang. Cambridge: Harvard UP, 1993. 43-70.

Eagleton, Terry. *The Ideology of the Aesthetics*. Cambridge: Basil Blackwell, 1990.

Egan, Michael. "Yu Dafu and the Transition to Modern Chinese Literature." *Modern Chinese Literature in the May Fourth Era*. Ed. Merle Goldman. Cambridge: Harvard UP, 1977. 309-24.

Fan Boqun, 范伯群 ed. *Bing Xin yanjiu ziliao*. 冰心研究資料 (Research Materials on Bing Xin). Beijing: Beijing, 1984.

Fan Jun 樊駿. "Mao Dun de *Shi*." 茅盾的蝕 (Mao Dun's *Eclipse*, 1955). Mao Dun yanjiu ziliao. Ed. Sun Zhongtian and Zha Guohua. Beijing: Zhongguo shehui kexue, 1983. Vol. 2, 145-81.

Feng Menglong. 馮夢龍 *Feng Menglong quanji*. 馮夢龍全集 (Complete Works by Feng Menglong). Nanjing: Jiangsu guji, 1993.

Feng Xuefeng. 馮雪峰 "Cong 'Menke' dao 'Ye': *Ding Ling wenji* houji 從夢珂到夜：丁玲文集後記 (From "Mengke" to "Ye": Postscript to *Ding Ling wenji*). *Ding Ling yanjiu ziliao*. Ed. Yuan Liangjun. Tianjin: Tianjin renmin, 1982. 292-300.

Feng Yuanjun. "The Journey." Trans. Jennifer Anderson and Theresa Munford. *Chinese Women Writers: Collection of Short Stories by Chinese Women Writers of the 1920s and 30s*. Hong Kong: Chinese Books and Periodicals, 1985. 168-78.

Feng Yuanjun. 馮沅君 "Lüxing." 旅行 *Chunhen.* 春痕 Ed. Ke Ling. 柯靈 Shanghai: Shanghai guji, 1997. 18–27.

Feng Yuanjun. "Separation." *Writing Women in Modern China: An Anthology of Women's Literature from the Early Twentieth Century.* Ed. and trans. Amy Dooling and Kristina Togeson. New York: Columbia UP, 1998. 101–14.

Feng Yuanjun. "Wubing sheyin" 無病呻吟 (Groaning without Ailment). *Feng Yuanjun chuangzuo yiwen ji.* Ed. Yuan Shishuo and Yan Rongxian. Jinan: Shandong renmin, 1983. 162–63.

Feng Zikai. 豐子愷 "Gao muxing." 告母性 (Call to Maternal Instinct). *Xin nüxing.* 新女性 (New Woman) 2. 12 (1927): 1378–79.

Feuerwerker, Yi-tsi M. "The Changing Relationship between Literature and Life: Aspects of the Writer's Role in Ding Ling." *Modern Chinese Literature in the May Fourth Era.* Ed. Merle Goldman. Cambridge: Harvard UP, 1977. 281–307.

Feuerwerker, Yi-tsi M. *Ding Ling's Fiction: Ideology and Narrative in Modern Chinese Literature.* Cambridge: Harvard UP, 1982.

Feuerwerker, Yi-tsi M. *Ideology, Power, Text: Self-Representation and the Peasant "Other" in Modern Chinese Literature.* Stanford: Stanford UP, 1998.

Feuerwerker, Yi-tsi M. "Text, Intertext, and the Representation of the Writing Self in Lu Xun, Yu Dafu, and Wang Meng." *From May Fourth to June Fourth: Fiction and Film in Twentieth-Century China.* Ed. Ellen Widmer and David Der-wei Wang. Cambridge: Harvard UP, 1993. 167–93.

Foucault, Michel. *The Archaeology of Knowledge.* Trans. A. M. Sheridan Smith. New York: Pantheon Books, 1972.

Freud, Sigmund. "The Most Prevalent Forms of Degradation in Erotic Life." Trans. James Strachey. *Sexuality and the Psychology.* Ed. Philip Rieff. Volume 11 of *The Standard Edition of the Complete Psychological Works.* London: Hogarth P, 1953. 58–70.

Frye, Northrop. *Anatomy of Criticism.* Princeton: Princeton UP, 1957.

Fu Sinian. 傅斯年 "Wan'e zhi yuan." 萬惡之原 (The Origin of Tens of Thousands of Evils). *Xin chao.* 新潮 (New Tide) 1.1 (1919): 127.

Gálik, Marián. *The Genesis of Modern Chinese Literary Criticism, 1917–1930.* London: Curzon, 1980.

Gálik, Marián, ed. *Interliterary and Intraliterary Aspects of the May Fourth Movement 1919 in China.* Bratislava: Veda Publishing House of the Slovak Academy of Sciences, 1990.

Gagnier, Regenia. *Subjectivities: A History of Self-Representation in Britain, 1832–1920.* New York: Oxford UP, 1991.

Geming wenxue lunzheng ziliao xuanbian. 革命文學論爭資料選編 (Selected Materials from the Debate on Revolutionary Literature). Beijing: Renmin wenxue, 1981.

Gerstlacher, Anna, Ruth Keen, Wolfgang Kubin, Margit Miosga, and Jenny Schor, eds. *Women and Literature in China*. Bochum: Herausgeber Chinathemen, 1985.

Girard, René. *Deceit, Desire, and the Novel: Self and Other in Literary Structure*. Trans. Yvonne Freccero. Baltimore: Johns Hopkins UP, 1965.

Goldman, Merle, ed. *Modern Chinese Literature in the May Fourth Era*. Cambridge: Harvard UP, 1977.

Gu Yeping. 辜也平 "*Jiliu sanbu qu yu Honglou meng* yitong lun." 激流三部曲與紅樓夢異同論 (On the Similarity and Difference between *Torrent Trilogy* and *Dream of the Red Chamber*). *Ba Jin yanjiu lunji*. Chongqing: Chongqing, 1988. 160–81.

Guo Moruo. 郭沫若 "Lun Yu Dafu." 論郁達夫 (On Yu Dafu, 1946). *Yu Dafu yanjiu ziliao*. Ed. Wang Zili and Chen Zishan. Tianjin: Tianjin renmin, 1981. Vol. 1, 91–101.

Han Liqun, 韓立群 ed. *Lu Xun zai Beijing*. 魯迅在北京 (Lu Xun in Beijing). Volume 3 of *Lu Xun shengping ziliao huibian*. 魯迅生平資料匯編 (Compilation of Materials on Lu Xun's Life). Tianjin: Tianjin, 1981.

Hanan, Patrick. *The Chinese Vernacular Story*. Cambridge: Harvard UP, 1981.

He Danren. 何丹仁 "Guanyu xin xiaoshuo de dansheng." 關於新小說的誕生 (On the Birth of New Fiction). *Ding Ling yanjiu ziliao*. Ed. Yuan Liangjun. Tianjin: Tianjin renmin, 1982. 246–51.

Hegel, Robert, and Richard Hessney, eds. *Expressions of Self in Chinese Literature*. New York: Columbia UP, 1985.

Hockx, Michel, ed. *The Literary Field of Twentieth-Century China*. Honolulu: U of Hawaii P, 1999.

Hsia, C. T. *A History of Modern Chinese Fiction*. New Haven: Yale UP, 1971.

Hsia, C. T., Joseph Lau, and Leo Ou-fan Lee, eds. *Modern Chinese Stories and Novellas 1919–1949*. New York: Columbia UP, 1981.

Hsia, Tsi-an. *The Gate of Darkness: Studies on the Leftist Literary Movement in China*. Seattle: U of Washington P, 1968.

Hu, Ying. *Tales of Translation: Composing the New Woman in China, 1899–1918*. Stanford: Stanford UP, 2000.

Huang Renpei, 黃仁平 ed. *Lu Xun Jing Song tongxin ji: Liangdi shu de yuanxin*. 魯迅景宋通信集：兩地書的原信 (The Correspondence between Lu Xun and Jing Song: the Original Letters of *Liangdi shu*). Changsha: Hunan renmin, 1984.

Huang Yixin, 黃一心 ed. *Ding Ling xiezuo shengya*. 丁玲寫作生涯 (The Writing Career of Ding Ling). Tianjin: Baihua wenyi, 1984.

Hyun, Sungjin. *In Search of the Meaning of Writing: A Study of Modern Chinese Diary Fiction*. Ph.D. dissertation, U of Michigan, 1997.

Jiang Guangci. 蔣光慈 "Guanyu geming wenxue." 關於革命文學 (On Revolutionary Literature). *Geming wenxue lunzheng ziliao xuanbian*. Beijing: Renmin wenxue, 1981. Vol. 1, 138–46.

Jiang Zengfu, 蔣增福 ed. *Zhongshuo Yu Dafu*. 眾說郁達夫 (People Talking about Yu Dafu). Hangzhou: Zhejiang wenyi, 1996.

Jin Ming. 錦明 "Dafu de san shiqi." 達夫的三時期 (The Three Periods [in the Writing Career] of Yu Dafu, 1927). *Yu Dafu yanjiu ziliao*. Ed. Wang Zili and Chen Zishan. Tianjin: Tianjin renmin, 1981. Vol. 2, 329–37.

Kahler, Erich. *The Inward Turn of the Novel*. Princeton: Princeton UP, 1973.

Kao, Yu-kung. "Lyric Vision in Chinese Narrative: A Reading of Hunglou meng and Rulin waishi." *Chinese Narrative: Critical and Theoretical Essays*. Ed. Andrew Plaks. Princeton: Princeton UP, 1977. 227–43.

Ko, Dorothy. *Teachers of the Inner Chamber: Women and Culture in Seventeenth-Century China*. Stanford: Stanford UP, 1994.

Kuang Yaming. 匡亞明 "Yu Dafu yinxiang ji." 郁達夫印像記 (My Impression of Yu Dafu). *Zhongshuo Yu Dafu*. Ed. Jiang Zengfu. Hangzhou: Zhejiang wenyi, 1996. 27–31.

Kumagaya Hideo. "Japanese Influences on Yu Dafu's Literary Thinking." *The Journal of the Oriental Society of Australia* 25–26 (1993–94): 128–49.

Kumagaya Hideo. "Quest for Truth: An Introductory Study of Yu Dafu's Fiction." *The Journal of the Oriental Society of Australia* 24 (1992): 149–63.

Larson, Wendy. *Literary Authority and the Modern Chinese Writer: Ambivalence and Autobiography*. Durham: Duke UP, 1991.

Larson, Wendy. *Women and Writing in Modern China*. Stanford: Stanford UP, 1998.

Larson, Wendy. "The Self Loving the Self: Men and Connoisseurship in Modern Chinese Literature." *Chinese Femininities/ Chinese masculinities: A Reader*. Ed. Susan Brownell and Jeffrey N. Wasserstrom. Berkeley: U of California P, 2002. 175–93.

Lau, S. M. Joseph, C. T. Hsia, and Leo Ou-fan Lee, eds. *Modern Chinese Stories and Novellas, 1919–1949*. New York: Columbia UP, 1981.

Lee, Leo Ou-fan. "Literary Trends I: the Quest for Modernity, 1895–1927." Volume 12 of *The Cambridge History of China, Republican China 1912–1949*. Ed. John K. Fairbank. Cambridge: Cambridge UP, 1983. 452–504.

Lee, Leo Ou-fan. "Modernity and Its Discontents: The Cultural Agenda of the May Fourth Movement." *Perspectives on Modern China: Four Anniversaries*. Ed. Kenneth Lieberthal, Joyce Kallyren, Roderick MacFarquhar, and Frederic Wakeman Jr. Armonk: M. E. Sharpe, 1991. 158–77.

Lee, Leo Ou-fan. *The Romantic Generation of Modern Chinese Writers*. Cambridge: Harvard UP, 1973.

Lee, Leo Ou-fan. "Romantic Individualism in Modern Chinese Literature: Some General Explorations." *Individualism and Holism: Studies in Confucian and Taoist Values*. Ed. Donald J. Munro. Ann Arbor: Center for Chinese Studies, U of Michigan, 1985. 239–55.

Lee, Leo Ou-fan. *Shanghai Modern: The Flowering of a New Urban Culture in China, 1930–1945*. Cambridge: Harvard UP, 1999.

Lee, Leo Ou-fan. "The Solitary Traveler." *Expressions of Self in Chinese Literature*. Ed. Robert Hegel and Richard Hessney. New York: Columbia UP, 1985. 282–307.

Lee, Leo Ou-fan. *Voices from the Iron House: A Study of Lu Xun*. Bloomington: Indiana UP, 1987.

Lee, Leo Ou-fan, ed. *The Lyrical and the Epic: Studies of Modern Chinese Literature*. Bloomington: Indiana UP, 1980.

Li Cunguang, 李存光 ed. *Ba Jin yanjiu ziliao.* 巴金研究資料 (Research Materials on Ba Jin). 3 volumes. Fuzhou: Haixia wenyi, 1985.

Li, Peter. "The Dramatic Structure of Niehai hua." *The Chinese Novel at the Turn of the Century*. Ed. Milena Dolezelová-Velingerová. Toronto: U of Toronto P, 1980. 150–64.

Liang Qichao. 梁啓超 "'Jie chanzu hui' xu." 戒纏足會敘 (Statement of the Society for the Prohibition of Foot-Binding). *Yinbing shi heji*. Shanghai: Zhonghua shuju, 1916. Vol. 1, 120–22.

Liang Qichao. "Lun nüxue." 論女學 (On Women's Education). *Yinbing shi heji*. Shanghai: Zhonghua shuju, 1916. Vol. 1, 1: 37–44.

Liang Qichao. "Lun xiaoshuo yu qunzhi de guanxi." 論小說與群治的關係 (On the Relation between Fiction and the Government of People). *Xin xiaoshuo.* 新小說 (New Fiction) 1 (1902): 157–61.

Liang Qichao. *Yinbing shi heji*. 飲冰室合集 (Complete Works of the Ice-Drinker's Studio). Shanghai: Zhonghua shuju, 1916.

Lieberman, Sally T. *The Mother and Narrative Politics in Modern China*. Charlottesville: U of Virginia P, 1998.

Lin, Yü-sheng. *The Crisis of Chinese Consciousness: Radical Anti-Traditionalism in the May Fourth Era*. Madison: U of Wisconsin P, 1979.

Lin, Yü-sheng. "Radical Iconoclasm in the May Fourth Period and the Future of Chinese Liberalism." *Reflections on the May Fourth Movement: Symposium*. Ed. Benjamin Schwartz and Charlotte Furth. Cambridge: Harvard UP, 1973. 23–58.

Link, Perry. *Mandarin Ducks and Butterflies: Popular Fiction in Early Twentieth-Century Chinese Fiction*. Berkeley: U of California P, 1981.

Liu, James J. Y. *Chinese Theories of Literature*. Chicago: U of Chicago P, 1975.

Liu, Lydia H. "Invention and Intervention: The Making of a Female Tradition in Modern Chinese Literature." *From May Fourth to June Fourth: Fiction and Film in Twentieth-Century China*. Ed. Ellen Widmer and David Der-wei Wang. Cambridge: Harvard UP, 1993. 194–220.

Liu, Lydia H. *Translingual Practice: Literature, National Culture, and Translated Modernity, China, 1900–1937*. Stanford: Stanford UP, 1995.

Liu Siqian. 劉思謙 *"Nola" yanshuo.* " 娜拉 " 言說 (Talking about "Nora"). Shanghai: Shanghai wenyi, 1993.

Lu, Tonglin, ed. *Gender and Sexuality in Twentieth-Century Chinese Literature and Society*. Albany: State U of New York P, 1993.

Lu Xun. 魯迅 "Bian" 扁 (Tablet, 1928). *Lu Xun quanji*. Beijing: Renmin wenxue, 1981. Vol. 4, 87–88.

Lu Xun. "*Chuguan* de 'guan'" 出關的關 (The "guan" in *Chuguan*). *Lu Xun quanji*. Beijing: Renmin wenxue, 1981. Vol. 6, 517–23.

Lu Xun. *Liangdi shu* 兩地書 (Letters between Two Places). *Lu Xun quanji*. Beijing: Renmin wenxue, 1981. 11.1–316.

Lu Xun. *Lu Xun quanji*. 魯迅全集 (Complete Works by Lu Xun). 16 volumes. Beijing: Renmin wenxue, 1981.

Lu Xun. *Lu Xun shuxin ji*. 魯迅書信集 (Anthology of Lu Xun's Correspondence). Beijing: Renmin wenxue, 1956.

Lu Xun. "Lun zhengle yan kan" 論睜了眼看 (On Looking Facts in the Face). *Lu Xun quanji*. Beijing: Renmin wenxue, 1981. Vol. 1, 237–41.

Lu Xun. "Moluo shili shuo" 摩羅詩力說 (On the Power of Satanic Poetry). *Lu Xun quanji*. Beijing: Renmin wenxue, 1981. Vol. 1, 63–115.

Lu Xun. "Nora zouhou zenmo yang" 娜拉走後怎麼樣 (What Happens after Nora Leaves Home). *Lu Xun quanji*. Beijing: Renmin wenxue, 1981. Vol. 1, 158–65.

Lu Xun. Qianji 前記 (Preface). *Wei ziyou shu* 偽自由書 (Book of False Freedom). *Lu Xun quanji*. Beijing: Renmin wenxue, 1981. Vol. 5, 3–6.

Lu Xun. "Qingnian bidu shu" 青年必讀書 (Must-Reads for the Youth). *Lu Xun quanji*. Beijing: Renmin wenxue, 1981. Vol. 3, 12–13.

Lu, Xun. *Selected Stories of Lu Xun*. Trans. Hsien-yi Yang and Gladys Yang. New York: Norton, 1960.

Lu Xun. "Ti Panghuang" 題彷徨 (Written for *Panghuang*). *Lu Xun quanji*. Beijing: Renmin wenxue, 1981. Vol. 7, 150.

Lu Xun. "Wo de shilian" 我的失戀 (My Disappointed Love). *Lu Xun quanji*. Beijing: Renmin wenxue, 1981. Vol. 2, 169–71.

Lu Xun. "Wo he *Yusi* de shizhong" 我和語絲的始終 (My Relationship with *Yusi*). *Lu Xun quanji*. Beijing: Renmin wenxue, 1981. Vol. 4, 164–75.

Lu Xun. "Wo zemo zuoqi xiaoshuo lai" 我怎麼做起小說來 (How I Started to Write Fiction). *Lu Xun quanji*. Beijing: Renmin wenxue, 1981. Vol. 4, 511–15.

Lu Xun. "Xuyan." 緒言 (Preface). *Zhongguo xinwenxue daxi (1917–1927)*. Ed. Zhao Jiabi. Hong Kong: Hong Kong wenxue yanjiu she, 1963. Vol. 4, 1481.

Lu Xun. "Ying de gaobie" 影的告別 (Farewell of a Shadow). *Lu Xun quanji*. Beijing: Renmin wenxue, 1981. Vol. 2, 165–66.

Lu Xun. "*Zixuan ji* zixu" 自選集自序 (Preface to Self-Selected Anthology Written by the Author Himself). *Lu Xun quanji*. Beijing: Renmin wenxue, 1981. Vol. 4, 455–58.

Lu Yin. "After Victory." Trans. Amy Dooling and Kristina Togeson. *Writing Women in Modern China: An Anthology of Women's Literature from the Early Twentieth Century*. Ed. and trans. Amy Dooling and Kristina Togeson. New York: Columbia UP, 1998. 135–56.

Lu Yin. 盧隱 "Chuangzuo de wojian." 創作的我見 (My Opinions on Creativity). *Xiaoshuo yuebao*. 小說月報 (*Short Story Monthly*) 12.7 (10 July 1921): 18–22.

Lu Yin. "Lishi de riji" 麗石的日記 (Lishi's Diary). *Lu Yin xiaoshuo quanji*. Ed. Li Jie. Changchun: Shidai wenyi, 1997. Vol. 1, 45–55.

Lu Yin. *Lu Yin xiaoshuo quanji* 盧隱小說全集 (Completed Fictional Works by Lu Yin). 2 volumes. Ed. Li Jie. 李傑 Changchun: Shidai wenyi, 1997.

Lu Yin. *Lu Yin xuanji* 盧隱選集 (Selected Works by Lu Yin). 2 volumes. Ed. Qian Hong. 錢虹 Fuzhou : Fujian renmin,1985.

Lu Yin. "My Opinions on Creativity." Trans. Paul Foster and Sherry Mou. *Modern Chinese Literary Thought: Writings on Literature, 1895–1945.* Ed. Kirk Denton. Stanford: Stanford UP, 1996. 235–37.

Lu Yin. "Sixiang de zhuanbian." 思想的轉變 (Transformations of My Thoughts). *Lu Yin xuanji*. Ed. Qian Hong. Fuzhou: Fujian renmin, 1985. Vol. 1, 591–95.

Lu Yin. "Yige Qingfu de riji" 一個情婦的日記 (Diary of a Mistress). *Lu Yin xiaoshuo quanji*. Ed. Li Jie. Changchun: Shidai wenyi, 1997. Vol. 1, 407–25.

Luo Jiongguang. 羅炯光 "Lun Feng Yuanjun de xiaoshuo chuangzuo" 論馮沅君的小說創作 (On Feng Yuanjun's Fiction Writing). *Zhongguo xiandai, dangdai xiaoshuo yanjiu* 中國現代當代小說研究 (The Study of Modern and Contemporary Chinese Fiction) 21 (1985): 73.

McLaren, Anne E., ed. and trans. *The Chinese Femme Fatale: Stories from the Ming Period.* U of Sydney East Asian Series, Number 8. Sydney: Wild Peony, 1994.

McMahon, Keith. *Causality and Containment in Seventeenth-Century Chinese Fiction.* Leiden: E.J. Brill, 1988.

Mann, Susan. *Precious Records: Women in China's Long Eighteenth-Century.* Stanford: Stanford UP, 1997.

Mao Dun. 茅盾 "Chuangzao" 創造 (Creation). *Mao Dun quanji*. Beijing: Renmin wenxue, 1984–1997. Vol. 8, 1–32.

Mao Dun. "Cong Guli dao Dongjing." 從牯嶺到東京 (From Gulin to Tokyo, 1928). *Mao Dun yanjiu ziliao*. Ed. Sun Zhongtian and Zha Guohua. Beijing: Zhongguo shehui kexue, 1983. Vol. 2, 2–10.

Mao Dun. "Dongyao" 動搖 (Vacillation). *Mao Dun quanji*. Beijing: Renmin wenxue, 1984–1997. Vol. 1, 101–258.

Mao Dun. "Du *Ni Huanzhi.*" 讀倪煥之 (Reading *Ni Huanzhi*, 1929). *Mao Dun quanji*. Beijing: Renmin wenxue, 1984–1997. 19.197–217.

Mao Dun. Hong 虹 (Rainbow). *Mao Dun quanji*. Beijing: Renmin wenxue, 1984–1997. Vol. 2, 1–270.

Mao Dun. "*Hong* ba" 虹跋 (Afterword to *Rainbow*). *Mao Dun yanjiu ziliao*. Ed. Sun Zhongtian and Zha Guohua. Beijing: Zhongguo shehui kexue, 1983. Vol. 2, 15.

Mao Dun. "Huanmie" 幻滅 (Disillusionment). *Mao Dun quanji*. Beijing: Renmin wenxue, 1984–1997. Vol. 1, 3–100.

Mao Dun. "Lu Yin lun." 盧隱論 (On Lu Yin, 1934). *Lu Yin zhuan.* 盧隱傳 (Biography of Lu Yin). Xiao Feng. 蕭鳳 Beijing: Beijing shifan daxue, 1982. 137–45.

Mao Dun. "Mao Dun huiyi lu" 茅盾回憶錄 (Recollections by Mao Dun). *Mao Dun yanjiu ziliao*. Ed. Sun Zhongtian and Zha Guohua. Beijing: Zhongguo shehui kexue, 1983. Vol. 1, 88–427.

Mao Dun. *Mao Dun quanji.* 茅盾全集 (Complete Anthology of Mao Dun's Works). 37 volumes. Beijing: Renmin wenxue, 1984–97.

Mao Dun. *Mao Dun wenyi zalun ji.* 茅盾文藝雜論集 (Anthology of Mao Dun's Miscellaneous Literary Discussions). Shanghai: Shanghai wenyi, 1981.

Mao Dun. "Nü zuojia Ding Ling." 女作家丁玲 (The Woman Writer Ding Ling, 1933). *Ding Ling yanjiu ziliao*. Ed. Yuan Liangjun. Tianjin: Tianjin renmin, 1982. 252–56.

Mao Dun. *Rainbow*. Trans. Madeleine Zelin. Berkeley: U of California P, 1992.

Mao Dun. "Tongxin." 通信 (Correspondence, 1922). *Yu Dafu yanjiu ziliao*. Ed. Wang Zili and Chen Zishan. Tianjin: Tianjin renmin, 1981. Vol. 2, 304.

Mao Dun. *Wo zouguo de daolu.* 我走過的道路 (The Path I Have Trod). Hong Kong: Sanlian, 1981.

Mao Dun. "Xie zai *Ye qiangwei* de qianmian" 寫在野薔薇的前面 (Written as Preface to *Wild Roses*). *Mao Dun yanjiu ziliao*. Ed. Sun Zhongtian and Zha Guohua. Beijing: Zhongguo shehui kexue, 1983. Vol. 2, 11–14.

Mao Dun. "Zhen you daibiao jiu wenhua jiu wenyi de zuoping mo" 真有代表舊文化舊文藝的作品麼 (Are There Really Works That Represent Old Culture and Old Arts? 1922). *Mao Dun quanji*. Beijing: Renmin wenxue, 1984–1997. 18.311–12.

Mao Dun. "Zhuiqiu" 追求 (Pursuit). *Mao Dun quanji*. Beijing: Renmin wenxue, 1984–97. Vol. 1, 259–422.

Mao Zedong. "Talks at the Yan'an Forum on Literature and Art" (1942). *Modern Chinese Literary Thought: Writings on Literature, 1895–1945*. Ed. Kirk Denton. Stanford: Stanford UP, 1996. 458–84.

Martin, Wallace. *Recent Theories of Narrative*. Ithaca: Cornell UP, 1986.

Martin-Liao, Tienchi. "Traditional Handbooks of Women's Education." *Women and Literature in China*. Ed. Anna Gerstlacher, Ruth Keen, Wolfgang Kubin, Margit Miosga, and Jenny Schor. Bochum: Herausgeber Chinathemen, 1985. 165–89.

Mei Jie, 梅節 ed. *Mei Jie chongjiaoben Jin Ping Mei cihua.* 梅節重校本金瓶梅詞話 (Mei Jie's Newly Edited Version of Plum in a Golden Vase). Hong Kong: Mengmei guan, 1993.

Mei Sheng, 梅生 ed. *Zhongguo funü wenti taolun ji.* 中國婦女問題討論集 (Anthology on the Discussion of the Chinese Woman Question). Shanghai: Xin wenhua, 1924.

Mencius. *Mencius.* Trans. W.A.C.H. Dobson. U of Toronto P, 1963.

Meng Yue 孟越 and Dai Jinhua 戴錦華. *Fuchu lishi dibiao: xiandai funü wenxue yanjiu* 浮出歷史地表：現代婦女文學研究 (Emerging from the

Horizon of History: A Study of Modern Chinese Women's Literature). Zhengzhou: Henan renmin, 1989.

Metzger, Thomas A. *Escape from Predicament: Neo-Confucianism and China's Evolving Political Culture.* New York: Columbia UP, 1977.

Mou, Sherry J. "Writing Virtues with Their Bodies: Rereading the Two Tang Histories' Biographies of Women." *Presence and Presentation: Women in the Chinese Literary Tradition.* Ed. Sherry Mou. New York: St. Martin's, 1999. 109–47.

Plaks, Andrew, ed. *Chinese Narrative: Critical and Theoretical Essays.* Princeton: Princeton UP, 1977.

Plaks, Andrew. *The Four Masterworks of the Ming Novel.* Princeton: Princeton UP, 1987.

Prasad, M. Madhava. *Ideology of the Hindi Film: A Historical Construction.* Delhi: Oxford UP, 1998.

Prusek, Jaroslav. *The Lyrical and the Epic: Studies of Modern Chinese Literature.* Ed. Leo Ou-fan Lee. Bloomington : Indiana UP, 1980.

Qian Qianwu. 錢謙吾 "Ding Ling." 丁玲 (1930). *Ding Ling yanjiu ziliao.* Ed. Yuan Liangjun. Tianjin: Tianjin renmin, 1982. 226–37.

Qian Xingcun. "The Bygone Age of Ah Q." Trans. Paul Foster and Sherry Mou. *Modern Chinese Literary Thought: Writings on Literature, 1895–1945.* Ed. Kirk Denton. Stanford: Stanford UP, 1996. 276–88.

Qian Xingcun. 錢杏村 "Mao Dun yu xianshi." 茅盾與現實 (Mao Dun and Reality, 1928). *Mao Dun yanjiu ziliao.* Ed. Sun Zhongtian and Zha Guohua. Beijing: Zhongguo shehui kexue, 1983. Vol. 2, 101–30.

Radtke, Kurt W. "Chaos or Coherence? Sato Haruo's Novel *Den'en no yûutsu* and Yu Dafu's Trilogy *Chenlun.*" *Literature, Visual Arts, and Linguistics.* Vol. 1 of *Rethinking Japan.* Ed. Adriana Boscaro, Franco Gatti, and Massimo Raveri. Sandgate, Folkestone, Kent: Japan Library Limited, 1991. 86–101.

Raphals, Lisa. *Sharing the Light: Representation of Women and Virtue in Early China.* Albany: State U of New York P, 1998.

Samei, Maija B. *Gendered Persona and Poetic Voice: The Abandoned Woman in Tang and Five Dynasties Song Lyrics (ci).* Ph.D. dissertation, U of Michigan, Ann Arbor, 1998.

Schor, Naomi. *Breaking the Chain: Women, Theory, French Realist Fiction.* New York: Columbia UP, 1985.

Schwartz, Benjamin. "The Limits of 'Tradition versus Modernity' as Categories of Explanation: The Case of the Chinese Intellectuals." *Daedalus* 101. 2 (Spring 1972): 71–88.

Smith, Sidonie. *A Poetics of Women's Autobiography: Marginality and the Fictions of Self-Representation.* Bloomington: Indiana UP, 1987.

Sommer, Matthew. "The Penetrated Male in Late Imperial China." *Modern China* 23.2 (April 1997): 140–80.

Su Xuelin. 蘇雪林 "Yu Dafu lun." 郁達夫論 (On Yu Dafu, 1934). *Yu Dafu yanjiu ziliao.* Ed. Wang Zili and Chen Zishan. Tianjin: Tianjin renmin, 1981. Vol. 2, 381–92.

Sun Fuyuan. 孫伏園 "Dangao zhizao fangfa de guanshu yu funü genben wenti de taolun." 蛋糕制造方法的灌輸與婦女根本問題的討論 (How to Make Cakes and the Discussion on the Basic Problems of Women). *Xin nüxing* 新女性 (New Woman) 6 (1926): 417.

Sun Zhongtian 孫中田 and Zha Guohua 查國華, eds. *Mao Dun yanjiu ziliao.* 茅盾研究資料 (Research Materials on Mao Dun). 3 volumes. Beijing: Zhongguo shehui kexue, 1983.

Swann, Nancy L. *Pan Chao: Foremost Woman Scholar in China.* 1932. New York: Russell and Russell, 1968.

Tötösy de Zepetnek, Steven. "From Comparative Literature Today Toward Comparative Cultural Studies." *Comparative Literature and Comparative Cultural Studies.* Ed. Steven Tötösy de Zepetnek. West Lafayette: Purdue UP, 2002. 235–67.

Tsu, Jing. "Perversions of Masculinity: The Masochistic Male Subject in Yu Dafu, Guo Moruo, and Freud." *Positions* 8.2 (Fall 2000): 269–316.

Wang, David Der-wei. *Fictional Realism in Twentieth-Century China: Mao Dun, Lao She, Shen Congwen.* New York: Columbia UP, 1992.

Wang, David Der-wei, and Ellen Widmer, eds. *From May Fourth to June Fourth: Fiction and Film in Twentieth-Century China.* Cambridge: Harvard UP, 1993.

Wang, David Der-wei. "Story-telling Context in Chinese Fiction: A Preliminary Examination of It as a Mode of Narrative Discourse." *Tamkang Review* 15.1–4 (1983): 133–50.

Wang Dehou. 王得後 Liangdi shu *yanjou.* 兩地書研究 (Study on *Letters from Two Places*). Tianjin: Tianjin renmin, 1982.

Wang Hui. 汪輝 "Lu Xun xiaoshuo de jingshen tezheng yu 'fankang juewang' de rensheng zhexue." 魯迅小說的精神特徵與反抗絕望的人生哲學 (The Spiritual Characteristics of Lu Xun's Fiction and his Life Philosophy of "Resisting Despair"). *Ershi shiji zhongguo wenxue shilun.* Ed. Wang Xiaoming. Shanghai: Dongfang chuban zhongxin, 1997. Vol. 1, 404–32.

Wang Xiaoming, 王曉明 ed. *Ershi shiji zhongguo wenxue shilun.* 二十世紀中國文學史論 (Discussions on the History of Twentieth-Century Chinese Literature). 3 volumes. Shanghai: Dongfang chuban zhongxin, 1997.

Wang Xiaoming. "Wufa zhimian the rensheng: Ershi niandai wanqi de Lu Xun sixiang." 無法直面的人生：二十年代晚期的魯迅思想 (The Life That Cannot Be Faced: Lu Xun's Thoughts in the Late 1920s). *Ershi shiji zhongguo wenxue shilun.* Ed. Wang Xiaoming. Shanghai: Dongfang chuban zhongxin, 1997. Vol. 1, 456–94.

Wang Zili 王自立 and Chen Zishan 陳子善, eds. *Yu Dafu yanjiu ziliao.* 郁達夫研究資料 (Research Materials on Yu Dafu). 2 volumes. Tianjin: Tianjin renmin, 1981.

Watt, Ian. *The Rise of the Novel.* Berkeley: U of California P, 1962.

Wolf, Margery. *Revolution Postponed: Women in Contemporary China.* Stanford: Stanford UP, 1985.

Woolf, Virginia. *A Room of One's Own.* New York: Harcourt Brace Jovanovich, 1981.

Widmer, Ellen, and David Der-wei Wang, eds. *From May Fourth to June Fourth: Fiction and Film in Twentieth-Century China.* Cambridge: Harvard UP, 1993.

Xiao Feng. 蕭鳳 *Lu Yin zhuan* 盧隱傳 (Biography of Lu Yin). Beijing: Beijing shifan daxue, 1982.

Xiao Qian. 蕭乾 "Ping 'Chubeng.'" 評出奔 (On "Escape," 1935). *Yu Dafu yanjiu ziliao.* Ed. Wang Zili and Chen Zishan. Tianjin: Tianjin renmin, 1981. Vol. 2, 394–99.

Xing Yi. 辛夷 "'Zhuiqiu' zhong de Zhang Qiuliu." 追求中的章秋柳 (Zhang Qiuliu in "Pursuit," 1929). *Mao Dun yanjiu lunji.* 茅盾研究論集 Ed. Zhuang Zhongqing. 莊鍾慶 Tianjing: Tianjing renmin, 1984. 96–107.

"Xuanyan." 宣言 *Xin funü.* 新婦女 (New Woman) 1 (1920): 1–6.

Yan Jiayan. 嚴家炎 *S huiguan yu wusi xin wenxue de qiyuan.* S 會館與五四新文學的起源 (The S Hostel and the Origin of May Fourth New Culture). Changsha: Hunan jiaoyu, 1991.

Yang, Shuhui. *Appropriation and Representation: Feng Menglong and the Chinese Vernacular Story.* Ann Arbor: Center for Chinese Studies, U of Michigan, 1998.

Ye Shaojun. 葉紹鈞 "Nüzi renge wenti." 女子人格問題 (The Question of Women's Character). *Zhongguo funü wenti taolun ji.* Ed. Mei Sheng. Shanghai: Xin wenhua, 1924. Vol. 5, 149–56.

Yeh, Michelle. "International Theory and the Transnational Critic: China in the Age of Multiculturalism." *Modern Chinese Literary and Cultural Studies in the Age of Theory: Reimagining a Field.* Ed. Rey Chow. Durham: Duke UP, 2000. 251–80.

"Yi jiu san er nian Zhongguo wentan niaokan" 一九三二年中國文壇鳥瞰 (Overview of the Literary Arena in 1932). *Ba Jin yanjiu ziliao.* Ed. Li Cunguang. Fuzhou: Haixia wenyi, 1985. Vol. 3, 5–7.

Yi Zhen. 毅真 "Ding Ling nüshi." 丁玲女士 (Miss Ding Ling, 1930). *Ding Ling yanjiu ziliao.* Ed. Yuan Liangjun. Tianjin: Tianjin renmin, 1982. 223.

Yi Zhen. "Jiwei dangdai zhongguo nü xiaoshuojia." 幾位中國當代女小說家 (Several Contemporary Chinese Women Fiction Writers). *Dangdai zhongguo nü zuojia lun.* 當代中國女作家論 (On Contemporary Women Writers). Ed. Gu Fengcheng. 顧鳳城 Shanghai: Guanghua, 1933. 1–36.

Yu Dafu. 郁達夫 "Chanyu dubai" 懺餘獨白 (Confessional Monologue). *Yu Dafu wenlun ji.* Hangzhou: Zhejiang wenyi, 1985. 465–67.

Yu Dafu. "Chenlun." 沉淪 (Sinking). *Yu Dafu xiaoshuo ji.* Hangzhou: Zhejiang renmin, 1981. Vol. 1, 16–50.

Yu Dafu. "'Chenlun' zixu." 沉淪自序 (Preface to "Sinking" by the Author Himself, 1921). *Yu Dafu xiaoshuo ji*. Hangzhou: Zhejiang renmin, 1981. Vol. 2, 816.

Yu Dafu. "Chunfeng chenzui de wanshang" 春風沉醉的晚上 (Intoxicating Spring Nights). *Yu Dafu xiaoshuo ji*. Hangzhou: Zhejiang renmin, 1981. Vol. 1, 237–49.

Yu, Dafu. "Class Struggle in Literature." Trans. Haili Kong and Howard Goldblatt. *Modern Chinese Literary Thought: Writings on Literature, 1895–1945*. Ed. Kirk Denton. Stanford: Stanford UP, 1996. 263–68.

Yu Dafu. "*Dafu zixuan ji xu*." 達夫自選集序 (Preface to the *Anthology Selected by the Author Himself*, 1932). *Yu Dafu xiaoshuo ji*. Hangzhou: Zhejiang renmin, 1981. Vol. 2, 835–37.

Yu Dafu. "Haishang tongxin" 海上通信 (Correspondence at Sea). *Yu Dafu xuanji*. Beijing: Renmin, 1982. 183–90.

Yu Dafu. "*Jilei ji* tici." 雞肋集題辭 (Words Written on *Anthology of Chicken Flanks*, 1927). *Yu Dafu wenlun ji*. Hangzhou: Zhejiang wenyi, 1985. 325–27.

Yu Dafu. "Riji wenxue." 日記文學 (Diary Literature, 1927). *Yu Dafu yanjiu ziliao*. Ed. Wang Zili and Chen Zishan. Tianjin: Tianjin renmin, 1981. Vol. 1, 255–61.

Yu, Dafu. "Sinking." Trans. Joseph S. M. Lau and C. T. Hsia. *Modern Chinese Stories and Novellas, 1919–1949*. Ed. S. M. Joseph Lau, C. T. Hsia, and Leo Ou-fan Lee. New York: Columbia UP, 1981. 125–41.

Yu Dafu. "Wenyi yu daode" 文藝與道德 (Literature and Morality). *Yu Dafu wenlun ji*. Hangzhou: Zhejiang wenyi, 1985. 544–46.

Yu Dafu. "Wuliu nian lai chuangzuo shenghuo de huigu." 五六年來創作生活的回顧 (Recollections on My Writing Career of the Past Five or Six Years, 1927). *Yu Dafu wenlun ji*. Hangzhou: Zhejiang wenyi, 1985. 331–36.

Yu Dafu. "Xueye: Riben guoqing de jishu zizhuan zhi yizhang" 雪夜：日本國情的記述，自傳之一章 (Snowy Night: One Chapter in My Autobiographical Records of the Milieu in Japan, 1936). *Yu Dafu yanjiu ziliao*. Ed. Wang Zili and Chen Zishan. Tianjin: Tianjin renmin, 1981. Vol. 1, 57–61.

Yu Dafu. *Yu Dafu wenlun ji* 郁達夫文論集 (Literary Criticism by Yu Dafu). Hangzhou: Zhejiang wenyi, 1985.

Yu Dafu. *Yu Dafu xiaoshuo ji*. 郁達夫小說集 (Anthology of Yu Dafu's Fiction). 2 volumes. Hangzhou: Zhejiang renmin, 1981.

Yu Dafu. *Yu Dafu xuanji*. 郁達夫選集 (Selected Works by Yu Dafu). Beijing: Renmin, 1982.

Yuan Jin. 袁進 "Juexing yu taobi: lun minchu yanqing xiaoshuo." 覺醒與逃避：論民初艷情小說 (Awakening and Escape: on Popular Love Stories in Early Republican Period). *Ershi shiji zhongguo wenxue shilun*. Ed. Wang Xiaoming. Shanghai: Dongfang chuban zhongxin, 1997. Vol. 1, 250–76.

Yuan Liangjun. 袁良駿 "Xin shiqi Ding Ling xiaoshuo yanjiu zonglun." 新時期丁玲小說研究綜論 (Comprehensive Discussion on Research about Ding Ling's Fiction in the "New Period"). *Ding Ling yanjiu wushi nian.* Ed. Yuan Liangjun. Tianjin: Jiaoyu, 1990. 133-57.

Yuan Liangjun, ed. *Ding Ling yanjiu ziliao.* 丁玲研究資料 (Research Materials on Ding Ling). Tianjin: Tianjin renmin, 1982.

Yuan Liangjun, ed. *Ding Ling yanjiu wushi nian.* 丁玲研究五十年 (Fifty Years' Research on Ding Ling). Tianjin: Jiaoyu, 1990.

Yuan Shishuo and Yan Rongxian, 袁世碩，嚴蓉仙 eds. *Feng Yuanjun chuangzuo yiwen ji.* 馮沅君創作譯文集 (Anthology of Feng Yuanjun's Writings and Translations). Jinan: Shandong renmin, 1983.

Yue Daiyun. 樂黛雲 "*Shi* he *Ziye* de bijiao fenxi" 蝕和子夜的比較分析 (Comparative Analysis between *Eclipse* and *Midnight*, 1980). *Mao Dun yanjiu ziliao.* Ed. Sun Zhongtian and Zha Guohua. Beijing: Zhongguo shehui kexue, 1983. Vol. 2, 182-204.

Yue, Mingbao. "Gendering the Origins of Modern Chinese Fiction." *Gender and Sexuality in Twentieth-Century Chinese Literature and Society.* Ed. Lu Tonglin. Albany: State U of New York P, 1993. 47-65.

Yü, Ying-shi. "The Radicalization of China in the Twentieth Century." *Daedalus* 122. 2 (Spring 1993): 125-50.

Zeng Pu. 曾樸 *Niehai hua.* 孽海花 (Flowers in the Sea of Sins). *Zhongguo jindai wenxue daxi* 中國近代文學大係 (General Compendium of Early-Modern Chinese Literature). Shanghai: Shanghai, 1991. 1-237.

Zhang Jinglu. 張靜廬 *Zai baojie ershi nian.* 在報界二十年 (Twenty Years in Journalism). Shanghai: Shanghai zizhi gongsi, 1938.

Zhang, Jingyuan. *Psychoanalysis in China: Literary Transformations 1919-1949.* Ithaca: Cornell U, East Asian Program, 1992.

Zhang Tianyi. 張天翼 "Bing Xin." 冰心 (Bing Xin). *Bing Xin yanjiu ziliao.* Ed. Fan Boqun. Beijing: Beijing, 1984. 194-95.

Zhang Xichen. 章錫琛 "Jiushi nüzi yu xinshi nüzi." 舊式女子與新式女子 ("Old woman" and "new woman"). *Xin nüxing* 新女性 (New Woman) 2.12 (1927): 1269-73.

Zhao, Henry. *The Uneasy Narrator: Chinese Fiction from the Traditional to the Modern.* Oxford: Oxford UP, 1995.

Zheng Boqi. 鄭伯奇 "*Hanhui ji* pipan." 寒灰集批評 (Critique of *Anthology of Cold Ashes*, 1927). *Yu Dafu yanjiu ziliao.* Ed. Wang Zili and Chen Zishan. Tianjin: Tianjin renmin, 1981. Vol. 2, 319-29.

Zhongguo xinwenxue daxi (1917-1927). 中國新文學大係 (General Compendium of New Chinese Literature). Hong Kong: Hong Kong wenxue yanjiu she, 1963.

Zhou Zuoren. 周作人 "Lun zaizuo jidangao" 論再做雞蛋糕 (On Making Cakes Again). *Xin nüxing* 新女性 (New Woman) 8 (1926): 560.

Zi Gang. 子岡 "Bing Xin nüshi fangwen ji." 冰心女士訪問記 *Bing Xin yanjiu ziliao.* Ed. Fan Boqun. Beijing: Beijing, 1984. 97-106.

Zito, Angelo, and Tani Barlow, eds. *Body, Subject, and Power*. Chicago: U Chicago P, 1994.

Zuo Qun, 左群 ed. *Lu Xun zishu*. 鲁迅自述 (Lu Xun's Words about Himself). Hong Kong: Wenxin, 1973.

Index

"After Separation," 132
"After Victory," 142, 145
Anderson, Marston, 82
Autumn, 95

Ba Jin, 25, 84, 129, 173
baihua, 44
Ban Zhao, 130
Bao Tianxiao, 27
Barlow, Tani E., 153
Bing Xin, 118, 127
Butterfly fiction. *See* Mandarin Duck and Butterfly fiction

Cai Yuanpei, 25
cainü. *See* talented woman
Call to Arms. *See Nahan*
CCP. *See* Chinese Communist Party
"A Certain Night," 187
Chambers, Ross, 16
Chatman, Seymour, 144
Chen Duxiu, 29
Chen Pingyuan, 25
Cheng Fangwu, 75
Chenlun, 26
Chinese Communist Party, 3, 24
Chow, Rey, 2, 63, 153
Chuangzao she. *See* Creation Society
Chuangzao zhoubao, 25
"Class Struggle in Literature," 75
"Cong yewan sao tainliang. *See* "From Night to Dawn"
congliang, 34
"Creation," 119
Creation Society, 23
Creation Weekly. *See Chuangzao zhoubao*

"Day." *See* "Ri"
"Dian," 88
"Diary of a Mistress," 142, 146
"The Diary of Lishi," 142
"Disillusionment," 102
"Dixiong," 49
Den'en no yuutsu, 72
Denton, Kirk, 22, 63
Ding Ling, 12, 149
Doleželová-Velingerová, Milena, 37
Dongfang wenku, 25

Eastern Han, 45

Eclipse Trilogy, 103
Ershi nian budu zhi guai xianzhuang, 36

Family, 84. *See also Jia*
"Farewell of a Shadow." *See* "Ying de gaobie"
"Father," 142
"Feizao," 51
Fen, 49
Feng Xuefeng, 189
Feng Yuanjun, 12, 126, 196
Feuerwerker, Yi-tsi, 171
Flames, 146
"From Literary Revolution to Revolutionary Literature," 75
"From Night to Dawn," 179, 184
Fu Sinian, 29
Funü pinglun, 28
Funü sheng, 28
Funü shibao, 28
funü wenti, 28
Funü zazhi, 28
Funü zhoukan, 28

"Gaolao fuzi," 51
"Gejue." *See* "Separation"
"Gejue zhi hou." *See* "After Separation"
Girard, René, 113
Gramsci, Antonio, 129
Great Proletarian Cultural Revolution, 3
"Gudu zhe," 49
guixiu pai, 127
Guiyan. *See The Returning Wild Goose*
Guo, Moruo, 75, 136
Guomin dang. *See* Nationalist Party
guomin xing, 40

"Haze," 119
He, Danren, 188
Hesitation. *See Panghuang*
Honglou meng, 36
Hsia, C. T., 118
Hu, Shi, 25
Hu, Yepin, 171, 181
Hu, Ying, 13
"Huanmie." *See* "Disillusionment"

"In the Hospital," 189
"Intoxicating Spring Nights," 62, 74
Ivory Ring, 146

Jia, 25. See also *Family*
Jiang Guangci, 75, 172
Jiliu, 88
Jin Ping Mei, 33
"The Journey," 132

Kang, Youwei, 18, 21

Larson, Wendy, 9
Lee, Leo, 27
"A Letter," 142
Li, Shizeng, 25
Liang, Qichao, 9, 18, 21
liangjia funü, 35
Liangyou huabao, 27
Libai liu, 26
Lieberman, Sally, 13
lienü zhuan, 32
The Light Is in Front of Us, 181
Lin, Yü-sheng, 3
Link, Perry, 112
Lisao, 48
Literary Research Association, 23
Liu, Lydia, 13, 42153
Love Trilogy, 88
Lu Xun, 23, 25, 26, 40, 189
Lu Yin, 12, 118, 126, 196
Lun zheng le yan kan, 40
"Lüxing." See "The Journey"

Mandarin Duck and Butterfly Fiction, 102. See also *yuanyang hudie pai xiaoshuo*
"Mangmang ye," 63
"Manli," 142
Mao Dun, 31, 101, 128, 140, 173, 177, 190
Mao Zedong, 193
May Fourth Movement, 2
McMahon, Keith, 34
"Mengke," 151
Metzger, Thomas, 4
Midnight, 122
min, 31
Ming, 9
"Miss Sophia's Diary," 151, 152, 177, 180
Mudan ting, 37
Muqin, 154

Nahan, 25
"Nanqian," 62
National Defense Literature, 191
Nationalist Party, 24

new woman, 1, 3, 5
New Youth. See *Xin qingnian*
Nie haihua, 35, 36
"1930 nian chun Shanghai (zhiyi, zhi'er)." *See* "Shanghai, Spring 1930, Part I and II"
"Nora zouhou zenmo yang." *See* "What Happens after Nora Leaves Home"
nü xuesheng, 2
Nü xuesheng, 27
Nübao, 28
Nüren de xin. See *A Woman's Heart*
nüxing de wenzhang, 45
Nüzi shijie, 28

"On the Satanic Power of Poetry," 44
Opium War, 21
Outlaws of the Water Marsh. See *Shuihu zhuan*

Panghuang, 25
Peony Pavilion. See *Mudan ting*
Plaks, Andrew, 35
Plum in a Golden Vase. See *Jin Ping Mei*
"Poetry and Prose," 119
Precepts for Women, 130
"Pursuit," 103

Qian Xingcun, 75
qianze xiaoshuo, 35
Qing, 9
Qu Qiubai, 174
Qu Yuan, 48

Rainbow, 118, 121
Realism, 101, 190
Refeng, 49
"Regret for the Past," 41, 189
The Returning Wild Goose, 140
Revolutionary Literature, 75, 141, 173
"Ri," 151

"Sanba jie yougan." *See* "Thoughts on March 8"
Sato Haruo, 72
Saturday. See *Libai liu*
Seaside Friends, 128, 140
"Separation," 132
"Shafei riji dier bu," 152
"Shafei nüshi de riji." *See* "Miss Sophia's Diary"
"Shanghai, Spring 1930, Part I and II," 152

Shanghai Commercial Press, 25
Shangshi. *See* "Regret for the Past"
Shangwu yingshu guan. *See* Shanghai Commercial Press
shidai xing, 104
Short Story Monthly, 102. See also *Xiaoshuo yuebao*
Shuihu zhuan, 97
Sinking. See *Chenlun*
"Sinking," 61, 62
Six Chapters of the Floating Life, 161
"Somebody's Sorrow," 142
Sommer, Matthew, 161
Song, 33
"Sophia's Diary (II)," 179, 180
The Sorrow of Young Werther, 26, 136
Spring, 95
"Suicide Diary." *See* "Zisha riji"
Sun Fuyuan, 30
Sun Society, 75

talented woman, 6, 9, 45, 161
"Talks at the Yan'an Forum on Literature and Art," 193
"Thoughts on March 8," 192
Three Cardinal Guides, 130
Tian'anmen Incident, 3
"Tianjia chong." See "Tianjia Village"
"Tianjia Village," 179, 186
tianren h yi, 21
Tötösy de Zepetnek, Steven, 17
Tsu, Jing, 63

"Vacillation," 103
"A Victim of the Times," 142

Wang, David, 118
Wang Jianhong, 174
Wang Yunwu, 25
Wanyou wenku, 25
watakushi shosetsu, 72
Way, 21, 38
wei rensheng de yishu, 44
Wenxue yanjiu hui. *See* Literary Research Society
wenyan, 6
"Wei Hu," 152, 173
"What Happens after Nora Leaves Home," 41, 45
"When I Was in Xia Village," 189
Wild Roses, 118, 119

"Wo de shilian," 44
woman revolutionary, 83
A Woman's Heart, 140
"Wu," 88
Wu Woyao, 36
Wu Zhihui, 25

Xiaoshuo yuebao, 25
Xin chao, 29
Xin funü, 28
xin guixiu pai, 127
xin nüxing, 1
Xin nüxing, 28, 30
xin nüxing pai, 127
Xin qingnian, 25
"Xingfu de jiating," 51
Xu Guangping, 45
Xu Zhenya, 26
Xuesheng zazhi, 102
"Xueye," 72

"Yang Ma de riji," 184
Yan, Fu, 21
Yan Jiayan, 118
Yan'an, 12, 188
Yang Xingfo, 25
yanqing, 27
"Yecao," 151, 165
Yecao, 49
Ye qiangwei, 118
"Ying de gaobie," 44
"Yinhuise de si," 62
"Yu," 88
Yu Dafu, 11, 23, 25, 60, 128, 173
Yu Dafu's Self-Selected Anthology, 76
Yü, Ying-shi, 21
yuanyang hudie pai xiaoshuo, 26
Yue, Mingbao, 8
Yuli hun, 26

Zeng Pu, 35
Zhaohua xishi, 49
Zheng Boqi, 81
zhishi fenzi, 21
Zhongguo funü wenti taolun ji, 28
Zhongguo jindai wenxue daxi, 35
Zhongguo xin wenxue daxi, 2
zhongjian wu, 44
Zhou Zuoren, 30, 44
"Zisha riji," 151, 165

www.ingramcontent.com/pod-product-compliance
Lightning Source LLC
Chambersburg PA
CBHW060949230426
43665CB00015B/2132